The Case for Christian Theism

The Case for Christian Theism

An Introduction to Apologetics

A. J. Hoover

BAKER BOOK HOUSE
Grand Rapids, Michigan 49506

The title of the first edition of this book,
Dear Agnos, accounts for the personal references throughout this book.

To Mother

PREFACE

When Peter commanded Christians to give a defense of their faith
(I Peter 3:15), he fated some of us to write books on apologetics. I think
every generation needs a single volume that gives a comprehensive
survey of the basic material for Christian evidences. I always like a
book one can hand to an unbeliever and say, "Here, read this and
you'll know *what* I believe and most of the good reasons *why* I believe
it."

Now that I've tried to write such a book, I can see the job was
harder than I thought. To be comprehensive and yet not write a book
as large as the New York telephone directory one must compress a
great deal and simplify a lot of problems. Along with simplification,
of course, goes the danger of oversimplification. In spite of this risk,
however, I hope I've written a book that can serve as a one-volume introduction to the evidences for this generation. I've tried to combine
the philosophical case for Christianity (chs. 1-8) with the historical
case (chs. 10-20), with chapter nine, "Why History?" bridging the two
major sections.

One important note: I feel one must steer a middle course on the
question of theistic arguments. I can't go with the Roman Catholics
and say the existence of God is demonstrable, but neither can I go
with Barth and say that apart from Christ I would be an atheist. To
me, the least one can be after hearing the arguments for God is a
perplexed agnostic. The most one can be is a deist.

I've addressed the reader (Agnos) in the first person and in an in-
formal tone because I feel that one should present apologetics in a
very existential mood. Witnessing for Christ is, after all, a very personal matter. When we say, "This is the evidence," we really mean,

"This is the evidence as I see it—hope you see it the same way." Apologetics is partly an art and partly a science. Each generation and each individual will have something unique to say in the way they contend for the faith.

Underneath the unique and the individual, however, lies a hard core of material that hasn't changed much since St. Augustine, indeed since the New Testament. Among contemporary apologists I'm very much indebted to thinkers of the Evangelical persuasion: Ramm, Carnell, Henry, Clark, Trueblood, Lewis, Schaeffer, Stott, to mention only a few.

I'm also indebted to my wife, Gloria, not only for proofreading the manuscript in all its stages but also for tolerating and encouraging my interest in apologetics these sixteen years of our married life.

CONTENTS

1

ATHEISM IS IMPOSSIBLE!

Dear Agnos,

I'm sure you're wondering why I call you "Agnos." Agnos is short for "agnostic," one who has suspended judgment on the question of God. An agnostic says he doesn't know whether or not God exists. He claims the evidence is inconclusive either way.

Now that I know how to address you, Agnos, I want to make clear my purpose in writing this book. I'm a Christian and I want you to become one also. Let's put all the cards on the table in the first chapter—I'm out to convert you to Jesus Christ. If you're afraid that the evidence for Christianity might be good enough to do that, put this book down right now! If you're honest enough to look at my case for Christianity, read on!

But you may say: "You're addressing the wrong person. I'm not an agnostic, I'm an outright atheist. I *know* there is no God." Do you really? Are you sure that you know that much? I think I can convince you that this dogmatic atheism is impossible. In fact, that's the purpose of my first chapter. It sounds strange, but my first chapter is to make you an agnostic—a reverent agnostic—and the rest of my book is to make you a Christian. If my reasoning is correct, we can start this intellectual odyssey with the thesis: *no one should be an atheist.* If you're not a theist, the most you can logically be is an agnostic.

If you're a typical atheist you probably subscribe to some basic propositions. You probably say that God doesn't exist, that the universe is wholly matter, that faith is a weak and shameful refuge for feeble-minded people, and that only the scientific method should be used by

13

a rational man. Let's use these propositions and prove that you're not an atheist.

A. YOU CAN'T BE A DOGMATIC ATHEIST.

Agnos, if you could know that God doesn't exist, you would have an exhaustive knowledge of all the facts of reality, for any one fact that you overlooked might be the fact in question, namely God's existence. God is a possible fact and when you say dogmatically that he doesn't exist you're really asserting knowledge of all facts. If you're acquainted with all of reality, the entire universe, all of being, then you can rightly assert that God isn't included in reality. But who in his right mind would claim to know all reality?

Suppose, for example, that you had a bag of marbles and wanted to prove that there were no black marbles in the bag. To do that, you'd need to see all the marbles in the bag and you'd need to see them all at once. Unless you met these conditions you could never prove your assertion. In this illustration, the bag is the universe and you're saying that there's no God in the bag. Do you know all there is in the bag?

Let's be ridiculous about it. Suppose you start hunting God on earth. You look under every flat rock on the planet—no God. Then you move to Mars—still no God. Then to Jupiter, to Neptune, Uranus, Pluto, then to all the Milky Way, then on to Andromeda, and so on throughout the universe. Still no God. Even then, would you know for sure there is no God? Suppose God had been just one jump ahead of you all the way, craftily evading your diligent search?

This sounds silly, I know, but I'm trying to make a very serious point: you would have to know everything, to be everywhere at every time in order to affirm apodictically, "I know there is no God." To be a genuine atheist you must be omniscient and omnipresent— attributes we usually associate with God. In short, you would have to be God, in order to say there is no God!

B. YOU REALLY BELIEVE IN THE SUPERNATURAL.

If you grant this point, Agnos, then I've got you on the next point. Once you deny your omniscience, I can also show you that you really believe in the supernatural. If you're a naturalist or a materialist, one who believes that nature or matter is all there is, you probably think this is a verbal trick. But consider this point: no one can deny that there is an unknown dimension that transcends our present knowledge of reality. If we use the word *nature* to mean the universe we have experienced up to now, then there is obviously a "supernature," because "super" just means "beyond" or "above." Supernature, then, simply refers to the whole range of facts, forces, entities, and laws that we don't know at the present time. Many unbelievers use the word "supernatural" to mean the fanciful, the occult, the mysterious, the impossible, and the imaginary but if we use it in the sense described here we can begin this study on a reasonable common ground.

Of course, a naturalist believes that there is a reality beyond the presently known world. He feels, however, that this reality beyond the known world is just like the known world. He believes it is still material or natural. He asserts that the whole universe is homogeneous throughout—the same substance from end to end: matter. But what right does anyone have to say what the unknown reality is like? How can you really know that much about the unknown? Wouldn't you need to experience the unknown reality to assert so confidently that it is just like the world we already know? Wouldn't you need to see the universe as a whole to affirm, "It is all matter"? Isn't it possible that the unknown is fundamentally different from nature? Isn't it possible that there exists something immaterial, superempirical, spiritual?

Note, dear Agnos, that the negative proposition, "There is no God," and the positive proposition, "All is matter," both require omniscience to prove. This leads us to the third assertion.

C. YOU REALLY HAVE SOME KIND OF FAITH.

If you deny your omniscience and admit the existence of the supernatural then you really have some kind of faith. It may not be religious faith yet, but it is a start, for even religious faith can begin with general faith. We'll spend an entire chapter on the nature of faith and an entire chapter on the problem of proof but for now we can define faith simply as assenting to a proposition we can't prove by direct methods. When we prove things by direct methods we call that knowledge; when we use indirect methods we call that faith or belief.

You should never define faith as a blind leap into the dark. It is, rather, a walk into the light. The light of faith may be a bit dimmer than what we call knowledge, but it isn't darkness. Faith must always be based on *some* evidence, though it may not be *perfect* evidence. Faith lies midway between certitude and credulity, between confidence and gullibility.

Thus defined, it is obvious that all men have faith of some kind. You can't live without it. You certainly can't have a philosophy without it. All men have beliefs, hypotheses, theories, explanatory postulates that they entertain about the whole universe, especially the unseen or unexperienced part of it. All men, in sum, have a *worldview* (there is really no substitute for that good old German word, *Weltanschauung)* and all worldviews transcend empirical reality. If you have any kind of general philosophy at all, Agnos, you already have more faith than you're willing to admit.

Hence, it is wrong to say that only the Christian has the problem of "faith versus reason." All thinkers have this problem—if they think at all! Even the unbeliever must grapple with the question: Where does knowledge end and faith begin in my worldview? If you acknowledge the existence of "the beyond" in your philosophy you must go on and tell us what its source and authority are. You must decide what you'll accept about the beyond and what the criterion of your acceptance will be. In this respect you're no different from the religious person. The problem of faith and reason is a general philosophical problem, one that must be negotiated in every worldview.

If my reasoning is sound so far, Agnos, you're not a flaming atheist, you admit the supernatural, and you agree that you have some kind of faith. All this doesn't make you a theist or a Christian yet, but it is a step in the right direction. You're now a "reverent agnostic," an "honest doubter," a person who doesn't know about God but who's willing to learn if there is adequate evidence. The rest of this book is about the evidence.

WHY ARGUE?

We are beginning a long intellectual journey, Agnos. Before we take a single step, it is imperative that we both have faith in thinking, in debating and argumentation. If you'll pardon the pun, *your mind matters!* If argumentation is fruitless we might as well not take that first step. Hence, the title of this chapter, "Why Argue?"

I use the word *argue* in the good sense of "discuss, dispute, debate, and dialogue," not in the bad sense of "wrangle, bicker, and fuss." I don't believe that a man can be "argued into belief"; I don't believe that the evidence for Christianity is perfect and demonstrative; but I do believe that the evidence is adequate and that argumentation, in the best sense of the word, is therefore a vital part of the Christian witness. Strange, but the first group I must convince is some Christians!

A. WHAT THE BIBLE SAYS ABOUT ARGUMENT.

It is a sad fact, Agnos, that some Christians, as well as many non-Christians, believe that the Bible is against thinking, that Christianity recommends blind faith, and that Christ taught a narrow religion of authority that denounces reason as evil and misleading. Listening to some people you'd think that the first and greatest commandment is, "Thou shalt not think."

Nothing could be farther from the truth. A brief survey of some Biblical passages will convince you that God never uttered such a commandment.

The apostle Peter commanded Christians to "be prepared to make a defense to any one who calls you to account for the hope that is in you" (I Peter 3:15). The Greek word for *defense* here is *apologia*, from which we derive words like "apologize," "apology," "apologetics." In Peter's day, an *apologia* meant a formal courtroom defense of your position.

Jude wrote his small epistle to urge Christians to "contend for the faith which was once for all delivered to the saints." He went on to explain that such defense of the faith was necessary because certain false teachers had slipped into the church, "ungodly persons who pervert the grace of our God into licentiousness and deny our only Master and Lord, Jesus Christ" (Jude 3, 4).

The apostle John warned Christians not to believe every message but to "test the spirits to see whether they are of God; for many false prophets have gone out into the world" (I John 4:1). John emphasized in both his gospel and his epistles that Christ, the heart of the faith, was a real historical figure whom many had seen, heard, and touched (John 20:27; I John 1:1). He ended his gospel on an apologetic note: "Now Jesus did many other signs in the presence of the disciples, which are not written in this book; but these are written that you may believe that Jesus is the Christ, the Son of God, and that believing you may have life in his name" (John 20:30, 31).

The apostle Paul complimented correct thinking on several occasions. He warned the Thessalonians to "test everything; hold fast what is good" (I Thess. 5:21). He praised the Corinthians by saying, "I speak as to sensible men; judge for yourselves what I say" (I Cor. 10:15). He prayed that the love of the Philippians might "abound more and more, with *knowledge* and all *discernment*" (Phil. 1:9).* He prayed that the Ephesians might acquire a "spirit of *wisdom* and revelation in the *knowledge*" of God and that God might *enlighten* the eyes of their hearts so that they might *know* the Christian hope (Eph. 1:17, 18). He explained to the Colossians that their new nature in Christ was "being renewed in *knowledge* after the image of its creator" (Col. 3:10). Finally, Paul told the Roman Christians that men who are ignorant of God are "without excuse," because "what can be known about God is plain to them, because God has shown it to them. Ever since the creation of the world his invisible nature, namely, his eternal power and deity, has been clearly perceived in the things that have been made" (Rom. 1:19, 20).

Jesus Christ himself, the heart of our faith, taught that the mind is a crucial part of man's total religious life. He told the Samaritan woman that men must worship God "in truth," that is, with their intelligence (John 4:24). In the Parable of the Sower he claimed that a

* Italics mine.

man must understand the gospel before he can accept it (Matt. 13:19). He commanded us not only to love God with all our heart, soul, and strength, but also with our *mind* (Luke 10:27). On many occasions Christ engaged in skilled disputation with his opponents, confuting them on such matters as paying tribute to Caesar (Matt. 22:21), the authority of John the Baptist (Matt. 21:24), the resurrection and the afterlife (Mark 12:18-27), and the relation between David and the Messiah (Luke 20:41-44). Even though he often accused his opponents of intellectual dishonesty (John 9:41), he seldom shunned a discussion with a serious and honest opponent. On one occasion, when he found such an opponent, he said: "You are not far from the kingdom of God" (Mark 12:34).

Even in the Old Testament, God showed the same respect for man's intellectual integrity. He required that Moses and Aaron give Pharaoh a miracle to prove themselves and their mission (Exod. 7:9). He commanded the Israelites to disregard a prophet whose predictions didn't come to pass (Deut. 18:22). He challenged the idols to do something to prove that they were divine. "Set forth your case, says the Lord; bring your proofs. . . . Tell us what is to come hereafter, that we may know that you are gods; do good, or do harm, that we may be dismayed and terrified." Because the idols did nothing to prove themselves, God rightly concluded: "Behold, you are nothing, and your work is nought; an abomination is he who chooses you" (Isa. 41:21-24).

Give a defense of your hope; contend for the faith; test the spirits; prove all things; love God with your mind; prove yourself by working a miracle; set forth your case—can you honestly read these verses and still say that the Bible is anti-intellectual, that God is against reason, or that Biblical faith is gullibility?

But there is another side to this coin. Someone may respond: "You have overlooked the verses that warn against human reason." Didn't Paul warn about "philosophy and empty deceit" (Col. 2:8)? Didn't he assert that God had made worldly wisdom look foolish and that the unregenerate man couldn't understand the things of the Spirit (I Cor. 1:20; 2:14)? Didn't he say that "the mind that is set on the flesh is hostile to God" (Rom. 8:7)? Yes, he did, and we must take such warnings seriously. We must look at this other side of the coin before we conclude that God has given human reason *carte blanche* in the religious life. Reason plays a role in Christian faith, a vital role, but it may not necessarily be a starring role; it may turn out to be only a supporting role. When we assert the *competence* of reason we don't mean *omnicompetence*.

The key to Paul's warnings about reason lies in the phrase, "mind that is set on the flesh." Paul doesn't condemn mind per se or mind that is set on the spirit, but mind that is set on the flesh. He doesn't condemn thinking in general, but thinking that disregards the truth of God and his revelation. The word *philosopher* originally meant "a lover of wisdom" (from *philos*, friend, and *sophia*, wisdom). Since a word like this changes a lot in centuries of usage, we have no right to assume that "philosophy" in Colossians 2:8 means the same as the word used in the catalogue of a modern university. Condemning philosophy in the first century isn't the same as saying, "Thou shalt not think."

When the Bible warns about human reason, I take it to mean autonomous reason, reason detached from God, detached from divine revelation. Why reason should never detach itself from God is, in a real sense, the theme of this whole book. My thesis reads: without God, reason can't make sense out of the universe.

Please do not panic, therefore, dear Agnos, when you hear me use the word *philosophy*. I mean nothing sinister by it, as you'll see in the coming chapters.

B. WHY THE CHRISTIAN NEEDS PHILOSOPHY.

The Christian needs philosophy. He needs logic, clear thought, right reason. Only harm can come to Christian theology when reason and religion are completely divorced.

We Christians need philosophy because God commands us to preach, to communicate our faith. We aren't allowed to remain silent, like the disciples of some Eastern religions. God requires us to speak, to explain our experience, to proclaim our hope. If the church were nothing but a huge Trappist monastery, where silence is the prime virtue, then we could neglect philosophy. We are fated to philosophical involvement by Christ, the divine Logos, who won't let us remain silent, but enjoins us to be his witnesses to the world (Acts 1:8). To be a witness requires intellectual baggage: logic, grammar, rhetoric.

If a Christian refused to philosophize, he might live out a long life in practical service to his fellow man but he couldn't think about his beliefs or express them in words to others. You can't write theology or defend religious doctrines without using logic. We would have none of those wonderful treatises on the Trinity, the Incarnation, and the Atonement from Origen to Augustine to Calvin to Barth if reason didn't play at least a supporting role in the drama of Christian theology.

The only way you can divorce reason from faith is to divorce faith from truth. Every human discipline must come to terms with truth, sooner or later, and theology is no exception. Hence, both reason and faith are sons of God, like Jacob and Esau, and neither should attempt to steal the other's birthright.

The Christian needs philosophy because only with right logic can the great Christian doctrines be expressed in times of historical necessity. Great Christian doctrines are usually hammered out in times when there are attacks on the faith. Nearly all the great creeds—the Apostles', the Nicene, the Athanasian—were formulated as apologetics. Nearly all the great defenders of the faith expressed their thinking in the prevailing philosophy of the day. St. Augustine used Plato's framework; St. Thomas Aquinas built on Aristotle; Bishop Butler followed Locke's empiricism; Emil Brunner borrowed heavily from Kierkegaard. Without philosophy, properly defined, the church could neither preach nor defend its faith.

Some human cultures (e.g., China) have had such an unbroken uniform philosophy of life that no one ever thought it necessary to formulate a creed. These people believe something, but they seldom reflect on their creed because no one ever attacks it. Their creed is a "given," not a "chosen." They know *what* they believe, but not *why* they believe. Once you attack their creed, you stimulate them to think, to defend their beliefs, to express their creed in rational terms.

This, Agnos, is why I see nothing wrong with honest doubt. Every reflective Christian knows about honest doubt. You can't defend your creed unless you have that very personal feeling that "I've got to prove it to myself first!" Sometimes the most cogent arguments you can fashion come when you feel that you're holding high debate with yourself. Philip Melanchthon once said: "A man often preaches his beliefs precisely when he has lost them and is looking everywhere for them, and, on such occasions, his preaching is by no means at its worst."

The Christian needs philosophy because only with right logic can he examine and evaluate the claims of other religions, other claimants to divine revelation. We've had many individuals in history claim revelation from God: Zoroaster, Moses, Christ, Mohammed, Joseph Smith, Father Divine. Not all of them can be right, because they make contradictory claims. How do we decide which one has the correct claim? By fighting? No, for that would prove only who is the strongest. By voting? No, for that would prove only what the majority opinion is. By right reason? Yes, for this is the common ground that unites rational men.

Christians believe that God is truly ready to take the risk of honest inquiry. We feel that only when all the cards are on the table does Christ get his true opportunity. Theologian John Baillie confessed: "My own testimony would have to be that in the long run nothing but harm has come to my faith from the many occasions on which I have yielded to the temptation of foreclosing my inquiries because they seemed to be leading me away from the faith rather than towards it."[1]

C. WHY THE UNBELIEVER NEEDS PHILOSOPHY.

Don't think, dear Agnos, that we Christians should do all the thinking. You need right logic also. I realize that philosophy and theology have a bad reputation at times. Some wit has said that philosophy looks for a black cat in a dark room when no cat is there but theology finds the cat anyway. This doesn't speak well of either philosophy or theology, but there is a small grain of truth to the witticism. Philosophy and theology often repel us by their obscurity, their hairsplitting distinctions, their bamboozling abstractions.

Yet it is nearly impossible to stop thinking about the problems discussed by philosophy and theology: God, freedom, immortality, ethics—subjects that empirical science can't handle. These are the "eternal questions" that demand an answer from us, no matter how shaky and unenlightened that answer may be.

Take, for example, the problem of life itself. If you're reading this page, Agnos, I assume you're still alive. Why are you still alive? Why haven't you committed suicide today? What purpose do you have in continuing to live? I assume you have some purpose, however feeble. But you can't answer the question, "Why live?" without getting into philosophy. We *must* philosophize, whether Christian or agnostic, because life requires thinking and the good life requires good thinking.

My motto on this question is: "I act, therefore, I hope." All of us act. Activity requiring decision fills the entire day. Decisions imply value judgments. You can't discuss values without philosophy. The fact that you continue to act shows that you really down deep believe in the validity of philosophy.

"I act, therefore, I hope." Hope what? I hope to know, to understand. I hope that my actions are correct. I hope my value judgments are right. You can't choose not to act, unless you become catatonic or commit suicide. Therefore, life per se requires philosophy. Action dooms you to think, to judge, to evaluate. Few sceptics allow their scepticism to keep them from acting.[2]

Now, if you admit that right logic is necessary, even in the unbeliever's life, you must finally conclude that truth exists, because

1. *Invitation to Pilgrimage* (New York: Scribner, 1942), p. 23.

2. Of course, I suppose I shouldn't overlook the possibility of some existential Tertullian who would say: "I act, because it is absurd!"

thinking can't go on without this postulate. We say we are beginning a journey to find the truth, but really you can't even begin such a journey unless you already have *some* truth. You can't seek truth without finding it in some sense. Of course, mere seeking doesn't prove that you have the *whole* truth about everything, but starting to seek does prove that you have some truth.

Ponder this question: With what do I seek truth? A proper method or an improper method? Hopefully with a proper method and thus if your method is proper you have some truth already. Even if you try to avoid truth you find it anyway. For you would have to ask: Did I avoid it *truthfully?* If you did, you have a measure of truth in your method. If not, then your avoidance wasn't successful and you found truth rather than avoiding it. Strange, isn't it? Even avoiding truth is a way of finding it.

What is this thing, truth, that you find even if you try to avoid it? It reminds me of God, the Hound of Heaven, who won't let you alone. It chases you day and night. There is no way to escape its vigilant pursuit, except by catatonia or suicide.

Another way of making this same point, Agnos, is to say that you can't possibly be a complete sceptic. A total sceptic must say: "There is no truth at all," which is impossible to affirm because the proposition itself claims to be true. You'd be saying: "It is a truth that there are no truths." If there are no truths, then the proposition as a whole is false. The assertion destroys itself. A sceptic can't even affirm his scepticism without undercutting himself.

What would you think, for instance, if a dog came up to you and said: "Dogs don't talk"? Immediately you would know something was wrong. How could a dog say anything if dogs don't talk? The proposition itself must be false in order for the dog to utter the proposition. The same is true for the total sceptic; his scepticism must be false in order for him to assert any true proposition. As Aristotle showed long ago, the most the sceptic can do, to remain consistent, is to believe his scepticism but to remain silent. The moment he begins to preach, he gets into trouble.

Note the similarity between the Christian and the sceptic: both have a viewpoint they think is true, both assert it, and both, because they preach, must accept the necessity of philosophy. Both are inconsistent if they preach while denying the need for philosophy.

Only the total sceptic, however, is guilty of contradiction. There is another brand of scepticism where a man says, "I know a little truth, but am very ignorant about many other things." Well, welcome to the club, Agnos! If this is your scepticism, then all of us are sceptics. This brand of scepticism is no different from the reverent agnosticism we complimented in the last chapter. Scepticism in this sense is an admirable starting point for our intellectual inquiry. Scepticism in this sense doesn't deny the need for philosophy.

You can't escape it, Agnos. *Life requires philosophy!* Socrates once said: "The unexamined life is not worth living." I agree, and I add: "The unexamined faith is not worth believing." Now that we both agree on the value of examination, let's press on and examine the problem of faith. Our motto from now on will be: "Come, now let us reason together, says the Lord" (Isa. 1:18).

Suggestions for Further Reading

E. J. Carnell, *An Introduction to Christian Apologetics* (Grand Rapids: Eerdmans, 1948), chs. 2, 3.

Rem B. Edwards, *Reason and Religion* (New York: Harcourt, Brace Jovanovich, 1972), chs. 3-5.

E. L. Miller, *God and Reason* (New York: Macmillan, 1972), chs. 1, 8.

Alan Richardson, *Christian Apologetics* (New York: Harper and Row, 1974), ch. 1.

David E. Trueblood, *Philosophy of Religion* (New York: Harper and Row, 1957; Baker, 1973 [reprint]), ch. 1.

Donald A. Wells, *God, Man, and the Thinker* (New York: Dell, 1962), chs. 6, 9.

THE ANATOMY OF FAITH

If my last chapter was a success, Agnos, we're now ready to argue. One of the most basic problems unbelievers face is the nature of faith—not just Christian faith but faith in general. If truth is possible and debate can help us reach it, one reasons, then we can have none of this irrational thing called faith. Faith always goes beyond proof; it is a leap, an unjustified leap, into a region where we know nothing for sure.

Our discussion must begin, therefore, with a careful definition of faith. The word has gotten into a lot of trouble lately, as words often do. "Faith" isn't a stained-glass word, reserved only for religious use. True, the word is essential to religion, but only because it is essential to life. In the last chapter we argued that life requires philosophy; in this chapter we argue that *life requires faith.*

A. THE DEFINITION OF FAITH.

It appalls me, dear Agnos, that the phrase "blind faith" is so popular among unbelievers. Few Christians would ever describe their faith as blind. For about 2000 years now the mainstream Christian view has been that faith is a reasonable trust, a sensible confidence in things like God, Christ, and the Bible. This trust is based on adequate evidence, though it may not be perfect or demonstrative.

An anonymous English schoolboy once defined faith as the "power of believing what you know ain't so." H. L. Mencken defined it as "an illogical belief in the occurrence of the improbable." Ambrose Bierce said it is "belief without evidence, in what is told by one who speaks without knowledge, of things without parallel." One anonymous writer called faith "the boast of a man who is too lazy to investigate." G. B. Shaw remarked: "People will believe anything that amuses them, gratifies them, or promises them some sort of profit."

Listening to these cute definitions you'd think that no sensible man would ever believe in anything. You'd also wonder why most world languages have words for faith and belief. Sadly enough, some Christians fall into the same error of defining faith as if it were credulity. When challenged to give a defense of their belief, as Peter commanded (I Peter 3:15), they reply: "I just accept it by faith."

I can't agree with this. Faith must never be used to cloak ignorance or excuse laziness. To devote your entire life to something you can't defend isn't faith but courageous nonsense. You can justify any system of thought in history—Communism, Fascism, Satanism— by saying, "I accept it by faith." We can never make an intelligent choice between worldviews unless we have some credentials for our various faiths. James Ross is correct when he says: "The widespread 'inadequate evidence' view of faith is entirely unfaithful to . . . the traditional teaching of Judaism and Christianity."[1]

What is the correct definition of faith? Faith is trust, informed trust, reasonable trust, trust based on some evidence. Words like "faith" and "knowledge" are always hard to define because their relation to each other is very flexible and varies slightly from one person to the next. You can define knowledge without introducing faith, but you can't define faith without mentioning knowledge, because faith implies something less than knowledge.

When we say a person knows something, we mean (loosely) that he holds to a truth he can prove in some direct way. We often exclaim: "I know it and I can prove it!" We seldom say: "I believe it, and I can prove it!" Hence, when a person asserts knowledge of something, we inquire into the grounds or reasons for the assertion, which usually turn out to be immediate sensations, direct experiences, or something like that.

But when we say a person believes something, we mean (loosely) that he holds to a proposition that he can't prove *directly*, but that has sufficient evidence of an *indirect* kind to justify the belief. In matters of faith, we usually say: "I believe it and can show good evidence for my belief." Strong words like "prove" and "demonstrate" we usually reserve for matters of knowledge.

1. *Introduction to the Philosophy of Religion* (London: Macmillan, 1969), pp. 84-85.

Hence, faith and reason are not opposites, though they differ in their method of operation. Both seek to discover truth or knowledge. Reason uses a more direct approach, seeking truth by direct perception, induction, necessary inference, controlled experimentation, and the like. Faith breaks into the region of the less certain and trusts indirect means of investigation to get at the truth, such as accepting the research and investigation of other people. Legitimate faith is always based on some evidence, though the evidence is never perfect. Reasonable trust doesn't require perfect evidence, else every law court and every newspaper in the land would have to stop. But faith must have some evidence or it ceases to be reasonable and degenerates into mere credulity and superstition. Faith must remain rooted to factual reality or the human imagination would run wild creating new propositions for the mind to believe.

It may help you to see the matter in graphic form. If you view the problem from the standpoint of truth or knowledge, you would say that faith stands midway between knowledge and ignorance, thus:

1. Knowledge—truth by direct proof.
2. Faith—truth by indirect proof.
3. Ignorance—no truth possible, because no data, direct or indirect, are available.

If you wish to view the matter from the standpoint of psychological certitude, you would say that faith stands midway between certainty and credulity or gullibility, thus:

1. Certainty—conviction based on direct evidence.
2. Faith—conviction based on indirect evidence.
3. Credulity—conviction based on no evidence.

Note, Agnos, that faith, by standing between knowledge and ignorance, certainty and credulity, in a sense partakes of the essence of both. It has some evidence, which relates it to knowledge, yet it has some uncertainty, because the evidence is indirect.

Now, in the interests of precision, I must point out that this whole scheme sketched so far is a bit too tidy. We should fog it up a little. We use the words "knowledge" and "faith" so loosely that no eternally precise definition can be given to them. You really can't draw a clear line between knowledge, faith, and ignorance. It is not at all unusual, for example, for the same proposition to be knowledge to one person and faith to another. In a court of law, events introduced into testimony are knowledge to the witness but faith to the jury. A trained scientist would demand much stronger proof for a proposition than (say) Sophie the scrubwoman. We would say that "Sophie believes too easily." Notice the pity implied when we say, "He was always so trusting."

Reason and faith form a continuum along a line we could call "methods of getting at the truth." They change slowly and by degrees; when you try to find the exact dividing point between them, all you really see is a foggy band. Thus, how you use these words, "knowledge" and "faith," depends on a number of factors: your natural cynicism, your credulity, your reflective temperament, your formal education, your interests.

B. WHAT IS THE BEST METAPHOR?

If the literal meaning of faith causes trouble, the symbolic uses of the concept cause just about as much trouble. Can we properly call faith a "leap"? This question boils down to a choice of metaphors and metaphors are largely a matter of taste. Metaphors don't prove your case; they illustrate what you have proved by other means. Thus, merely calling faith a leap doesn't prove it irrational, if my notion of faith is correct.

Those who call faith a leap are trying to symbolize one genuine aspect of belief: the idea of *momentous decision*. It is true that faith is never forced by the evidence, as is usually the case when we speak of knowledge. Since faith operates in a region where the evidence is less certain, the factor of choice is engaged; the will becomes a participant in the drama. In matters of faith, you decide to trust a certain proposition or person because the evidence is adequate. And since religious faith involves such crucial consequences (eternal life) we seem all the more justified in calling religious faith a leap.

Yet momentous decision is only one aspect of faith, even of religious faith. Another aspect is adequate evidence. Even when you're leaping it is good to "look before you leap." It is very misleading to say that faith is a leap into the dark or into the unknown. As Elton Trueblood argues, you could just as easily say that faith is a walk into the light, the light we have. The light of faith may be a bit dimmer than that of knowledge but it isn't complete darkness. Yet it seems to me a bit tame to call faith a "walk." Walking doesn't convey the serious deliberation involved in religious faith.

Is there a metaphor between walk and leap that combines both aspects of faith, both the evidence and the voluntary decision? Jump? Stroll? Run? Perhaps "venture" is the best alternative to leap, but nothing will probably replace leap in the popular parlance. I think I'll keep using leap—provided you don't say that it is a blind leap into the dark. Faith is a venture based on evidence, evidence adequate enough to justify the decision to leap, evidence adequate enough to create hope in the success of leaping.

At this point, Agnos, I can introduce my philosophy of apologetics. Christian Apologetics is the discipline that seeks to prove the truth of the Christian religion. "Prove" doesn't mean to establish as knowledge, but to show evidence adequate enough to encourage the venture of faith. Using the leaping metaphor, I would say that my job as an apologist is to encourage responsible leaping. I try to show that the leap is not hopeless, that you can reach the other side, that many have done it before you, that the dangers below aren't as great as you think. Beyond this, however, the apologist can't go. You can lead a horse to water but you can't make him drink. I present the evidence; you must decide to leap.

C. THE ORIGINAL LEAP OF FAITH: PHILOSOPHICAL REALISM.

I insist that faith is a perfectly respectable operation of the human intellect. You use it every day and probably don't even notice it. The human mind has a large element of trust in it. It's not stupid to trust, nor is it stupid to demand reasons why we should trust. If you consider children and precivilized men you'll see that the natural attitude of the human mind is, "I'm ready to believe almost anything, since life is so full of interesting possibilities." Of course, as one grows older or more educated he'll say, "I must gradually discard certain beliefs because they fail to harmonize with my experience as a whole." But we never reach the point where we can say: "I never accept anything on faith!"

One of the most trusting leaps we make every day of our lives is in a very sensitive area of philosophy: epistemology. Epistemology studies the grounds for valid knowledge. One of the first problems epistemology deals with is: How do you know there is a world at all outside of your own mind? Another aspect of the same problem is: How do we know that other minds, like our own, exist? We couldn't have social life if we didn't believe that each different person behind his exterior body enjoys a conscious life of his own, an area of privacy into which no one else can wholly enter. I would feel no compunction at all about killing you if I thought that "Agnos" was only an unconscious mechanism or merely a blob of colored shapes flitting momentarily across my own private range of vision.

But the problem is: How do we know this? More accurately, how do *I* know this, since "we" implies you, and I'm not sure you exist yet!

How would one prove the existence of the world and other minds? I mean prove it so that it becomes a matter of knowledge?

The solipsist answers: you can't prove it. Solipsism is the belief that nothing exists except the conscious ego of the person doing the thinking. He argues that it is possible for the entire world to be an illusion which takes place entirely within the ego alone. I myself constitute the whole of reality, he says.

René Descartes thought he had arrived at the absolute bedrock of all philosophy when he reasoned, *Cogito Ergo Sum*, "I think, therefore, I exist." But David Hume went him one better and argued that we must keep doubting and eliminate that "I" and thus reach an even more fundamental thesis, "I think, therefore, thinking exists." Danish biologist Hans Driesch went them both one better and argued that the most we can be absolutely sure of is, "I am something (I can't be sure what) at this very moment when I raise the question." And this, dear Agnos, is the only self-evident truth I suppose that man can have, the only proposition that makes no assumptions, involves no faith.

Thus, solipsism is rationalism *ad absurdum*; the solipsist is so determined not to believe anything except what is obviously self-evident that he ends up accepting the existence of nothing but himself and he is only certain of that one second at a time. I doubt if you are a solipsist, however, because most people are realists. Realism, the opposite of solipsism, is the conviction that the world is really "out there," an independent, non-self entity, outside your mind. Most people are realists by habit, but how can you ever prove perfectly the conviction of realism? You can't, you just assume it because it works and it makes so much sense—much, much more sense than solipsism. But *assuming* it because it explains is what I mean by faith—proof by indirect methods. Thus, realism is an act of faith, a responsible leap, a sensible trust. It is perhaps the first and most primitive leap we ever make. Someone has well said: "Faith is blended with the baby's first food."

Keep this in mind, Agnos. You reject solipsism, but not because realism is self-evident. In the coming chapters I'm going to argue for Christianity the same way you reject solipsism.

D. FAITH: BEFORE AND AFTER KNOWLEDGE.

As we explore the nature of faith, we find it necessary to look at another widely held notion: that faith always comes *after* knowledge. Find out all you can know, and then draw the line between knowledge and faith—this seems to be the popular conception. Get all the facts you can, and then press cautiously into the unknown.

First, let me concede that, in many general ways, faith, informed trust, comes after knowledge. I mean that most people, when they go into a subject seriously, get all the *direct* evidence they can for their propositions and assertions and then make cautious judgments and predictions about the rest, the indirect evidence. However, I can't accept the thesis that faith comes only after knowledge; it comes both before and after knowledge. Knowledge starts in reasonable trust. We have just pointed out that knowledge of the world couldn't even begin if we didn't make a primitive leap of faith and postulate the existence of a world at all, apart from the consciousness of the individual.

Any psychologist knows that all of us have a highly complex filtering system that screens incoming sense data and organizes experience according to an *a priori* pattern. One of the commonest myths we have to demolish when we study epistemology is the idea that there is a *purely given* experience—undistilled, uninterpreted sense data from the outside world. This simply isn't true. Experience doesn't enter the head naked; facts aren't simply given to us on a platter. That thing out there called "world" is all "a blooming, buzzing confusion" until you reduce the buzzing to some kind of order with a presensory filter. All men must learn by attention, discrimination, trial and error, selection and rejection, to put some principle of order into the manifold of sensation.

Even the world of ordinary sense perception is a habit of interpretation, an acquired habit. Your picture of the world is an interpreted world. If you go on to ask, "What is the world really like in itself?" you may never be able to answer that question fully. In the past, physicists said the "real" or uninterpreted world lacks many of the traits we usually ascribe to the world: color, sound, taste, smell. They said these are all "subjective" aspects of reality, i.e., they exist in the perceiving person, not in the perceived object. We lost quite a lot giving up all those subjective aspects, but perhaps, thought some, we were compensated by finally tracking down reality to its lair.

Now, psychologists call this *a priori* filtering system your "perceptual set." All you need do to prove its existence is to go to Australia and compare your picture of the world with that of an aborigine. Or, compare your picture with that of medieval people or ancient people. You'll be amazed at how differently you see that mass of data out there in the world. People in other times and other places will pay attention to things in experience that you don't consider important at all.

This perceptual set, this biased filter, is *a matter of faith*. I mean, it is accepted when you're very young and incapable of verifying it objectively; then it is reinforced and molded in later years by your society.

But you may respond: "My perceptual set, however, is true, and that of the aborigine is distorted." But how do you know? It all depends on your viewpoint. Who are you to say that he pays attention to unimportant things? You may say: "My perceptual set produces truth about the physical world and his produces falsehood." That is a debatable assertion, but even if I grant the point, you certainly didn't have the ability to make that evaluation when you first started using your perceptual set. When you first started using it, you accepted it on trust, not knowledge. Thus, trust precedes knowledge, not the other way around. It is meaningless to say that our "experience" comes before our trust; the reverse seems to be the case. Your knowledge of the world could never have begun without a perceptual set accepted by faith. Faith precedes knowledge and makes knowledge possible.

St. Augustine once said something just like this: "I believe in order to understand." Far from opposing reason, faith allows reason to begin operating. I'm sure that Augustine had many different meanings in mind when he made this statement, but certainly among them was this: you can never know anything from this buzzing mass of detail called "experience" until you introduce a principle of order into the data. Another way of stating the same truth, from a different angle, is to say that you can never verify a complex hypothesis about a mass of data unless you provisionally accept it as true and then test it to see if it unifies the data.

To "believe in order to understand" means to "give the theory a chance" and see if it can make a reasonable case for itself. Data never organize themselves; only a mind with a theory can organize data. In a law court the defense attorney says, in effect: "Let us believe for a moment that my client is innocent and see if that hypothesis helps us understand the facts of this case better than the hypothesis of his guilt." Only if the people in the jury box imagine the hypothesis of his innocence to be true can the defendant get a fair trial. Justice, therefore, requires faith!

Even in psychotherapy the principle "believe in order to understand" operates. Viktor Frankl, the famous Viennese psychologist, once told a girl that "intellectual achievement is preceded by existential commitment." When the girl insisted on a rational explanation for the meaning of her life and her daily tasks, Dr. Frankl challenged her to be mature and to endure the struggle for a while without any clear-cut answers. "If you cannot grasp it intellectually," he said, "then you must believe in it emotionally. As long as I have not found the supra-meaning but have only an inkling about it, I cannot wait until I am 80 years of age and only then dedicate myself to it, but must rely on my vague inkling and commit my heart to serving it."[2] Even in psychotherapy, commitment and trust often precede knowledge and certainty. "I act, therefore, I hope to know."

St. Augustine and Viktor Frankl both had a keen appreciation of the fact that *scepticism really destroys life*. Faith promotes living; doubt destroys it. If you did only what could be proved or what couldn't be doubted, you probably wouldn't even get out of bed in the morning. Your whole existence would be paralyzed. You'd be catatonic. As stated before, the consistent sceptic either goes insane or commits suicide.

E. FAITH AND SCIENTIFIC DISCOVERIES.

Faith, or proof by indirection, is especially workable in the world of science. Scientists suspect the existence of many things long before they actually see them. For example, if for some reason our moon was totally invisible, you could still postulate its existence because it has other, indirect ways of impinging on our consciousness. You could infer from the behavior of the tides and the eclipses of the sun that a body of some kind was just beyond the earth, even if you were always prevented from observing it directly.

Drawing some illustrations from the actual history of science, we note that atoms were postulated long before they could be examined in a direct way. Scientists believed in atoms, not because they could see these basic units on the microscopic level, but because the suggestion that matter is atomic explained a great deal that they observed on the macroscopic level. Genes were inferred the same way. Long before the development of the electron microscope, biologists had postulated the existence of these carriers of heritable material to explain what happens in reproduction. But not until this powerful new eye was developed were they able to actually see the genes strung out along the length of the chromosome. The germ theory has a similar history. Louis Pasteur believed in bacteria long before he proved they existed; he believed in them because of their explanatory power. Two centuries before Pasteur an Italian physician by the name of Francostoro had hypothesized that plagues were caused by unseen "seeds of contagion."

We find a most striking example of proof by indirection in the discovery of the planet Neptune. After English astronomer Sir William Herschel discovered Uranus in 1781, astronomers noted that

2. See Robert C. Leslie, *Jesus and Logotherapy* (New York: Abingdon Press, 1965), p. 62.

the planet didn't follow the orbit they had mapped out for it. They observed that Uranus traveled faster and farther between the years 1800 and 1810 than between 1830 and 1840. They reasoned that this could only be explained by the pull of a then unknown planet, which accelerated the motion of Uranus from 1800 to 1810 and retarded it from 1830 to 1840. Thus, the position of the hypothetical planet was predicted independently by two astronomers, Frenchman Urbain J. J. Leverrier and Englishman John Couch Adams. A German, Johann Galle, made the final discovery in the Berlin Observatory, September 23, 1846. Newtonian mechanics celebrated its greatest triumph.

Pierre and Marie Curie used the same reasoning in isolating and extracting radium from pitchblende and chalcocite. Up until their time, pitchblende was known to contain two radioactive elements: uranium and thorium. But Marie Curie kept observing that something in pitchblende was giving off stronger radiation readings than either uranium or thorium. She and her husband first isolated polonium, which is 400 times more radioactive than uranium. They kept working and finally obtained a quantity of pure radium, 900 times more radioactive than uranium. It would have been easy to ignore the variant radioactive readings and explain them away, but the Curie team held to the faith that has sustained scientists for centuries: *when something exists, it gives off readings of some kind.*

I think you can see from these examples, Agnos, that science couldn't exist without faith, properly defined.

F. THE TWO EXTREMES: RATIONALISM AND FIDEISM.

Sometimes a thing can best be described by the extremes on either side. Often in human thought the truth on a certain question tends to be in the middle path. I feel this is true of faith. Because faith is reasonable trust, thinkers have tended to overemphasize either the reason or the trust. Historically, faith is usually flanked by two ugly gutters on each side. Using Hegel's terminology, we would say that faith is a synthesis between the antithesis of rationalism and the thesis of fideism.

1. **The fallacy of rationalism** lies on one extreme. The rationalist believes that all knowledge is homogeneous, the same throughout, consisting solely of combining what is self-evident. Geometry gives us the best model for rationalism, because there you have the passage from self-evident truths (axioms) to necessary conclusions by way of valid logical operations. Deduction is the rule of the game; squeeze out necessary inferences from necessary truths. It is an exercise in tautology; your conclusions are inescapable.

When rationalism becomes extreme (I call it "compulsive rationalism"), it develops a neurotic passion to make everything in the world a "clear and distinct idea." To use G. K. Chesterton's words, the rationalist "lives in the clearly lit prison of one idea." His mind moves in a perfect circle, but it is a very narrow circle.[3] If knowledge is monolithic, there is no continuum involved, no change in the degree of certitude. Thus, for the rationalist, the unpardonable sin is faith, the tendency to accept things with less than perfect evidence, the proclivity to talk about probability and reasonable doubt. He can't accept something unless it is based on direct evidence: definite truths, definite sensations, clear experiences, or inescapable inferences drawn from them.

Jesus said you can move a mountain with faith the size of a mustard seed (Matt. 17:20). The rationalist inverts the metaphor and insists that you need faith as big as a mountain to move a mustard seed!

2. The fallacy of fideism[4] goes to the other extreme and urges that true faith needs no evidence at all. The fideist scorns all attempts to give even a partially rational basis to faith; he denounces philosophy and human reason as devices of the devil. He insists that religion requires absolute certainty and that human logic can never impart such certainty. Faith is therefore a radical trust in God, not a reasonable trust based on indirect evidence.

It is interesting to note that rationalism and fideism often occur together in Christian history; the extremes seem to breed each other. Tertullian of Antioch (c. 160-230) felt constrained to oppose the Greek philosophy of his time. He said of the Resurrection: "I believe it because it is absurd; it is certain because it is impossible."[5] Later, St. Bernard of Clairvaux (1091-1153) reacted to the rationalism of Peter Abelard (1097-1142) and accused him of "lusting after proof." Luther and Erasmus revolted against the hairsplitting scholasticism of their day.[6] Sören Kierkegaard reacted to the rationalistic pantheism of Hegel. Drawing inspiration from Kierkegaard, Barth and Brunner in our own time have reacted to the rationalistic optimism of the nineteenth century. All the great fideists of Christian history

---

3. *Orthodoxy* (Garden City, N.J.: Doubleday, 1969), p. 20.

4. "Fideism" translates roughly as "faithism." Two other words used in the same way are "pietism" and "mysticism."

5. Some scholars doubt that Tertullian uttered such a ridiculous statement. I agree with Nietzsche when he says that anyone who would assert such a thing really means, "I believe because *I* am absurd."

6. One of the most delightful satires on rationalism is Erasmus' *Praise of Folly*, trans. Leonard F. Dean (New York: Hendricks House, 1946), pp. 95ff.

would agree with Pascal that "the heart has its reasons which are unknown to reason."

I always feel a bit sheepish, Agnos, when I criticize fideism, because people think you're attacking faith per se, when you're really only attacking uninformed faith. "Faith in faith" is not Biblical faith, any more than being "in love with love" is Biblical love. You can't love love; you love some object, some person, e.g., a woman. If you love a woman it is because you're attracted to something objective—her beauty, intelligence, grace, dignity, wit, charm. The same is true of faith. When you speak of faith you immediately imply an object—faith *in* something. And the object must be described by reason, at least in the beginning stages of faith.

And what about the ending stages? Well, that's why I feel sheepish when I criticize fideism. All the great fideists in history make a good point: that religious faith finally transcends (though still includes) the rational, objective, scientific categories of thought. One of the greatest women that ever lived, Helen Keller, was sustained through all her hardships by such a simple, unreflective faith. "A simple, childlike faith in a Divine Friend," she said, "solves all the problems that come to us by land or sea." Many people of like mind assume that Christ recommended this childlike faith as the prime condition for salvation.

The truth is that Christ did *not* command us to have a childlike faith. What he said was: "Whoever humbles himself like this child, he is the greatest in the kingdom of heaven" (Matt. 18:4). Humility isn't the same as credulity or naivete. St. Paul clearly told the Corinthian Christians not to be like children in their thinking: "Brethren, do not be children in your thinking; be babes in evil, but in thinking, be mature" (I Cor. 14:20).

The danger in recommending childlike faith is that children are easily led astray. Their critical faculties aren't developed enough to evaluate dictators, charlatans, and religious pretenders. If the simple *attitude* of faith is all that matters and the *content* or *object* of faith is unimportant, then there is nothing to keep a deeply religious man from worshipping whatever object he sincerely chooses: Moloch, Zeus, Satan, Hitler, Communism, or merely money.[7] If the object *is* important, then you've brought reason back into the picture (I said reason, not rationalism!). If reason is irrelevant, then all we can do is compare leaps of faith. "My leap is better than your leap."

---

7. Here one is reminded of the celebrated phrase of Kierkegaard that a man who worships an idol passionately is superior to a Christian who worships the true God without passion.

G. A BALANCED COIN:
THE DIALECTICAL NATURE OF FAITH.

It turns out, therefore, Agnos, that genuine faith is dialectical, that is, it is a battleground for two opposing forces. It strikes a delicate balance between rationalism and fideism, reason and trust, evidence and commitment, head and heart, logic and axiologic, fact and value. There are several ways you can express this balance. You can say we must seek to be both tender-minded and tough-minded. We should avoid both an undevotional theology and an untheological devotion. Commitment without reflection is fanaticism, while reflection without commitment is the paralysis of all action. Using Kantian terms, we can say that reason without faith is empty and faith without reason is blind.

The rationalist has such an impossible standard of proof that he believes in almost nothing. The fideist has such a permissive standard of proof he (logically) could believe in anything. In the middle stand those who have a reasonable standard of proof and believe in something—that is, they believe in something believable!

The rationalist says: "Cursed are the leapers!" The fideist says: "Blessed are the leapers!" I say: "Blessed are the critical leapers!"

In saying this, I feel certain that I'm in the mainstream of Christian thought. For two thousand years now the bulk of Christian thinkers have held that faith and reason must embrace each other fervently if they are to survive. This was the basic view of Clement of Alexandria, Augustine, Anslem, Aquinas, and Calvin. Our century has seen an imposing phalanx of fideists—Barth, Brunner, Tillich, Bultmann—but I honestly think that their separation of faith and reason can't stand. I think Christians in the main will always come back to the delicate balance I've described in this chapter and will try to work out in this book.

If faith has this dialectical interplay, this constant tug of opposites within its breast, our duty in preaching may vary from century to century. In ages of fideism, for example, we perhaps ought to point out to the complacent people who believe too easily that the things they believe aren't necessarily self-evident, that they are accepted on trust and are proved by indirect methods. In ages of reason and religious doubt, on the other hand, we must shout from the housetops that faith is not blind credulity but reasonable trust based on adequate evidence, that science and reason do not have the key to all mysteries, and that a reasonable man can be a Christian without crucifying his intellect.

If faith is dialectical, we should avoid the fallacy of reductionism, which is the error of saying that something is *simply* this or *merely* that. A rationalistic theologian might say that religion is pure dogma or mere doctrine, while a fideist might say it is merely feeling. I doubt if we could ever prove that there is a "mere idea" or a "mere feeling." Human nature is so complex that it may be impossible to boil it down into anything "mere." I really wonder if any idea we have is totally distinct from feeling. Philip Wheelwright argues that every idea has a "feeling-tone" as a natural part of itself. In the case of abstract ideas, like those of mathematics, the feeling-tone is rather slight. But in the case of ethical ideas (e.g., "justice") the feeling-tone may be very marked. When we think of justice we usually conjure up images of equity in the courts, fair distribution of goods, civil rights. Wheelwright says, "When such feeling-tone is quite lacking, then the so-called idea is little or nothing more than a sense of the words being formed in the throat or being heard in the ear."[8]

Now God is one of those ideas that has a very strong feeling-tone. Anyone who believes only in the "mere idea" of God doesn't really believe in God.

H. CONCLUSION.

The rest of this book, Agnos, is to convince you that the Christian venture of faith is reasonable, that it is based on adequate, though indirect, evidence. In the final analysis Christian faith is the response of the whole personality to the Person of God in Christ. Faith is far more than mental assent to a few doctrines about Christ; it is the "yes" of the total individual to Christ.

When we talk of faith it means something different when used of facts and when used of persons. When used of facts, faith connotes doubt, conjecture, or uncertainty. For example, when you say, "I believe it will snow today," you mean you really don't know but that it is possible or probable. But when used of a person, faith expresses confidence. If you were to receive a bad report on John and say, "I believe in John," it would be an affirmation of trust in John. "I trust the person John, regardless of this report."

Of course, there *is* a connection between the facts of John's life and your trust in him. You *grew* to trust him because in the past he had trustworthy behavior. Most of us don't trust total strangers, sight unseen. However, once you've learned to trust someone, it is considered bad taste to accept a negative report about him.

8. *The Way of Philosophy* (New York: Odyssey Press, 1954), pp. 412-13.

The same is true of Christ. Trust in Christ is based on good, factual objective, historical evidence, but Christian faith is more than the objective evidence. Christian theology treats both kinds of faith, but sadly enough, apologetics emphasizes primarily the factual basis of faith, since most unbelievers think that faith has no objective evidence. This is unfortunate, because the apologist is really trying to lead you to total commitment.

After all the facts are in, Agnos, you still have the final decision. Whether you can step out of the light of knowledge into the dimmer light of faith is your choice. Emerson once wrote to Carlyle: "Faith and love are apt to be spasmodic in the best minds. Men live on the brink of mysteries and harmonies into which they never enter, and with their hand on the doorlatch they die outside."[9]

I hope, good friend, that you don't die outside!

Suggestions for Further Reading

Edwards, *Reason and Religion*, chs. 3-5.

John Hick, *Faith and Knowledge* (Ithaca, N. Y.: Cornell University Press, 1957).

E. L. Miller, ed., *Classical Statements on Faith and Reason* (New York: Random House, 1970).

Richardson, *Christian Apologetics*, ch. 10.

Trueblood, *Philosophy of Religion*, chs. 2, 3.

9. Emerson, letter to Thomas Carlyle, March 12, 1835.

4

THE PROBLEM OF PROOF

When you set out to prove something, Agnos, you need first to discuss a theory of proof itself. Like every game, the game of proof has rules. There is no simple answer to the question, "How do you prove something?" Proof in court may differ from proof in geometry and proof in science may differ from proof in theology. Many thinkers say that "theological proof" is a contradiction in terms, but they're usually the same people who say that faith is a blind leap. If faith is a responsible leap, as we argued in the last chapter, then it's my duty to show that religion can use proof in the same way as other branches of learning. Let's begin by inspecting the most certain form of proof—deduction.

A. PROOF BY DEDUCTION.

If there is such a thing as "perfect proof," it surely lies in deductive operations. Perfect proof means that the proposition you assert, your conclusion, follows necessarily from the reasons (premises) you give. It means that there is no doubt, reasonable or otherwise, about the conclusion.

The word "deduce" comes from a Latin root meaning "to lead from." In deduction you reason from the general to the specific, from the universal to the particular, as in the following model syllogism:

1. All crows are black.

2. Jack is a crow.

3. Therefore, Jack is black.

By studying this model syllogism you can see the three characteristics of deduction that give it its "certain" conclusions:

1. Your conclusion is inescapable if the premises are true and if the
    syllogism is put together correctly (i.e., if it is valid).

2. Your conclusion is already implicit in the premises.

3. No new discovery in the world of fact would alter the truth of
    the conclusion, if the premises are true and the syllogism is
    valid.

If you grant the first two premises of our model syllogism there is no
way you can deny the conclusion without self-contradiction, because
the conclusion is already implicit in the premises. You need only
squeeze it out and make it explicit. Deduction is thus an exercise in
tautology; you work out the necessary meaning of sentences placed
together in a valid pattern. If you had really proved that "all crows
are black," you would have counted every possible crow, and if Jack
is really a crow, he would have been one of those you counted, and
hence you would know he is black without even writing up this
syllogism. Why go through a syllogism to prove something you know
by direct experience? Deduction is based on premises, which, if actually true, make deduction seem unnecessary. Its usefulness, however, can be subtly appreciated only after we have considered the
other method—induction.

You needn't consult the empirical world to use deductive operations. In deduction you can play with symbols all your life and never
tell what they symbolize and still get inescapable conclusions. In
math, which is severely deductive, $2 + 2 = 4$ regardless of conditions in
the world of empirical fact. You can close your eyes, stop up your ears
and nose, tape over your fingers and tongue, dismantle all your senses
and still say: $2 + 2 = 4$. It is certain regardless of whether it is two of
one thing or two of another thing. That's why in mathematics you can
print the answers in the back of the book; there's only one right
answer to a deductive operation. If you get an answer other than the
correct one you missed the problem.

You're now prepared to appreciate a very crucial distinction in
logic: the difference between *validity* and *truth*. People use the word
"valid" loosely to mean correct or true, but in formal logic it means
only that the syllogism has the correct *form*. Validity doesn't prove
that the syllogism as a whole is reliable. Take, for example, the following syllogism:

1. Anyone who eats seaweed is crazy.

2. All apologists eat seaweed.

3. Therefore, all apologists are crazy.

Now, this syllogism is valid, i.e., the conclusion is properly inferred from the premises and the conclusion would be reliable *if* the premises were true. However, both premises are false and thus the conclusion is unreliable, even though the syllogism as a whole is valid. To check validity you need only reduce the syllogism to symbols:

1. All S are C.
2. All A are S.
3. Therefore, all A are C.

Once you reduce a syllogism to symbols to check its validity, you separate deductive operations from the world of actual fact. Now we can see that the vaunted certainty of deduction is a deceptive certainty. It's a built-in certainty, like a self-fulfilling prophecy. You *know* the conclusion will be what it is because the terms of the problem are rigged in advance. If $2x = 10$, you know for sure that $x = 5$ because given the meaning of 2 and given the meaning of 10 and given the nature of integers, x can only be 5. To say something else would be to contradict yourself, and the Law of Contradiction is the basis of all meaningful argument and communication.

The certainty of deduction is like saying that "all good men are men." Nothing in the sentence really startles us because the predicate is already in the subject. When you have a sentence where the predicate is already implicit in the subject we call that an "analytical proposition." Such propositions are true by definition. They are absolutely certain but singularly uninformative. You really don't learn much about the world by listening to redundant statements like "bachelors have no wives," "widows have no husbands," "blind men can't see," and "deaf men can't hear."

There have been thinkers all through history (especially rationalists) who felt that this mathematical-deductive method is the only way to prove anything. They didn't realize that with deduction you never really prove anything in the realm of matters of fact. As Russell and Whitehead argued in *Principia Mathematica*, pure mathematics is certain only because it is a special case of deductive logic and both logic and mathematics derive from tautological, definitional axioms. Logic is very important in giving *form* to the content supplied by the senses, but you can't use logic to prove in advance what the *content* of reality will be. To have reliable syllogisms you must have proper form, true, but you must have truthful premises also. This pushes the inquiry to the crucial question: How do you prove the premises to begin with?

B. PROOF BY INDUCTION.

You prove premises by induction. The word comes from the Latin root, "to lead to." Induction reasons from the specific to the general, from the individual to the universal. It gets down into the grass and counts all those hundreds and thousands of individual cases which make up the evidence for the grand universal premises used in deduction, "all men are mortal," "all crows are black."

The premises in induction are not sweeping generalizations but discrete, atomistic units of observation. Suppose you wanted to prove that the premise used in our model syllogism (all crows are black) is true. You'd need to go out and start looking at specific crows. Your record of observation might look something like this:

1. Crow #1 . . . . black.
2. Crow #2 . . . . black.
3. Crow #3 . . . . black.

    and so on . . . .

In other words, every crow you encountered was black. Would you then be justified in drawing the conclusion that "all crows are black"? Keep in mind that there is a big difference between "all crows are black" and "all crows I have counted are black." To go from the latter to the former is called "inductive leap"—similar to the leap of faith. You can't possibly see all the crows now in existence on any given day, much less all the crows in the past and in the future. Therefore, you have no right to draw the conclusion that "all crows are black." You may assert it as a belief, but your premises didn't force the conclusion. So, in induction,

1. Your conclusion is never forced by the premises.
2. Your conclusion isn't already implicit in the premises.
3. A new discovery would affect the truth of the conclusion (e.g., if you found a white crow it would destroy the conclusion).

We seem driven to a sad observation, Agnos: induction deals with the real world, but can't give us certain conclusions. Deduction gives us certain conclusions but avoids the real world. It has been well said that "deduction has no right to its premises and induction has no right to its conclusions." How, then, do we humans ever get any genuine truths? George Meredith wrote the lines:

> Ah, what a dusty answer gets
> the soul
> When hot for certainties in
> this our life!

Actually, things aren't as bad as they seem; we still get along surprisingly well and survive our threescore and ten years and learn a lot about the world in the process. But we do it by giving up that fantastic ideal of absolute, deductive truth! We survive by learning to believe, to make inductive leaps, to trust reality and our fellow man. If we had to prove everything deductively it would close all law courts, destroy all newspapers, stop all history writing, and terminate all scientific research. *The world runs on probability and faith, Agnos, not on deductive certainty.*

As I argue for Christianity, Agnos, I shall use these guidelines: truths about matters of fact, about the empirical world, are never logically necessary, because logic can't totally anticipate the nature of reality. You can always imagine the contrary of a matter of fact. But the bare logical possibility of error doesn't mean that we should really doubt a highly probable empirical proposition, else we could never argue for any proposition in the world of fact. What we really want, when we ask for proof of a factual proposition, is not a demonstration of its logical impossibility, but a degree of evidence which will exclude reasonable doubt.

So, friend Agnos, you really haven't scored a hit against Christianity at all by simply proving that the evidence for it isn't deductive. No matter of fact is deductive, because in deduction you're only comparing ideas with ideas (A = A, 2 + 2 = 4). But in induction you get into the world of real things—sticks, stones, people, lamb chops. In this world things aren't so certain. When you frame assertions about the world outside the mind, instead of relating one idea to another idea you're matching an idea with an object. Getting an idea to correspond to an object is a lot harder than making it correspond to another idea. Most of the things we argue about in this life aren't deductive—for there is little argument in deduction. Most of our arguments concern the objective world and how to relate ideas to it.

C. COHERENCE AND CORRESPONDENCE.

You can see the distinction between deduction and induction more clearly if we change terms and use "coherence" and "correspondence." In most logic texts you'll find the "Correspondence Theory of Truth" contrasted with the "Coherence Theory of Truth." Correspondence uses induction, while coherence uses deduction.

Perhaps the oldest and most popular definition of truth is the correspondence definition. It says that a sentence is true if and only if what the sentence talks about exists in the world as described in the sentence. Truth is a property of assertions which correspond to the real world. A true proposition imparts reliable information about the state of affairs outside of the sentence. The Correspondence Theory says, "Check the referent to see if the sentence is true." Most of us feel that unless a fact or an event has impinged on some human consciousness it's not truly real. A fact must be caught in the circuit of an ego, it must irritate a mind, before we grant it status as reality. As far as man is concerned, nothing is real unless it belongs to conscious experience.

The Correspondence Theory is the theory of common sense; we use it every day of our lives. Without it we would have no factual knowledge. All the great champions of empirical epistemology— Aristotle, Aquinas, Locke, Russell—have defended it with great acumen. Nevertheless, it has certain difficulties. To begin with, when we say that "a true statement must correspond to reality" that sounds lofty and subtle but it conceals two assumptions: (1) that human observation agrees on most things, and (2) that human observation, even when in agreement, is an accurate reflection of reality. Both assumptions are open to debate. We seem to be at the mercy of our senses and our perceptual sets.

But a far greater limitation to the Correspondence Theory is the simple fact that there is much of reality with which we can't directly "correspond." You simply can't "check the referent" every time you wish. Much, maybe most, of reality outruns our direct investigative powers. Not being omniscient, we must close the knowledge gap with another method of truth-finding.

Enter the Coherence Theory! If we can't correspond with all reality, the only way we can ever escape the tyranny of the immediate and have a worldview—a view of the entire universe—is to round out the Correspondence Theory with the Coherence Theory. (Note the similarity to rounding out knowledge with faith.) It would be wonderful if we could correspond directly with every entity in the cosmos, but we can't. Our only hope seems to be to correspond with some reality directly and the balance indirectly.

The Coherence Theory says that a proposition is true if it is consistent with a long list of already coherent propositions, many of which (hopefully) have been proved already by correspondence. Coherence claims that the ultimate test of truth lies in consistency or harmony within the whole realm of rational ideas. We use the Coherence Theory when we say that a theorem in geometry is true since it fits into a system of other theorems, axioms, and definitions.

Proof by coherence is very useful in a number of human endeavors. In a court of law, for example, neither the jury nor the judge may be able to verify by direct observation the indictment against the defendant ("Jones killed Brown"), but it could be shown that this hypothesis is the only one consistent with all the testimony and the circumstantial data of the case. When the prosecuting attorney proves to the jury that "Jones killed Brown," he, in a sense, makes them "see" the murder, because the murder must have happened if all the true propositions in the case are to remain coherent with each other.

Proof by coherence is absolutely indispensable in confirming scientific hypotheses. The astronomers who discovered Neptune combined both facts of correspondence and predictions based on coherence. They reasoned that since there was a perturbation in the orbit of Uranus and since Newtonian mechanics explained the motion of all moving bodies, there therefore must be another planet out beyond Uranus to explain the perturbation. They found it exactly where it was supposed to be. Notice the interlocking dependence of correspondence and coherence: a known fact, combined with a theoretical belief, led to another known fact.

The Coherence Method allows you to venture with some assurance into realms not subject to direct observation. You can see by now that the difference and the interlocking dependence between coherence and correspondence are similar to the difference and the interlocking dependence between reason and faith described in the previous chapter.

But coherence has its limitations also. Anyone who would stop with correspondence alone is timid, but anyone (like Hegel) who would use coherence irresponsibly is too bold. Coherence alone can't give you a complete worldview, just as deduction alone can't anticipate the content of reality. It is possible for you to build an elaborate system of propositions that are all coherent but false. Coherence must forever remain wedded to correspondence, just as faith must remain wedded to reason. In case of divorce, we have no dependable worldview.

D.   HOW DO YOU PROVE A WORLDVIEW?

Since Christianity is a view of the entire universe, we're vitally concerned with the question: "How do you prove a worldview?" Immediately a chorus of venerable voices—Kantians, Pragmatists, Existentialists, Logical Positivists—shriek and groan and cry, "You can never prove anything in metaphysics, because it goes beyond experience." I admit that we should venture beyond direct experience only with great caution, but I believe that all the serious questions about life finally involve metaphysics. Life requires philosophy; life requires faith; life requires metaphysics. You can't deal with origin, destiny, purpose, meaning, ethics, values, God, or any really vital issue without going into metaphysics sooner or later.

If you try to handle such matters without venturing beyond direct experience you deceive yourself and those ignorant enough to follow you. If coherence works in law courts, science, and in other fields I see no good reason why it shouldn't work in metaphysics also. Those who say that metaphysical assertions are totally untestable in experience overstate the case; one should say metaphysical assertions aren't *as* testable as scientific statements. The line between science and metaphysics, like the line between reason and faith, turns out to be a foggy band instead of a line.

Realizing how cautious we must be in venturing beyond experience, I feel constrained to offer some guidelines for evaluating and choosing worldviews.[1]

1. We must realize that there's no such thing as a "neutral worldview," a metaphysic that all would agree to as "basic" to anything else. Worldviews may cover the same data, but qua worldviews they are mutually exclusive. There's no way to have a synthesis between (say) theism and naturalism; they are eternally antithetical.

Further, there's no such thing as a "lowest common denominator" worldview, a boiled-down objective view of the phenomenal world that "all thinkers really believe in." Worldviews are like glasses and we all have a pair in front of our eyes, through which we view the cosmos. Take off your glasses and all you see is a big blur, thousands of bare facts in a mass, with no meaning. Reality resembles "a blooming, buzzing confusion" if you try to see, philosophically or scientifically, without any glasses.

Remember our discussion of the "perceptual set," Agnos? No one sees everything in the world outside; what you select to see is determined by your individual perceptual set. And there is no "neutral" set, because this would mean a set that lets in everything without discrimination. The best we can do is compare our worldviews with each other, not with some mythical neutral metaphysic.

2. A good worldview should have a high degree of coherence or internal consistency. One of the quickest ways to kill a system is to show self-contradiction, as we did with total scepticism. It's like being killed with a hatpin stuck through the heart; the wound is tiny but death is just as certain. If, for example, your system affirms both

1. It would be nice if we had a verb to stand for the phrase, "go into metaphysics." Maybe we should coin one, like "metaphysicize" (the "c" is pronounced hard, like a "k").

determinism and free will you have a problem; you'll need some fancy footwork to show how both can be true at the same time.

I say a good worldview should have "a high degree of consistency"—why not say "perfect consistency"? I'm not sure any mortal could ever achieve perfect consistency, especially in dealing with the whole universe! Emerson once quipped: "A foolish consistency is the hobgoblin of little minds, adored by little statesmen, philosophers, and divines. With consistency a great soul has simply nothing to do."

This is much too strong. If by "foolish consistency" Emerson meant "perfect coherence" then I agree. But I hesitate to demean consistency altogether, for it is a prime criterion of truth. Thinkers have tried to work out many alternative logical systems since Aristotle, but none has come up with one that could dispense with consistency. The Law of Contradiction is basic, even to discussing worldviews; I really don't think we can ever transcend it. If I find an egregious contradiction in a system, this makes me want to look at another system. Christianity has some incoherent portions, I admit, but I hope to reduce some of them to paradoxes and show that the others are relatively unimportant.

3. **A good worldview will have a strong foundation in correspondence; it will have factual support.** Furthermore, it will include all kinds of data. It will seek to *consider* and *explain* facts from all areas of reality. It will show no favoritism by preferring physical facts to psychological facts, or objective data to subjective data, or material reality to spiritual reality. For a metaphysician to write off an entire bloc of reality as irrevelant would be as reprehensible as a defense lawyer saying to the jury, "Anyone who testifies against my client is by definition a liar!"

We have no right to prejudge the case by saying that one particular kind of fact is more important or more fundamental or more true or more real than another kind of fact. A good worldview will seek to integrate all kinds of data into a meaningful, coherent picture. If we subordinate one area of reality to another, we must give a very good reason for doing so. We must prove that subordination makes sense, i.e., creates a more coherent view of all the data.

4. **A good worldview has explanatory power.** You needn't *see* a theory for it to be a good theory; you need only see that it integrates and explains the facts you *can* see. We never have progress in knowledge until we go beyond the facts to explanatory postulates, theories, hypotheses that unite the facts. A good scientist is a thinker who is able to get on top of the facts; he constructs a vision, a model, a

picture, a paradigm, a scheme of interpretation that shows us what the bare facts prove. Facts never really "speak for themselves," as our cliché has it; facts speak only for a theory.

When you get to metaphysics, the subject is so vast and the problem is so far removed from simple observations and simple control of the data you become poignantly aware of the need for the Coherence Method. Metaphysics will never be as certain as physics, but this doesn't mean that metaphysicians just take wild shots in the dark. We accept metaphysical systems because of their explanatory power, not because the systems themselves can be perfectly verified. Worldviews recommend themselves by their clarity, consistency, coherence, and power to interpret. A Marxist historian would say that Marxism helps him make more sense out of history than any other view. A Freudian psychologist would say that Freud's view of man gives him a deeper and more consistent insight into man than competing views.

I'm a Christian, Agnos, because Christian theism illuminates more of reality for me than naturalism. As C. S. Lewis well observed, we Christians believe in God for the same reason we believe in the sun—not because we can see it directly, but because without it we can't see anything at all.

5. All worldviews use circular reasoning sooner or later. On the metaphysical level circular reasoning isn't a fallacy, as it is on the physical level.[2] Building a worldview is like proving a case in court—the whole point is to prove what you originally assumed. Both the lawyer and the metaphysician are *given* a thesis to defend to see if it unites and explains a complex web of data. Thus, to end up with the thesis you started with is certainly not fallacious; in fact, it's a basic rule of the game. As A. N. Whitehead said, "The true method of philosophical construction is to frame a scheme of ideas, the best that one can, and unflinchingly to explore the interpretation of experience in terms of that scheme."[3]

In many philosophical discussions we must beg *some* questions. This means simply that most of our arguments begin with premises. Unless something is self-evident then nothing can ever be proved and argumentation on any question can never begin. You can never prove even the simplest thing in life from scratch. Just try it and see if you don't wind up appealing to something "behind" or "under" the thing you try to prove. It isn't wrong to start an argument with unproved

2. A common instance of circular reasoning is called "begging the question," which is assuming the thing to be proved as proof of itself. Often it consists of merely restating in the premises what is already in the conclusion (e.g., "this is good because it's not bad").

3. *Process and Reality* (New York: Macmillan, 1967), p.x.

premises or assumptions; what is wrong is to hold to them even when they've proved to have poor explanatory power. It's not wrong to grind your ax; what is wrong in this serious game of worldviews is to keep on grinding it after you know that your poor metal won't sharpen.

6. **A good worldview will avoid two extremes:** *Occam's Razor* and *Reductionism.* This means a good worldview will be neither too simple nor too complex. Late medieval philosopher William of Occam (1300-1349) is supposed to have said, "Do not multiply entities without necessity," which means, "Don't make your explanatory postulate too complex." If your theory gets too complex, Occam's Razor will cut it off. This is surely a good rule to follow—up to a point. We should never conjure up unnecessary things to explain a body of data when a simpler theory will integrate the data just as well.

But you can carry this "principle of parsimony" too far, because simplicity isn't the only criterion for a good hypothesis. Comprehensiveness is also important. If your theory is so simple that it leaves some data totally unexplained then your razor has overreacted. For example, let's describe something simple, like an apple. Think of all the features of an apple and then look at the following descriptive sentences:

1. An apple is a round object.
2. An apple is a round, slick object.
3. An apple is a round, slick, sweet object.
4. An apple is a round, slick, sweet, red object.

Now, statement #4 is obviously the most reliable description of the apple—yet it's also the most complex. Statement #1 is the simplest—yet the most inadequate! It commits the Fallacy of Reductionism, the extreme to Occam's Razor. You commit the Reductive Fallacy when you "reduce" a complex set of data to only one aspect, thus neglecting or leaving unexplained a portion of the facts. An apple clearly has more qualities than just roundness. Christians feel that man is more than just a "mere animal," or a "blob of matter," and hence we feel that naturalism is guilty of reductionism when it asserts this. In the coming chapters I'll try to prove (1) that naturalism commits the Reductive Fallacy and (2) that Christianity doesn't run afoul of Occam's Razor.

7. A good worldview is established, not by one line of evidence, or by one knock-out argument, but by cumulative evidence, by converg-

ing lines from several sources of data. A skillful metaphysician builds up his case by showing that his theory explains material from several divergent sources. Like the separate strands of a rope, his converging lines of evidence combine to strengthen the central theory. The view that has the most strands, other things being equal, is the strongest view.

To vary the metaphor, a good worldview resembles a stage production and the metaphysician is the stage manager. One by one, he clicks on a series of cross-lights, placed at different angles around the stage. The full illumination from all of the lights falls on the center of the stage. When all the lights are on, you're supposed to "see" his assertion in the center of the stage.

8.   A good worldview does not have to be perfect to be held by reasonable men. There is no perfect worldview; they're all more or less adequate explanations of reality. Like Plato, we must take the best and most irrefragable of human theories, and let this be the "raft" upon which we sail through life.[4] Every worldview has a few loose ends, a few bits of data left unexplained, just as every big court case has a few uncoordinated facts scattered here and there. What British lawyer John Sparrow wrote of court cases can also apply to worldviews:

> Every lawyer knows that in a big and complicated case there is always, at the end of it, a residue of improbable, inexplicable fact. You do not invalidate a hypothesis by showing that the chances were against the occurrence of some of the events that it presupposes: many things that happen are actuarially improbable, but they happen.[5]

If you decide not to choose a worldview until a perfect one comes along, then you'll never choose one. You'll have to lapse back into agnosticism. You'll be inconsistent, of course, because life still requires action, action requires valuation, and valuation requires metaphysics.

**9.   **Finally, it's imperative for us to note that a good worldview is neither established nor falsified by mere experience or mere details—necessarily. I'm not saying that experience and detail don't help verify a worldview—they do. I'm saying that, even after you've confronted

---

4. *Phaedo*, 85b.

5. *After the Assassination: A Positive Appraisal of the Warren Report* (New York: Random, 1969), pp. 13-14. This work studied the evidence gathered by the Warren Commission after the assassination of President John F. Kennedy.

an opponent with a superior theory, he can hold to an inferior theory because he (for some reason) fails to see the superior explanatory power of your theory. When he does change (convert), it sometimes resembles "scales falling from the eyes." The conversion occurs all at once and he may exclaim: " I just never looked at it that way before!"

You can see this principle in European intellectual history. Herbert Butterfield points out that modern scientific mentality was born not because a mass of new data forced people to look at the universe in a way different from medieval people. No, long before the telescope and the microscope were invented, the big change had already taken place inside the scientists' mind, the change of perspective. "Of all forms of mental activity," says Butterfield,

> the most difficult to induce even in the minds of the young, who may be presumed not to have lost their flexibility, is the art of handling the same data as before, but placing them in a new system of relations with one another by giving them a different framework, all of which virtually means putting on a different kind of thinking-cap for the moment.[6]

Put on a different thinking cap—for the moment! That's perhaps the most basic rule in the game of choosing worldviews. Or, to use my favorite metaphor: try on another set of glasses. See if my spectacles make more sense of the world than yours. Assume, for the span of this book, that Christian theism is true and see if it makes a better case for all the facts than naturalism. The rest of this study, Agnos, will be devoted to marshalling evidence for the Christian glasses. Please keep reading, because if you stop now you may never know what reality would look like through another set of glasses.

Suggestions for Further Reading

Gordon Clark, *Christian View of Men and Things* (Grand Rapids: Eerdmans, 1947).

D. M. Emmet, *The Nature of Metaphysical Thinking* (London, 1945).

Harold Larrabee, *Reliable Knowledge* (Boston: Houghton Mifflin, 1945).

Ernest Mortenson, *You Be the Judge* (New York: Longmans, Green, and Co., 1940).

Bernard Ramm, *The God Who Makes a Difference* (Waco: Word Books, 1972), chs. 2-4.

W. H. Walsh, *Metaphysics* (New York: Harcourt, Brace and World, 1963).

Wells, *God, Man, and the Thinker*, ch. 9.

---

6. *Origins of Modern Science* (New York: Free Press, 1957), p. 13.

A GLANCE AT NATURALISM

Before we look through the Christian glasses, Agnos, it would be in keeping with a rational inquiry to compare the glasses of another worldview, naturalism. Knowing about naturalism in advance will allow us to make some helpful comparisons and contrasts later when we unfold the view of Christian theism. Both naturalists and theists have a bad habit of presenting their views as if they were physics and not metaphysics, knowledge and not faith. A. N. Whitehead called this the "Fallacy of Misplaced Concreteness," which is the tendency to treat our theories as if they were as directly evident to us as the facts they claim to explain. From my own experience I can say that naturalists tend to commit this fallacy more than theists. The primary purpose of this chapter is to present the tenets of naturalism and to show that naturalism is a worldview, not a simple fact of laboratory science, a metaphysic, not physics.

A. THE ANATOMY OF NATURALISM.

There is a logical reason for glancing at naturalism first; it is a simpler hypothesis than theism. It affirms nature or matter and then stops; the theist adds God to nature. Quite naturally, then, if naturalism commits a fallacy it will be the Reductive Fallacy; and, if theism has a problem, it will be with Occam's Razor. It makes sense, therefore, to look at the simpler worldview first.

There are many ways to analyze a worldview, but perhaps the best is to show how it answers certain basic metaphysical questions. Metaphysics is a study of reality as a whole, the science of being per se. Any worldview will provide answers to such broad questions as: What is being? What are its features? Where did it come from? What will it become? What are the processes that transpire within it? and What causes these processes? Let's take up some of these questions and see how naturalism seeks to answer them.

1.   **What is being?** A naturalist feels that nature is the whole show. All reality is simply and merely nature. Negatively, this means that there is no super-nature or extra-nature, no realm that escapes or transcends nature. The universe of nature is the sum of reality and there is no "other universe."

But this sounds as if you're talking in circles and saying, "Reality is reality," "Being is being." You need another feature of nature to bring precision into this picture. I can believe in God and still say, "All reality is nature." All I need do is to define God in such a way as to be a part of nature, as some pantheists do. The simple assertion, "Reality is nature," doesn't really exclude God.

The naturalist, warming to his task, improves his definition by saying that nature is the space-time universe. But even this added characteristic doesn't suffice to absolutely exclude God. Some systems of pantheism and panentheism easily include space and time in their definitions of God. Maybe the second question will be more exclusive.

2.   **Where did being come from?** The naturalist answers: from nowhere, or, better, from itself. He says the natural universe is eternal. When we call something eternal we mean it is uncreated, pre-existent, self-sufficient, indestructible. Something eternal needs no explanation; its origin is itself. So, you need no supernatural being to create nature, since nature accounts for itself. Something exists, and this something could not have come from nothing; therefore, it has always existed. Both naturalism and theism usually agree with this argument. The naturalist says the Eternal Something is nature; the theist says it is God.

But we still haven't defined reality tightly enough to exclude God. If God is eternal and a part of nature (being) then we can still have him as a possibility. Perhaps question three will be more exclusive.

3.   **What about the processes of reality?** The naturalist further tightens his case by asserting that all events in this natural universe are natural events (how could they be anything else if all is nature?). Every occurrence in the space-time cosmos is caused by an antecedent space-time event. In other words, there are no miracles or special acts of God.

But even this qualification doesn't exclude God. It can't exclude the brand of theism called deism, because the deist denies that God works miracles in the first place. Even many who believe in miracles would deny that a miracle is caused by some "unnatural" process; God's way of working miracles is just as "natural" as his way of causing a normal event. A Christian can say, "Natural events have natural causes," and still not become a naturalist! No, it's only when we reach question four that a genuine exclusion of God occurs.

4. What are the features of being? Naturalism says that all of nature is impersonal and non-axiological.[1] This definitely excludes God. There is no mind or designer either within or outside of nature. Whatever order, symmetry, or teleology nature may have comes solely from within nature. Furthermore, whatever values men may cherish are strictly human; the universe as a whole is non-axiological. The cosmos as a whole is neither good nor evil, beautiful nor ugly. The naturalist warns that we must beware of anthropomorphism in metaphysics; we mustn't attribute anything to nature that comes solely from human experience: love, morality, intelligence, or purpose. Nature as a whole has no personality traits.

I want you to note carefully, Agnos, that naturalism couldn't frame a definition that absolutely excluded God until it came to question four and then denied personality and axiology to the whole universe. The consequences of this denial will become clear later.

So far we see that naturalism affirms that (1) nature is the whole of reality, (2) nature is eternal, (3) natural events have natural causes, and (4) nature is impersonal and non-axiological. These four principles define, very broadly, the family traits of naturalism. We should note also that naturalism favors a particular epistemology, as do most worldviews. Naturalists usually feel that the scientific method is the only rational method for finding truth. Moreover, the only kind of truth a naturalist will usually admit into his worldview is scientific truth.

But exactly what is the scientific method and what is a scientific truth? We get no consistent answer to these questions from naturalists. Some take a narrow, empirical definition of science, while others have a broader meaning that allows more speculation, imagination, and coherence. As I argued in the previous chapter, the only way you can really discuss worldviews is to take the broader definition of

---

1. Axiology, one of the major branches of philosophy, is the study of values. It has two major subdivisions, ethics, the study of normative behavior, and aesthetics, the study of beauty.

scientific method, which includes both correspondence and coherence. Then the phrase, "only scientific method produces knowledge," means something so broad that it's roughly equivalent to "you must be rational." Broadly defined, science means simply knowledge, achieved by all legitimate means.

B. ARGUMENTS FOR NATURALISM

Many great and impressive thinkers through history have been naturalists: Democritus, Lucretius, Santayana, Russell, Dewey, Randall, Hook, Marx, Hobbes. One would think that the evidence for naturalism was well-nigh demonstrative. When you look at some of the arguments given, however, you realize that it is just another worldview, assumed because of its explanatory power. "I believe in order to understand." What are some of the arguments for naturalism?

1. Naturalists sometimes like to assert, or at least imply, that their worldview is scientific, that it has the support of empirical investigation, while any form of theism outruns experience. They picture naturalism as a slightly speculative generalization of science. The conviction is widespread among naturalists that "science is on our side."

The man in the street often agrees with this conviction. He has seen a bewildering succession of scientific "miracles" in the last century: the light bulb, radar, moon rockets, laser beams, the atomic bomb. These are his signs, just as Christians have their signs. "The man in the street," writes Bett, "would be as contemptuous of Einstein and relativity as he generally is of philosophy and theology except for this—he sees all around him the marvels of applied science. Here is real and wonderful evidence of what science can do, and therefore he is ready to take the word of scientists for abstract theories that would otherwise seem ridiculous."[2]

Agnos, a careful thinker *must not* be impressed by irrelevant arguments. *The miracles of science are irrelevant to the truth of naturalism as a metaphysic.* The idea that nature is the sum of reality, that it is impersonal and non-axiological, and that it is eternal can't be proved empirically by any single science or by any combination of sciences or by all the sciences put together.

Any science on earth can be pursued just as well under the worldview of theism as under naturalism, as you can see from the fact

2. Henry Bett, *The Reality of the Religious Life: A Study of Miracle, Providence, and Prayer* (New York: Macmillan, 1949), p. 90.

that most of Europe's first great scientists (Galileo, Newton, Coper-
nicus, Kepler) were Christians. *Not a single science is obligated to
presuppose the principles of naturalism in order to function!* How
could physics, chemistry, or biology have anything to assert about
naturalism when these sciences have nothing to say about the universe
as a whole? Each science deals with only a limited portion of reality.
None of them in isolation makes a worldview; even taken together
they still don't constitute a metaphysic. Where is that science or that
combination of sciences that proves naturalism to be the "scientific
worldview"?

2. Closely related to this first argument is the assertion that theism
can't be tested at all by the scientific method and thus, says the
naturalist, it lacks the evidence from correspondence naturalism has.

But here again the assumption is made that there is somewhere an
experiment or a set of experiments of such a nature that when they are
performed, we can see that naturalism is the only scientific possibility. *What are these experiments?* I can't imagine an experiment whose
performance would verify an entire worldview! The reason I can't
imagine it is that the notion of a "worldview-verifying experiment" is
a self-contradiction. A worldview says something about the whole
universe; but if you had an experiment the result of which would say
something about the whole universe, who would perform it? The experiment couldn't say something about the whole universe because
you, the performer, would be *outside* the experiment. It would be like
saying that you could see *all* of reality under a microscope; how could
you, when you and the scope are also part of reality?

I'm not just carping, Agnos, this is a crucial point. When the
naturalist claims to tell me something about nature as a whole, I must
know how he came by that assertion—scientifically. If you reject
theism because you can't prove it by use of the scientific method, then
you must in all fairness give up naturalism also, as well as all
worldviews. By definition, science can study only occurrences within
nature; it can't investigate nature *in toto* since the whole of space-time
is not an event within space-time.

3. Many naturalists argue that since you can't defend theism by
legitimate scientific evidence, and since the proofs for God aren't persuasive, naturalism therefore wins the metaphysical contest by default. When you have only two worldviews, they argue, and one fails
to establish itself you must accept the other.

This argument has two faults. First, it's wrong to say there are only
two worldviews; between theism and naturalism stand agnosticism

and positivism, positions which say that all metaphysics is vain speculation. Naturalism certainly can't win over them by default, because they place the burden of proof on anyone who has anything specific to affirm about the entire universe.

A greater fault, however, lies in the assumption that one theory can win over another by default, even if you have only two theories. In logic this is known as the fallacy of *Argumentum ad Ignorantiam*, "argument advanced to ignorance." You commit this fallacy when you assume that the failure to establish one side of an issue automatically establishes the other side. For example, if medical research hasn't been able to isolate the virus of a particular disease, it doesn't follow that the disease is caused by something other than a virus. We can only say we don't know the cause at this time. Lack of evidence for one view doesn't establish the opposite view—it establishes nothing.

4. By this time the naturalist may feel a bit frustrated and blurt out: "Well, at least the world of nature as I see it is known by everyone through firsthand, direct, empirical evidence, and that's more than I can say for your God!"

Careful! You're treading on slippery philosophical ground when you say this. You're assuming a simple common sense realism that is highly controversial. Many great thinkers in history (Augustine, Kant, Leibnitz) would argue that space and time are not basic features of the outside world but are imposed by the mind on the data of experience. The common notion that we exist in space-time isn't self-evident; it needs philosophical proof. And the proof of this assumption isn't simple, scientific, laboratory proof; it is highly complicated epistemological analysis.

But, further, this argument again makes the false assumption that something in the empirical world necessarily establishes naturalism. Theists also believe that the world exists, even the hard, concrete, physical world. How could the mere existence of the world ever settle the dispute between the naturalist and the theist? Naturalism asserts much more than the bare idea, "The world exists." It goes beyond this to the metaphysical assertion: "Only the world exists and it is eternal, impersonal and non-axiological."

The theist and the naturalist don't differ on *whether* the world exists, but its *mode* of existence, theism saying the world is created and contingent, naturalism saying it is eternal and self-explanatory. Anytime you have two theories competing to explain the same body of data, the simpler of the two can always say, "Well, at least my hypothesis doesn't go much beyond the bare facts." Of course not, but the whole problem is, can you just stop with the bare facts? Bare facts by themselves don't require you to go beyond them; it's the mind that wants to get "behind" the facts to their meaning.

5. By this time, I think we've thrown the naturalist off his vaunted "scientific approach." If my arguments so far have been correct, he should be ready to admit that you can only argue for naturalism as you would for any other metaphysic. You can't invoke any mystical aura of science to verify naturalism; the theory will have to fight it out in the metaphysical arena.

One legitimate argument a naturalist *can* make is that naturalism seems to be a simpler hypothesis than theism, and thus Occam's Razor would cut off any kind of supernatural entity as unnecessary to explain the data of reality. This is a very possible argument, *if* we know in advance that naturalism is also comprehensive enough to explain all the data. Simplicity alone isn't the only criterion for a good theory, as we argued in the previous chapter; a good worldview will also be comprehensive. Any description of an apple that ignores its color and taste is inferior, though simpler, to one that includes them. The naturalist is now arguing:

1. A simple worldview that adequately explains the data of reality is superior to a more complex worldview.
2. Naturalism is such a worldview.
3. Therefore, naturalism is superior to the more complex worldview of theism.

Of course, I deny premise two. I say naturalism commits the Reductive Fallacy. I think naturalism has reacted to Occam's Razor so violently that it has fallen into Procrustes' Bed! In the coming chapters I'll try to delineate the material that, I think, naturalism overlooks and doesn't explain, material which necessitates the more complex hypothesis of theism. In a sense, the rest of this study is directed against this fifth argument for naturalism.

C. WHERE IS THE ETERNAL NATURE?

You need to realize, Agnos, how very difficult it is to prove naturalism. Something in this universe has to be eternal because something exists right now and something can't come from nothing. Now, if you don't believe in an eternal God, then you must say that some section of nature is eternal, which means it is everlasting, self-sufficient, self-explanatory, self-generating, self-everything!

Where in nature can you find such an eternal entity? Empirical science hasn't yet seen any kind of everlasting entity. Where could I

look to find a self-explanatory part of nature? Sticks, stones, mountains, rivers, islands, oceans, men, nations, civilizations, stars, solar
systems, galaxies—all of these things die, rust, fade, decay, wear
down, burn up. All reality known to the senses appears to be contingent, not eternal, limited, not everlasting.

The naturalist pulls a disappearing act on us to find the indestructible nature. He goes underground. He's been doing this for several centuries now. In ancient Greece the atomists like Democritus and
Epicurus affirmed that all macroscopic reality—men, trees, stones—
are but composite arrangements of invisible units called atoms. The
word "atom" means literally "uncuttable," hence the atom was
thought to be *the* basic unit of all reality. Collections of atoms are
temporal, said Democritus, but the atoms themselves are eternal.

Modern physics has destroyed this belief in the unity of the atom.
We've split the unsplittable. We now know that the atom itself is
made up of such things as electrons and protons and that they, too,
can suffer a mysterious kind of transformation into . . . . yes, into
what? Here we seem to reach the ultimate limits of human knowledge.
The naturalist must affirm that somehow under the elementary
subatomic particles lies a kind of amorphous pure energy and that
this finally is the "eternal nature."

But how can you really say that there is such an entity and that it is
eternal? If all the things that arise out of it are contingent, what right
do you have to say that this pure energy is eternal? Isn't this notion of
a pure, formless energy too abstract to handle—at least handle empirically? Edwards goes straight for the jugular vein when he writes:

> What exactly is energy that is so pure and formless that it
> is neither atomic energy nor heat energy nor light energy
> nor any other identifiable kind of energy? . . . . The
> energy of which [the naturalist] speaks cannot be any
> definite *kind* of energy, which is contingent on the rate of
> molecular movement, nor atomic energy, which is con-
> tingent on the fission disintegration of subatomic par-
> ticles, or any other definite or identifiable kind of
> energy.[3]

Naturalists often scoff at theists because they can't prove God scientifically, but can the naturalist prove his eternal nature scientifically?
No—we find him finally believing in order to understand, just like the
theist. He postulates a pure energy which no one can see to account
for the universe he can see. Whether we eventually come to believe

---

3. Edwards, *Reason and Religion*, pp. 268-69. Edwards' chapter on naturalism is one
of the best brief critiques you can find.

that such energy exists or not will depend, not on the empirical evidence for it, since this is impossible to obtain, but on whether the postulate itself can win over its opponent in the metaphysical arena, where clarity, consistency, coherence and explanatory power must arbitrate the contest.

It is time now to look at the theistic hypothesis and see if we can improve on naturalism. There is a story that Napoleon once asked a famous French scientist, Pierre Laplace (1749-1827), how God fitted into his scientific thinking. Laplace replied: "Sire, I have no need of that hypothesis," a fitting reply for a naturalist. From now on, my contention will be: "Sire, I need that hypothesis."

Suggestions for Further Reading

W. E. Hocking, *Types of Philosophy* (New York: Scribner's, 1929), chs. 3-6.

Y. H. Krikorian, ed., *Naturalism and the Human Spirit* (New York: Columbia University Press, 1944).

EVIDENCE FOR GOD
FROM THE WORLD

I ended the previous chapter, Agnos, by showing how difficult it is to prove naturalism. Science hasn't yet found the Eternal Something in nature. The naturalist ends by postulating a pure energy at the base of all reality, energy no mortal has yet observed, to account for the reality that we experience. It's now time for the theist to offer a counter-postulate to see if he can improve on naturalism.

The question of God's existence is without doubt the greatest question of history. In the *Syntopicon* to the *Great Ideas* program, a guide to the series *Great Books of the Western World*, the editors note that the section on God (ch. 29) is the largest of all the sections, having selections from nearly all of the authors of the great books. "The reason is obvious," say the editors. "More consequences for thought and action follow from the affirmation or denial of God than from answering any other basic question."[1]

There are three ways you can argue for the existence of God: from the world, from man, and from God by way of revelation. These are sometimes known as (1) the *a posteriori*, where you suggest God to explain some features of the universe, (2) the *a priori*, where you suggest God to explain unusual features of man's nature, and (3) the revelational, where God comes to man directly and makes himself known. The first two ways use the Coherence Method; the third claims direct correspondence. The next two chapters are devoted to the first two methods.

1. Vol. I, pp. 543ff.

A. THE COSMOLOGICAL ARGUMENT.

Perhaps the oldest known way of arguing for God is the Cosmological Argument. The argument has many forms, not all of them equally persuasive, but the form which stresses contingency seems to be the most fundamental.[2] Let us state the argument first in the form of a hypothetical syllogism:

1. If there is contingent being, then there is a necessary being.

2. A contingent being exists (the universe).

3. Therefore, there is a necessary being.

This syllogism is valid since it employs a legitimate operation of the hypothetical syllogism—asserting the antecedent. Premise two appears to be certain, and thus the only problem is in proving the first premise.

We can begin the proof of premise one by noting that you must have a necessary being in order to explain anything at all. We are dealing here with the most basic question of all metaphysics: "Why is there something at all rather than nothing?" All things we experience are obviously contingent, that is, they can't possibly explain their own existence; they could just as easily not-be. But something that can possibly not-be can't explain what exists, because it is incapable of accounting even for its own existence.

If something could account for its own existence, then it wouldn't be possible for it not-to-be. Therefore, if we're to have any rational account of things that can both be and not-be (contingent things), it must be by relating these contingent creatures to something which is *incapable of not being*. But this phrase—"incapable of not being"—is just a cumbersome expression for the Eternal Something, Eternal Nature, or the Necessary Entity.

If you deny this reasoning, you're driven to say either (1) that contingent being explains itself for all eternity or (2) that something can come from nothing. The first alternative would be equivalent to saying that something existed before it existed, which is absurd. If you choose the second alternative you've cut the taproot of all philosophy, all reason, all science. You would have to abandon both science and philosophy, for both are searches for explanations and you have rendered such a search impossible. You have violated the Law of Contradiction and we might as well stop arguing, for this Law is the basis of all meaningful discourse. If you honestly think that the world is ra-

2. The first three of St. Thomas' "Five Ways" are all forms of the Cosmological Argument—from motion, from efficient cause, and from contingency. See *Summa Theologica*, First Part ("Treatise on God"), Question 2, Article 3. See also the discussion by Edwards, *Reason and Religion*, p. 263.

tional, intelligible, and explicable, then you can't consistently argue that *everything* that exists is also capable of not-being.

Some timid souls wish to admit the contingency of the cosmos and stop there, but they can't escape the implications of contingency. It would be like admitting the smile but denying the face. It would be like a defense lawyer admitting several bits of incriminating evidence against his client and then saying: "Of course, we need not explain these facts." If you agree that the cosmos we experience is contingent, you are driven to ask: *"Contingent on what?"* Contingency means dependency, and you need to explain on what the universe is dependent. Only when you have identified this is the process of rational explanation complete.

You may ask: "Is there any scientific evidence for this contingency?" Yes, there is, because contingency implies temporality and in the last century scientists have accumulated some very persuasive evidence for the temporality of the universe. I refer specifically to the Second Law of Thermodynamics, also called the Law of Entropy. The Second Law must be understood in the light of the First Law, the Law of Conservation of Energy. The First Law says that neither matter nor energy is being created or destroyed at the present time (the law stops short of a metaphysical assertion). Hence, the quantity of energy in the universe is constant at the present but it is continually changing in form. The quantity of energy is constant, but this doesn't mean that energy is always available.

Now, the Second Law of Thermodynamics says that energy is constantly being diffused or dissipated, that is, progressively distributed throughout the universe. Some bodies are hotter than others, and heat is constantly flowing from the hotter ones to the cooler ones. Heat spontaneously flows from a hot body to a cold body, not the reverse. If this process goes on for a few billion more years—and scientists have never observed a restoration of dissipated energy—then the result of the process will be a state of thermal equilibrium, a "heat death," a random degradation of energy throughout the entire cosmos and hence the stagnation of all physical activity. Entropy says, in effect: let things alone and they will go from bad to worse—iron will rust, flowers will wither, colors will fade, men will die, the sun will burn out, everything will degenerate.

Some thinkers try to escape the effects of Entropy by arguing that a living organism, like man, is a case of counter-entropy, or of increasing order. But a man's life is only a momentary flicker of order, and even it produces more disorder than it creates. To maintain life you must supply it with energy and raw materials from the environment. You must manufacture food, clothing, shelter; you must burn fossil fuels to provide heat and cook food. All this results in an increase of disorder. Minutes after a man dies the cosmos is more disordered than before he was born.

Some thinkers feel that photosynthesis contradicts the hypothesis of increasing disorder, because plants can convert small molecules into large, highly organized molecules. But even here the gain is deceptive. You can't have photosynthesis without solar energy and to get solar energy you need nuclear fission reactions, which result in tremendous amounts of heat dissipation. The tiny increase in order represented by life on earth is purchased at the price of massive increases of disorder in the universe.

British astronomer Fred Hoyle was driven to believe in "continuous creation" (creation of matter out of nothing, also known as the Steady State Theory) by evidence similar to that for Entropy. You must believe in some kind of creation, he argues, because the only alternative to it would be to say that the material of the universe is infinitely old, a thesis impossible to hold when one looks at the problem of hydrogen in the universe. If the universe were infinitely old there would be no hydrogen left, because hydrogen is being steadily converted into helium throughout the universe and this conversion is a one-way process, that is, hydrogen can't be produced in any appreciable quantity through the breakdown of other elements. If matter were infinitely old, the universe couldn't consist chiefly of hydrogen as it does.[3]

What does all this imply, Agnos? It suggests that naturalism is a weak hypothesis. If the universe is running down, then it couldn't have existed forever. Naturalism can't explain why the universe is running down, except by postulating an unseen pure energy, the eternity and necessity of which are under grave suspicion if everything that arises out of it is temporal and contingent. I think you can see by now that the theistic hypothesis has powerful explanatory value. In the past, naturalism has recommended itself to people because they felt that nature needed no explanation; she was a self-fueling machine for all eternity. But it's difficult to hold this doctrine if Entropy is irreversible.

What can a naturalist say to this evidence for contingency? As always, he can fall back into scepticism or agnosticism. Or, he may argue that even though science has never observed energy being restored, it's possible that the present scheme of things with its entropic

3. See Chapter 6, originally entitled "The Expanding Universe," of Hoyle's book, *The Nature of the Universe* (New York: Harper and Brothers, 1950). Even Bertrand Russell, writing in 1931, admitted that this evidence from contingency strongly supports the hypothesis that the cosmos had a beginning at some definite date (*The Scientific Outlook* [London: George Allen and Unwin, 1931], p. 122).

diffusion is only one stage in a huge cycle of expansion and con-traction. Perhaps in a billion years we'll observe the process reversing itself. If he argues this way I can only ask: "Who is using faith now, the theist or the scientist?" All the evidence we have—all of it, mind you—points to a heat death for the universe. If you think this will someday be reversed, then your faith has not a single observation to support it. It's your duty to frame a worldview that explains *presently known facts*, not possible future facts. You can prove any theory on earth by appealing to future facts.

So, we have one argument for God; one cross-light is now burning. Do you see anything, Agnos? Perhaps not, but don't despair, we have more lights. Even with this one light, however, you can't deny that our belief has a good explanation of contingency. We feel that God, the Necessary Entity, the Eternal Something, explains how everything that could possibly not-be came to be. You can also appreciate why we love the story told in the third chapter of Exodus. When Yahweh told Moses to lead Israel out of Egypt, Moses complained by asking, "What will I tell the people your name is?" God replied:

> I AM; that is who I am. Tell them that I AM has sent you to them. . . . You must tell the Israelites this, that it is JEHOVAH the God of their forefathers, the God of Abraham, the God of Isaac, the God of Jacob, who has sent you to them. This is my name for ever; this is my title in every generation. (Exod. 3:13-15, NEB)

The name Yahweh (or Jehovah) comes from the same Hebrew root as the phrase here translated "I AM." Thus the very name of the He-brew-Christian God reflects his non-contingency, his everlasting quality. The great gulf that exists between Yahweh, the Eternal Being, and the created universe, the contingent being, is expressed poetically in Psalm 102:

> Of old thou didst lay the foundation of the earth,
>   and the heavens are the work of thy hands.
> They will perish, but thou dost endure;
>   they will all wear out like a garment.
> Thou changest them like raiment, and they pass away;
>   but thou art the same, and thy years have no end.

How appropriate, also, that this God should first appear to Moses in a burning bush—a bush, however, that would not be consumed. In all the earth fire is a universal symbol for destruction, decay, mutability. Yahweh, however, comes to Moses in the form of a bush that will not burn up, thus illustrating his quality of immutability.

B. OBJECTIONS TO THE COSMOLOGICAL ARGUMENT.

1.   Who made God? This is a very common retort to the Cosmological Argument. "If everything has a cause, then so must God." The person making this objection hasn't really grasped the argument yet. If God had to be made, then he would be, by definition, contingent; he couldn't be the cause of things that come into being and thus would not at all be what we mean by "God." Hence, to ask, "Who made God?" would be like asking, "Who made the unmakable being?" To ask who made a necessary entity is to talk nonsense.

2.   More serious is the objection that the Cosmological Argument commits the Fallacy of Composition, which is assuming that what's true of the part is necessarily true of the whole. For instance, it doesn't follow that just because every man has a mother that the whole human race has a mother. Likewise, it doesn't follow, says this objector, that nature as a whole is contingent, just because each of the parts of nature is contingent.

The key to the Fallacy of Composition lies in the word "necessarily." The fallacy is a warning not to pass uncritically from the parts to the whole, not to assume that what's true of the parts individually is necessarily true of the whole. But the fallacy doesn't say that it's *always* wrong to pass from the parts to the whole. Many times you can draw from the parts a legitimate inference regarding the whole. If each and every thread in a carpet is blue, then the carpet as a whole is blue. If all the parts of a machine are metal, then the whole machine is metal. If each and every part of the universe is contingent, then the whole of nature is contingent. The Cosmological Argument has the same form as these legitimate inferences from the parts regarding the whole.

3.   More serious still is the objection brought by David Hume, who denied the idea of causality altogether. The Cosmological Argument assumes the concept that "every event has a cause" and if this is destroyed the argument will be weakened. Hume argued that causation is a psychological, not a metaphysical principle. Its origins lie in the human propensity to assume necessary connections when all we really see is contiguity and succession. Hard on the heels of Hume came Kant, who argued that causation is a category built into the mind as one of the many ways in which we order our experience. Kant argued that God transcends time and space and we therefore have no right to

apply the concept of causality to him. We can only use the concept of cause to order data drawn from the senses.[4]

How can you prove that causality applies to everything in the universe? You can't prove it deductively, but you can point out that if you jettison the idea you destroy not only metaphysics but science as well. When you attack causality you attack much of knowledge per se; without this principle the rational connection in much of learning falls to pieces. Of course, that wouldn't have bothered Hume, since he was a sceptic anyway.

Moreover, Hume contradicted himself when he attacked causation. He couldn't even discuss the issue without framing the question in this form: "What causes our notion of causation?" Now if Hume ends up denying causation, it makes you wonder if he didn't also deny this denial. If causation has no grounding in the nature of things, then you can't ask any question beginning with the words, "What is the cause of . . . ?"—not even a question about the origin of causation. As W. T. Jones says,

> The argument that purports to prove that inductive inference cannot be rationally justified rests—covertly, to be sure—on inductive inferences about human nature and workings of the mind. Hume's critique of science cannot apply to the science of psychology, though there are no logical grounds for exempting this science from the general critique.[5]

Like all sceptics, Hume could have escaped this contradiction by simply being silent. But then there would have been no attack on causation to answer! So, it appears that we have either a non-existent attack on causation or a self-contradictory one. Either way, it's not a real attack.

4. The Logical Positivist argues that any metaphysical assertion of the existence of God is meaningless, since the assertion has no empirical situation in which it may be verified. In reply, I simply deny this allegation and affirm that empirical verification is certainly used in the Cosmological Argument.

Return, first, to the original syllogism: (1) if there is a contingent being then there is a necessary being; (2) there is a contingent being; (3) therefore, there is a necessary being. As is often true with a hypothetical syllogism, we use empirical evidence to prove the second

4. See Hume, *A Treatise on Human Nature*, ed. L. A. Selby-Bigge (Oxford: Clarendon Press, 1896), pp. 77ff.; Kant, *Critique of Pure Reason*, trans. Norman Kemp Smith (London: Macmillan and Co., 1929), p. 44.

5. *History of Western Philosophy* (New York: Harcourt, Brace, and World, 1952), III, 348.

premise. We establish the first premise by logical analysis, using the Law of Contradiction, which even the Logical Positivists accept. We use empirical evidence (Entropy) to establish premise two, and thus the argument does have an empirical situation in which it may be verified.

I think the trouble comes because the Positivist wants a single limited experience to verify the argument. What he must realize is that *all* being, or at least all contingent being, is a part of the verifying experiment. Because all things in the world are contingent, all observations of them ultimately imply the existence of the Necessary Entity. If the statement, "all being in the world is contingent," is empirically meaningful, then so also is the statement, "a necessary being exists," because on the basis of the syllogism the second is the unavoidable conclusion drawn from the first.

5. The Cosmological Argument, in isolation, doesn't prove that God is personal, intelligent, or moral. The Necessary Entity could be an impersonal being, such as that taught by Spinoza and some mystic pantheists.

This is a valid objection. The most that this argument proves, by itself, is that a Necessary Entity of some kind exists. He *could* be personal, intelligent, and moral, but all this argument proves, if sound, is that he is eternal, non-contingent. None of the proofs from natural theology can establish the perfect God of traditional religion. It will take several strands to make our rope, several cross-lights to illuminate our stage.

C. THE TELEOLOGICAL ARGUMENT.

The Cosmological Argument argues from the *fact* of a contingent universe. The Teleological or Design Argument argues from the *form* of the universe. If anything at all exists you can make the Cosmological Argument, but to make the Design Argument you must have two or more things in a *relation* to each other, a relation that suggests rational ordering by a purposive intelligence. As such, the Design Argument does not claim to prove the eternity of God, but rather the trait of intelligence.

We should note at the outset, Agnos, that the Design Argument is only an inference; it derives its strength from the Method of Coherence. No theistic teleologist ever intended to affirm that he had found God directly and confirmed his existence. The teleologist assembles a mass of orderly phenomena or orderly events and then argues that the theory of a designer is coherent with the phenomena and events. This means that another hypothesis might explain the facts just as well. Each person must make his own evaluation of the evidence. The Design Argument is one of the oldest and most popular proofs for God, and, for some strange reason, even its most avid critics, Hume and Kant, expressed a certain respect for it.

It has been said that the Design Argument is more like a chain-armor than a chain. If you destroy a single link in the armor, we have thousands more to offer. You can only destroy the argument by attacking the armor as a whole. The thousands of links in the armor are the thousands of instances of (seeming) purposive arrangement among the elements and events of the universe.

Just about everywhere you turn in this cosmos you meet instances of natural law and order. In general, the universe seems to be basically friendly to life, mind, personality, and values. Life itself, for example, is a cosmic function. That is, a very complex arrangement of things both terrestrial and extra-terrestrial must be obtained before it can subsist. The earth must be just so far from the sun to achieve the optimum temperature; the atmosphere must be just the right combination of breathable gases; the crust of the earth must be just so thick; the ratio between land and water must be just right, and so on.[6] One could multiply such instances, as I have said, into the thousands, perhaps millions.

A good question comes to mind: Is this type of teleological explanation valid in areas other than theology? Does it work in more mundane matters? The answer is yes. We use teleological explanations in several important areas of life.

1. We use the teleological explanation when we infer the existence of other minds, the original leap of faith. We *must* use it, or else we have no right to believe that persons are anything more than mindless automata. You never experience directly the operations of a person's mind, his emotions, plans, intentions, or purposes; you experience directly only the external behavior of other people. If you deny the teleological principle you can never attribute personality or free will to persons, except yourself. That means that if you deny the principle in an argument with someone, you will be guilty of self-contradiction. If there is no mind or person behind the body, why argue? What are

6. For more detailed treatments of such instances, see L. J. Hendersen, *The Fitness of the Environment* (New York: Macmillan and Co., 1913); *The Order of Nature* (Cambridge, Mass.: Harvard University Press, 1917); A. Cressy Morrison, *Man Does Not Stand Alone* (Old Tappan, N.J.: Revell, 1944); Lecomte du Nouy, *Human Destiny* (New York: David McKay, 1947); William Paley, *Natural Theology*, ed. F. Ferré (New York: Library of Liberal Arts, 1962).

you arguing with? Doesn't argument imply that you (instinctively) believe in the teleological principle?

2. We also use teleology in psychoanalysis. A good psychiatrist assumes that behind the aberrant behavior of his patient lies an unconscious purpose or drive or passion, a purpose that even the patient himself can't recognize or evaluate. If you deny the teleological principle (as behavioristic psychology does), then you can only say that the external behavior is mere objective phenomena with no internal process to give it meaning. The fact that psychoanalysis results in many cures implies that behaviorism is wrong on this point.

3. We use teleology when we interpret artifacts, especially those fashioned by people of ancient times. An archaeologist digging in a Stone Age site may come across a weapon that vaguely resembles a tomahawk, but only if the teleological principle is valid can he ascribe the tool to human ingenuity. In fact, one of the earliest known tools, the eolith (literally, "dawn stone"), is very difficult to distinguish from a rock shaped by natural forces. Most people have such an instinctive use of teleology that they apply it unreflectively to human tools, no matter how crude.

4. It sounds strange, Agnos, but in this case for design science is our star witness. Every time science advances our understanding of the universe, it adds a new link to the chain-armor. Why? Because science assumes that there is a correspondence between the mind and the universe, between intelligence and nature. Our intellects can interpret nature and so nature must, in some sense, be intelligible. A totally absurd entity would resist intelligent interpretation. Just as the speech of a madman would be meaningless to a sane person, so also would an absurd universe defy rational analysis. Science couldn't "decode" or "read" or "translate" nature if natural events were just random occurrences exemplifying no general principles.

Immediately you object that this sounds too anthropomorphic, that it imposes an interpretation on nature that is purely human. True, but doesn't science do the same? Science assumes that nature is rational— but isn't reason a human faculty? We predict eclipses by using mathematics—but isn't math based on deduction, which is a process of human thought? Science is just as anthropomorphic as the Design Argument; in both cases human reason claims to find its own rational constitution mirrored in external reality. The only alternative to this view is to say that there is no real order in the world about us, but that we impose our own orderly thoughts upon the world. This alternative view would destroy not only the Design Argument but also science.

But if you accept the only remaining position—that the world is really constructed rationally—then you can't escape the strong possibility that your mind and the world were made by another thinker, who bound the two together. Since there is this correlation between the intelligible world and the interpretive intellect, it is possible that they embody one and the same intelligence. If nature is, in a sense, like a language which we must decode, then it is very possible that it was created by a mind similar to our own. Usually intelligence can only interpret something created by another intelligence.

Agnos, a good theory not only explains the facts but also has heuristic fallout, that is, it opens up new areas of investigation that permit you to find more facts, which in turn tend to confirm the original theory. The teleological assumption not only unites and explains a vast body of data; it also leads to new discoveries in science. For example, some of our chemical elements were discovered by a man who assumed that all chemical elements were related to each other in a rational, coherent pattern of classification. In 1869, the Russian chemist Dmitri Ivanovich Mendeleev took the sixty-three elements then known to science and arranged them according to their similarities. By thus comparing the elements according to their patterns of similarity, he discovered that their properties were periodic functions of their atomic weights, that is, that their properties repeated themselves periodically after each seven elements.

Using this teleological hypothesis, Mendeleev was able to correct the assigned atomic weight of certain elements. His corrections were upheld by later research. He also predicted rather brashly that the gaps in his classification system would someday be filled. He even predicted the new elements by name: eka-boron, eka-aluminum, and eka-silicon. All three were discovered in just a few years. If the ability to predict is the sign of a good scientific theory, then the teleological explanation seems to be a good theory.[7]

D. OBJECTIONS TO THE TELEOLOGICAL ARGUMENT.

As stated before, Agnos, the Design Argument is a chain-armor and you must attack the entire armor, not the individual links. Remember also that it doesn't claim to be deductive. Any argument with empirical material in the premises can never be more than highly prob-

7. See Bernard Jaffe, *Crucibles: The Story of Chemistry from Ancient Alchemy to Nuclear Fission* (New York: Simon and Schuster, 1951), p. 208.

able. Critics like Hume have done a masterful job of analyzing the argument, so let's turn to some of their objections.[8]

1. It is objected that any universe at all would have *some* form, that is, the parts would have some relation to each other. How can you be sure that this universe bears the marks of special design? Would not any conceivable universe take on the appearance of organization?

It's true that any universe would have some organization, but it's not true that any conceivable universe would be as orderly as this one. I can imagine a universe that is nothing but a giant garbage dump, or a giant insane asylum, or a giant latrine, or a giant torture chamber. Or worse, a universe where life, mind, and personality could never possibly emerge. To say that any universe would be ordered doesn't explain why the world has the order it does instead of these conceivable alternates.

2. The theory of evolution takes most of the wind out of the Design Argument. It claims that the marvelous design in living organisms came about not by intelligent creation, but by slow adaptation to the environment.

It's true that evolution has weakened the argument somewhat, but it would be rash to say it has destroyed it altogether. First, evolution, even if accepted, would explain only the design in *organic* processes; it wouldn't explain the instances of purposive intelligence in the *inorganic* world. Second, evolution may even help the argument, if certain adjustments are made. George Mavrodes states this point well:

> A person may initially think that a wristwatch is so complex and purposive an object that it must have been made by a human craftsman. It is conceivable, however, that watches could be produced in a completely automated factory with no human intervention and that our hypothetical person could be convinced of this. But it does not follow that he should therefore give up his interest in the designer. For if he thought a watch was wonderful, what must he think of the factory which produces watches? Must it not suggest a designer even more forcefully?[9]

Many religious people who hold to the theory of evolution insist that evolution has enlarged rather than diminished their view of intelligent design in the universe. The thesis of purposive intelligence is not

---

8. Hume uses most of the following objections against the Design Argument. See his *Dialogues Concerning Natural Religion*, ed. Henry D. Aiken (New York: Hafner, 1948).

9. *The Rationality of Belief in God* (Englewood Cliffs, N.J.: Prentice-Hall, 1970), p. 10.

destroyed by the fact (if it is a fact) that it took millions of years rather than six days to produce the result.

3. We have studied only a very small portion of the universe and therefore we must be careful in drawing conclusions about its origins.

A good point, but a bit irrelevant. We are obligated to build our worldview on the evidence we presently have. Scientists do it; why can't philosophers and theologians? When he made this objection, Hume contradicted himself (again), for he later attacked miracles on the assumption that the universe was well known in all its parts. In his essay on miracles he displayed no reverence at all for the magnitude of the unknown universe. He claimed that the known universe was orderly and constant in its operations, so orderly that any account of a miracle, a violation of natural law, would be automatically rejected by any rational man.

You can't have it both ways. Either (1) the universe is largely unknown and thus the Design Argument is too ambitious but miracles are possible, or (2) the universe is well known and miracles are impossible but the Design Argument is a strong possibility. As we shall see later, even Hume's argument against miracles misfired.

4. The universe as a whole is unique and without parallel. Its creation is not something we could experience, not even once. No one has ever seen a cosmos being made, so we can hardly compare it with a watch. Inferences as to the causes of things must be based on our experience and the Design Argument violates this canon.

A valid objection, but all it shows is that the Design Argument, like all teleological explanation, is based on analogy. It is based on coherence, not correspondence. But then, so is the belief in other minds, so is the interpretation of artifacts, so is the process of psychoanalysis. If you personally have never constructed a watch, if all watches you have known are products of other minds, then you have never once experienced the connection between mind and product for a simple thing like a watch!

How then could you make the simplest teleological explanation? You couldn't; you would have to be a solipsist and believe that the only time a mind designed something was *when you personally designed something!* If you never made a watch, then you really couldn't tell us that a watch is different from a stone. If you find this position uncomfortable, then you need to show us the point where teleological explanations become invalid.

5. It is possible that chance caused all of the order and design in the universe. In eternity, all combinations are possible, and so it is not only possible but probable that in eternity the elements of the universe would arrange themselves as they are at the present.

The big flaw in this objection is the assumption that you have an eternity in which to arrange the present order. If Entropy is any guide, then you have a limited span of time to get the present arrangement. If you say that the present complexity and order were brought about in only six or eight billion years, you are asserting something that is extremely improbable, comparable to drawing all the cards of one suit from a deck in a single hand. Biologists estimate that the possibility of a barrel of dirt eventually developing into a horse by random mutation is $(10^3) \, 10^4$. This figure runs into millions of zeroes.

Agnos, there is something in most of us—call it dumb instinct—that revolts against the idea of chance being the cause of order. How, in the first place, could chance be a *cause* of anything? Doesn't chance imply that you really don't know what will happen? You can't know what chance will produce, yet it produced law and order, life and mind, personality and values! Is this really rational? When a scientist explains an immediate event, he operates on the assumption that this is a regular universe where everything occurs as the result of the orderly procession of cause and effect. Yet when some thinkers come to metaphysics, to the origin of the entire cosmos, they abandon the principle of order and assume that the cause of everything is an unthinkable causelessness, chance or fate. They assume purpose and direction everywhere except at the beginning of the universe. They start out saying everything has a cause and end by saying nothing really has a cause. Theism seems much more rational than this.

Is this perhaps why science gets into trouble when theism is given up? Can science continue to live, cut off from its original roots in theism? Only God gives meaning and order to the cosmos; science must have meaning and order to operate; mustn't science, therefore, have God?

6. Why not several gods? Many men work on a ship and a house. Why not postulate a family of deities to work on the universe?

This is a valid objection. The Design Argument doesn't prove conclusively the unity of the Designer. Unity and plurality are both possible theories. I would point out, however, that we have the same problem with other kinds of teleological explanation. For example, it would be just as difficult to rule out a "plural personality" theory to account for the erratic behavior of our fellow men. As a matter of fact, we usually hold on to a unified personality theory in relating to our friends, until their actions become so dichotomous that we feel compelled to believe in schizophrenia. Science seems to show that this is a *uni*verse we live in, not a *multi*verse, and if scientists can propose Unified Field Theories for the entire cosmos then the postulate of a single designer isn't too farfetched after all.

7. The Design Argument doesn't prove that the Designer is perfect, omniscient, or omnipotent. You need not have an omnipotent being to account for the finite universe; he need only be potent.

This also is a valid objection. Occam's Razor will prevent us from ascribing any more qualities to the cause than are minimally necessary to explain the effect. In fact, there is no argument or combination of arguments from natural theology which will give you the one hundred per cent perfect Yahweh of the Hebrew-Christian revelation. The Biblical God can only be established by Biblical evidence, which we shall cover later.

8. Finally, the best objection of all is the existence of evil in the universe. Evil is a clear case of undesign or antiteleology. One could scarcely infer, says the critic, that this world was created by a compassionate intelligence.

This too is a valid objection, so valid, in fact, that it deserves a complete chapter to itself, which will be found at the end of this work (ch. 17). If the Christian can't defuse the problem of evil, then his whole case is in jeopardy.

E. CONCLUSION.

In spite of all these objections, Agnos, I feel that theism gives a better explanation of both contingency and design than does naturalism. We have two cross-lights burning now. Maybe you can see something, maybe not. I see something, though I admit that it's just a silhouette so far. We need more lights, and we have more. But even if we stop with these lights, I would prefer theism.

You might say that our problem resembles a big court case. The evidence is massive, the analysis is intricate, but when it is all over, I still vote guilty. I say the universe is guilty of design and guilty of harboring a Necessary Being. The defense attorney (Hume *et al.*) has done a truly masterful job of defending his client against the charges of design and contingency, but in the end we all have to vote. After years of meditation and reflection on the mass of data, I still vote God.

Suggestions for Further Reading

Donald R. Burrill, ed., *The Cosmological Arguments* (Garden City, NY: Doubleday, 1967).

Carnell, *Introduction to Christian Apologetics*, chs. 7-10.

Anthony Flew, *God and Philosophy* (New York: Dell, 1966).

John Hick, *The Existence of God* (New York: Macmillan and Co., 1964).

_____, *Philosophy of Religion* (Englewood Cliffs, NJ: Prentice-Hall, 1963).

Sterling Lamprecht, *The Metaphysics of Naturalism* (New York: Appleton-Century-Crofts, 1967).

Alvin Plantinga, *God and Other Minds* (Ithaca, NY: Cornell University Press, 1967).

Bernard Ramm, *God Who Makes a Difference*, chs. 5, 6.
Protestant Christian Evidences (Chicago: Moody Press, 1954), ch. 2.

Robert Schafer, *Christianity and Naturalism* (New Haven, CN: Yale University Press, 1972).

A. E. Taylor, *Does God Exist?* (London: Macmillan and Co., 1945).

F. R. Tennant, *Philosophical Theology* (New York: Cambridge University Press, 1969), vol. II, ch. 4.

Trueblood, *Philosophy of Religion*, chs. 6, 7.

EVIDENCE FOR GOD FROM MAN

I'm ready to click on another light, Agnos, a brighter light, I feel, than the Cosmological and Teleological Arguments. We sometimes call it the Anthropological Argument, the argument from man. Our thesis is that *naturalism fails to explain man adequately*, just as it fails to explain the contingency and design of the universe. To introduce this chapter we need to discuss the problem of human nature.

The primary problem regarding God is whether he exists or not. The problem regarding man is his nature. Is he totally material, natural, physical? Or does something in his make-up transcend natural categories? How exactly does he differ from the lower animals which he resembles in so many anatomical ways? In 1967 Mortimer Adler gave the world what is probably the most learned discussion of this problem, *The Difference of Man and the Difference It Makes*. Adler lists seven aspects of man that differentiate him from the animals:

1. Only man employs a propositional language, only man uses verbal symbols, only man makes sentences; i.e., only man is a discursive animal.

2. Only man makes tools, builds fires, erects shelters, fabricates clothing; i.e., only man is a technological animal.

3. Only man enacts laws or sets up his own rules of behavior and thereby constitutes his social life, organizing his association with his fellows in a variety of different ways; i.e., only man is a political, not just a gregarious animal.

4. Only man has developed, in the course of generations, a

cumulative cultural tradition, the transmission of which constitutes human history; i.e., only man is a historical animal.

5. Only man engages in magical and ritualistic practices; i.e., only
    man is a religious animal.

6. Only man has a moral conscience, a sense of right and wrong,
    and of values; i.e., only man is an ethical animal.

7. Only man decorates or adorns himself or his artifacts, and
    makes pictures or statues for the non-utilitarian purpose of en-
    joyment; i.e., only man is an aesthetic animal.[1]

I will use these human features as I develop my case for the theistic
interpretation of man. When you read this list, your first question is:
so what? What do these differences imply? Can we draw any
metaphysical implications from them? I believe we can. In this
chapter I will propose a model for the interpretation of man. I will
argue that my model is coherent with these unusual features of man's
nature and that naturalism is an inferior model. The feature I take up
first is the one that to me is the most impressive: man's moral nature.

A. THE MORAL ARGUMENT FOR GOD.

The Moral Argument is similar to the Design Argument. In discussing the Design Argument we noted that science is possible only if we
assume a correspondence between man's reason and the rationality of
the universe. A totally absurd entity would resist rational interpretation. In similar fashion, the Moral Argument postulates a correspondence between man's moral constitution and the constitution of
the universe. Without this correspondence, a successful moral life
would be difficult; ethical man lives in an ethical universe.

How do I prove this? Well, I can start the proof by showing that
man has a "moral experience" which is just as real as his experience
of objects in the physical world. Why do you, Agnos, believe that the
book you're now holding is real and objective? Because you see it and
it causes pressure on your fingers. Now, I feel the "pressure" of moral
duty every day of my life. Just as I find myself in a sensible world, conditioned by objects outside me and to which I can only respond
passively, so also do I find myself in a moral world, conditioned by an
objective *something* out there that really seems to be more than my
opinions and inclinations. This feeling of ethical compulsion is just as

1. (New York: Holt, Rinehart, and Winston, 1967), p. 91. Most sociologists and anthropologists would agree with this list, with the possible exception of numbers 2 and 7.
Primatologists, those who study the primates, claim to detect an inchoate technological
and aesthetic capacity in certain primates.

real as the stone against which I stumble, and it can "stop me in my tracks" just as effectively. Being "struck by my duty" is a common feature of the moral experience.

At first you may balk at this notion that moral experience is as real as sensory experience. You ask, what is causing the pressure? We will answer that in a moment, but the important thing now is to note that there is a peculiar pressure on man to do his duty, to perform normative actions, to engage in proper conduct. If you flatly deny this pressure, then we'd just say you are a moral cretin, that you completely lack the moral faculty. It would be exactly like saying that you deny the physical world; we'd say you lack the faculty with which to apprehend it. You can be a solipsist in anything, if you wish. In other words, the argument for both the physical world and the moral world is circular, that is, it rests on a special faculty of apprehension, in one case of the empirical object, in the other of a moral right.

You can see additional evidence for the moral experience in the positive and negative feelings you have when you fulfill or violate the moral code. If you do something good like playing the Good Samaritan, sacrificing something, helping someone in need, or forgiving some cruel offense, it gives you a strange feeling of exhilaration, what religious people call beatitude. On the other hand, if you do something against your moral code, if you lie, cheat, steal, or hurt, you have feelings of guilt, remorse, and shame. Such positive and negative feelings seem to be universal. World literature testifies to the universality of the moral experience. It is the soul of much of man's greatest literature.

Moralists feel that the laws of this moral realm you experience are just as binding as those of the physical realm. If a man is crazy enough to believe that the law of gravity is open to subjective interpretation and if he thinks he has the freedom to ignore it, he soon learns to his destruction that he can't violate the structure of the physical world without paying a price. In the moral realm also, the rules aren't open to subjective interpretation. If you violate the rules of morality, which govern the relations of free persons, you suffer in the long run a set of consequences.

The most peculiar thing about moral experience is the unconditional claim that duty makes on us when we make moral decisions. Moral choices are decisions, not inferences, either inductive or deductive. If I reason, $2x = 10$, therefore $x = 5$, that is deduction. But if I observe, "I must help my neighbor," that isn't deduction. I don't deduce from certain premises that my neighbor has a claim on me, rather I "see" that he does. I don't create the moral canon, I acknowledge it. When poets write odes to duty and hymns to love, it is this element of unconditional claim they have in mind. When a moral person decides he must do his duty, he says: "I should, regardless of the consequences."

If moral experience is real and objective, we must then ask: What is the source of this pressure? Where does this claim to duty come from? The claim seems to involve the assertion that there are laws, norms, canons to which we are responsible for our behavior. But how can a moral law exist? And where does it exist? If we are not to dismiss the experience as an illusion, we must identify some entity causing the experience.

Could a moral law subsist in a material entity? No, because moral laws are norms chosen by intellectual beings. How could a rock or a tree exert moral pressure on me? Further, if the moral law subsisted in material things then there would never be any crime, since material things don't *choose* to go contrary to their nature. It seems far more rational to say that moral laws can exist only in and for free minds or persons. But we're still not out of the woods, for there are three possible types of minds: the mind of the individual, the mind of the group, and the mind of God.

1. The moral law can't exist in the mind of the individual, because this wouldn't at all explain the moral experience. When you experience the pressure of duty, it impels you to do the right even when it is against your inclinations. We often do things that cause us personal shame and remorse, but at the time we did them we chose to do them and wanted to do them. This doesn't fit with the idea of *individual subjectivism*, where my own private whim is the norm for morality. If the individual alone determined the moral law, you couldn't explain shame or guilt.

2. *Social subjectivism* also fails to explain where the moral law exists. I know the norm can't exist in the group because the group (nation, race, tribe) often sins just like the individual. There is no moral guarantee in numbers. Some of the greatest moralists in history gave their lives testifying to a moral ideal that the group had ignored or rejected. If the group determines morality, then you have no right to condemn the racial policies of Nazi Germany or the practice of slavery in the American South before the Civil War.

3. If morality can't subsist either in the mind of the individual or of the group, what kind of mind is left? Only the mind of God, it would appear. But before we can draw this conclusion, we hear an objection from a certain quarter: why not just stop with an impersonal moral

order? Do you really need to press on and conclude a personal moral God to explain ethics? Wouldn't Occam's Razor prevent this?

A good question. I sympathize with the objection because it comes from one who has at least admitted that morality is objective. I can't agree, however, that we can stop short of God in fully explaining morality; else we would be guilty of reductionism. To say that we must go beyond man and society but stop short of God still leaves the problem hanging. You still haven't answered the question: *Where is the moral law?* If you say that we have an "eternal moral realm" or a "spiritual principle" or a "dimension of values," I still can't understand the locus of morality. Is this realm mental or spiritual? If so, is it then a mind or a spirit? How then is it different from my mind, or from God's mind? To insist on an impersonal mind or spirit seems a contradiction in terms to me.

If you tell me that the reality which constrains me to do my duty is an *impersonal* reality, I can only say that this doesn't at all explain the constraint *I* feel. How could an impersonal reality possibly make me feel duty-bound to be kind and helpful, truthful and loving? I can't see how a *thing* could possess a moral and spiritual claim over me, a *person*. This is why pantheism is offensive to so many sensitive moral individuals. As Emil Brunner said, "A God who is neuter makes no claims."

This means, Agnos, that the only rational locus for the moral law is a person, a superhuman mind, God. We've seen that it must be mind, and we've seen that it must be a mind that is greater than the individual or the group. If God is the rationale for the moral law then my moral experience becomes crystal clear; if not, the experience leaves me profoundly puzzled. It is the duty of a good theory to clarify, not puzzle.

Of course, there are a number of objections to the Moral Argument, and we can clarify the argument by now considering some of them.

1. Most people who deny this reasoning will say, "Morality is so relative from place to place and time to time that you can hardly think there is a common moral law for all men. Ethical judgments are all relative."

First, I'm not arguing that all moral codes on earth agree, though I believe there is a larger amount of agreement than you think. I'm arguing that all men have a basic concept of normative conduct. They have a built-in *should* or *ought principle.* In its most general terms it says: "Do what you consider right and avoid what is forbidden." Even this minimum moral concept shows that man isn't a mere animal, that he transcends mere instinctual behavior. Is there any

other animal that can choose to pattern his behavior after an objective code? G. K. Chesterton puts the point well:

> We talk of wild animals; but man is the only wild animal. It is
> man that has broken out. All other animals are tame animals;
> following the rugged respectability of the tribe or type. All other
> animals are domestic animals; man alone is ever undomestic,
> either as a profligate or a monk. . . . It is exactly where biology
> leaves off that all religion begins.[2]

Second, I deny that morality is so relative. On the surface ethical
codes seem very different, but when you take a closer look you see
more agreement than many sociologists and anthropologists would
admit. C. S. Lewis writes:

> If anyone will take the trouble to compare the moral teaching of,
> say, the ancient Egyptians, Babylonians, Hindus, Chinese,
> Greeks, and Romans, what will really strike him will be how
> very alike they are to each other and to our own. . . . Men have
> differed as regards what people you ought to be unselfish to—
> whether it was only your own family, or your fellow coun-
> trymen, or everyone. But they have always urged that you ought
> not to put yourself first. Selfishness has never been admired.[3]

Historian Will Durant agrees:

> A little knowledge of history stresses the variability of moral
> codes, and concludes that they are negligible because they differ
> in time and place, and sometimes contradict each other. A
> larger knowledge stresses the universality of moral codes, and
> concludes to their necessity. Moral codes differ because they ad-
> just themselves to historical and environmental conditions.[4]

There is something strange in saying, "All morality is different." If
two moralities can be entirely different, why call them both
moralities? It would be like saying, "All chairs are unique." If the inductive units making up the generalization are really unique, how
could you speak of "all chairs" or "all morality"? When the relativist
uses the same word we suspect that he really knows there is something
common to all moralities.

Agnos, I think people really don't reflect on the consequences of
moral relativism. If the statement, "Murder is wrong," amounts to no
more than my subjective feelings about murder at the time, then a

2. *Orthodoxy*, p. 144.

3. C. S. Lewis, *Mere Christianity*, rev. ed. (New York: Macmillan and Co., 1952), p. 5.
For a short compilation of comparative moral codes illustrating the wide agreement on
basic ethical canons, see the Appendix of Lewis' *Abolition of Man* (New York: Macmillan and Co., 1947).

4. Will Durant, *The Lessons of History* (New York: Simon and Schuster, 1968), p. 37.

number of unlikely consequences follow: (1) it would be impossible for any of us to ever be mistaken in our ethical judgments; (2) our ethical judgments would never mean the same thing twice, because feelings vary; (3) no two people would ever agree on ethical judgments.

These consequences would render a huge sector of human life utterly meaningless. Look at any newspaper, tune in on any radio or TV broadcast, listen in on any conversation, and note the frequent moral judgments you hear. Note the words like: "should," "should not," "must," "must not," "ought," "ought not," "responsible," "blameworthy," "reprehensible," "obligatory." Everywhere you find the concept of duty tacitly assumed when people relate to each other. Morality may be ontologically peculiar, you may not like the fact that it isn't empirical and can't be handled by the scientific method, but its reality is hard to deny.

The greatest flaw, however, in ethical subjectivism is that it is self-contradictory. The old hatpin in the heart again; the wound is tiny but death is just as certain. You can't even discuss morality without assuming morality, and therefore anyone who affirms moral relativism contradicts himself. Suppose someone denies the moral experience altogether and asks me: "How do you know there are any moral laws binding all humans together?" I would answer: "What right do you have to ask? Doesn't your question imply that we *should* have evidence for what we assert? Where did you get the value premise that allows you to ask me the question? You seem to be saying: '*You ought to have evidence for oughts!*' But this is the same as saying: 'You ought to consider the possibility that there is no ought,' which is a self-contradiction. If there are no oughts, I don't have to consider anything if I care not to." When a man says we mustn't believe in morality without evidence, he is tacitly assuming that the "necessity of evidence" is itself a moral requirement.[5]

It turns out then that morality, or at least one moral principle, truth-telling, is innate. Even when a person asserts that all morality is relative, he thinks I ought to accept the proposition because it is true. The same process occurs when you establish the Law of Contradiction. When Aristotle tried to refute the sceptics, he argued that you must *use* the Law of Contradiction to even *deny* it, which proves it is self-evident. But Aristotle found out that his opponents refused to see

---

5. I recently received an advertisement from an audiovisual company in New York promoting a slide program for the humanities called "Sound Filmstrips Dealing with Contemporary Issues and Values." The envelope had stamped on it: "We can't teach values, but we must discuss them." If we can't teach values, I wonder what the "must" in the sentence could possibly mean!

this inconsistency. After a frustrating experience, the great philosopher decided that only men of character can apprehend the rational ultimates of philosophy. As always, the most honest thing for a sceptic to do is to remain silent. The Law of Contradiction and the rule of truth-telling both seem to be built into all thinking and into all communication.

When a man won't see his own contradiction, Agnos, he has committed the ultimate fallacy—Pigheadedness. A pigheaded person can't be convinced of a proposition even when the evidence is adequate. His fallacy is therefore moral and not intellectual.

2. Some people argue that since we come to believe in our values by learning and conditioning, values must therefore be relative.

The hidden assumption here is that anything true, absolute, or binding can not or need not be taught because it is innate, possessed by all minds *a priori*, before experience. We believe that there is a presensory moral capacity in man, but even in spite of this admission the objection still doesn't score. The fact that something is taught and learned is hardly evidence against its objective validity. For example, we don't come into the world knowing the scientific method, but that doesn't affect its validity. If this objection is taken seriously, we would have to compare the newborn infant with the educated adult, take everything the adult had acquired by education, and then declare it worthless!

3. The evolutionist has a similar objection. He tries to deflate the Moral Argument by saying that all morality is merely a gradual growth from a foundation of animal instincts. Men gradually work out their ethical systems by living together in social communities.

This objection commits the "Genetic Fallacy," which is a variation of the Reductive Fallacy. You commit the Genetic Fallacy when you assume that something which grows and develops is never more than its original state. For example, a full-grown man starts out as a single fertilized egg cell, but it would be ridiculous to say to a fifty-year-old man, "You're nothing but a fertilized egg cell walking around!"

When the evolutionist affirms that morality is nothing but a development from animal instincts, he assumes that he has destroyed its objective, binding quality. But he has destroyed reason by the same argument. For the evolutionist also contends that the human intellect developed from the physical brain of the primates, yet he assumes that the intellect is trustworthy. If not, what was it that just framed this objection? What was it that constructed the theory of evolution? If the mind, though evolved from lower forms, is entitled to trust, why not also the moral nature?

Furthermore, this objection overlooks the big difference between human morality and animal instincts, a distinction that is crucial to my case for the transcendence of man. No evolutionist has yet given a satisfactory explanation of how a *social instinct* developed into a *social conscience*. Animal instincts are biologically inherited patterns of behavior, and they are carried out automatically without a conscious purpose. Human morality is something very different. Go back as far as you wish in human history, and you'll find that men are always governed by complex codes of behavior.

Now, these rules of behavior aren't instinctive—that is, they're not biologically inherited. Separate a person from the social group and he'll never develop them. Most human behavioral patterns are passed on in social institutions. When you inquire into the origin of these institutions, you are referred to some remote ancestor. These codes are passed on by education, not heredity.[6] You must use human language to teach them. They belong, therefore, not to the realm of instinct, but the realm of mind. You can no more teach a dog the principles of ethics than you can teach a horse higher calculus or make a weasel appreciate classical music. Morality is peculiarly human.

B. THE AESTHETIC ARGUMENT FOR GOD.

You recall, Agnos, that axiology, the study of values, has two divisions: ethics and aesthetics. If you can make a Moral Argument for God, it stands to reason you can also make an Aesthetic Argument. The same God who gives meaning to the moral realm illuminates the aesthetic realm. We could put the two together and call it the Axiological Argument. We needn't go into great detail in this argument since the principles are the same as those of the Moral Argument.

As in the Moral Argument we began with moral experience, here we begin with the fact of aesthetic experience. All men have a "sense of beauty" and they make aesthetic judgments from time to time. If this isn't true, then we have an amazing coincidence on our hands, for millions of humans agree that certain things are beautiful and certain things are ugly. It would be difficult to find anyone, for example, who would seriously affirm that the Grand Canyon, the Swiss Alps, or the English lakes are ugly. It would be difficult to find anyone who would affirm that Homer, Dante, Shakespeare, and Goethe wrote trash, or

6. See the excellent discussion by Benjamin Farrington, *What Darwin Really Said* (New York: Schocken Books, 1966), p. 75.

that Rembrandt, Raphael, and van Gogh painted ugly pictures, or that the statues of Phidias, Michelangelo and Bernini have no more beauty than a dung heap.

Of course, you can be a solipsist in aesthetics as well as in science and morality. You may say that aesthetic judgments are purely subjective, that they correspond to no objective situation in the world. "Beauty is merely in the eyes of the beholder." You may say that, but if you do you drive yourself to the same consequences as those who follow moral subjectivism: (1) one would never be mistaken in an aesthetic judgment; (2) our aesthetic judgments would never mean the same thing twice because our feelings vary; (3) no two people would ever agree on aesthetic judgments.

If you seriously believe that there is nothing in the objective world that gives content to our word "beauty," we would simply conclude that you are an aesthetic cretin, that you completely lack the faculty that enables most people to see beauty, just as a moral cretin is unable to feel the pressure of the moral law. To you, the Golden Gate Bridge would be no more lovely than a crushed beer can; Michelangelo's *Pietà* would be on a par with a child's mud pie; Beethoven's Fifth Symphony would be no more beautiful than radio jamming noises. Most people would find these consequences rather uncomfortable.

I must admit that art sometimes seems to be subjective; beauty seems to be at the mercy of fashion and fashions always change. But this is a superficial view of art. All you need to do is compare several histories of art, and you will see that there is a strikingly large amount of agreement in aesthetic judgment. Any history of western art that left out Michelangelo, Raphael, Phidias, or Rembrandt would be considered incomplete. It is usually with contemporary art that judgment is still in flux. A modern artist may be struggling for recognition, but Raphael needn't struggle for recognition! Sometimes it takes longer for the aesthetic judgment to become stable when compared with morality, but in the end it is hard to dislodge the classic art works and the old masters. Great works of art have more security than many scientific theories.

We will never achieve complete agreement on aesthetics just as we will never reach complete agreement on ethics, but the large amount of agreement we have is hard to explain if aesthetic experience is merely subjective. If art is merely taste, then the large amount of agreement we have is almost a miracle of coincidence.

When you really appreciate ethics and aesthetics, Agnos, you can see how defective an empirical epistemology really is. If the human mind is nothing but a *tabula rasa*, a blank slate, then we would never have any right to prefer one action to another or pronounce one thing beautiful and another thing ugly. If man is just an empty, passive mind with a machinery of sensation to bring in the data, then you could never have any philosophical basis for ethics and aesthetics. Many of the animals have keener senses than we—why can't they make truth judgments, ethical judgments, and aesthetic judgments? Why can't a weasel appreciate Beethoven's string quartets? He has all the sense organs he needs, if sensation is all there is to aesthetics. If the aesthetic capacity is genuine, then man must have something that the weasel doesn't have.

Empiricism, by accepting the data of sensation only, is incapable of establishing norms for anything, much less morality and beauty. G. E. Moore made this point well in his *Principia Ethica* (1903) when he spoke of the "Naturalistic Fallacy," the attempt to derive an "ought" from an "is." Epicurus and John Stuart Mill tried to build ethical systems by assuming that because men do in fact desire something, they ought to desire it. Values, however, can't be established by appeals to empirical data, for such data give only *what* men do, not what they *ought* to do. The norm must come from inside the mind or you really have no norm.

If beauty is objective we are driven once more, as in the Design and Moral Arguments, to certain metaphysical implications. Once we truly understand the aesthetic experience, it appears that we must introduce mind to explain it. Human artistic productions are understood and appreciated only when we feel we have "read" or "translated" the purpose of the artist. Sensitive artists and poets have said the same things about natural beauty. In *Tintern Abbey* William Wordsworth wrote:

> For I have learned
> To look on nature, not as in the hour
> Of thoughtless youth; but hearing oftentimes
> The still, sad music of humanity,
> Nor harsh nor grating, though of ample power
> To chasten and subdue. And I have felt
> A presence that disturbs me with the joy
> Of elevated thoughts; a sense sublime
> Of something far more deeply interfused
> Whose dwelling is the light of setting suns,
> And the round ocean and the living air,
> And the blue sky, and in the mind of man:
> A motion and a spirit, that impels
> All thinking things, all objects of thought,
> And rolls through all things.

If this universe is the creation of an Infinite Mind, a Mind who created both the beauty in the world and the faculty in me for appreciating beauty, then my aesthetic experience is adequately explained. Once again, Agnos, if theism is true, my desire to understand a crucial dimension of experience isn't left unsatisfied.

C. MAN THE THINKER.

The argument gets rather sticky from this point on, Agnos, so please read and think carefully in this section.

My thesis here says that human thinking can't be adequately explained by naturalism or materialism. Just as morality is more than stimulus or instinct, and beauty is more than taste or preference, so also thinking is more than neurology. If you consider man as merely a natural, material entity, you'll never explain human reason.

As an analogy, take the difference between plane and solid geometry. Plane geometry considers only two dimensions in its figures—length and width. Solid geometry adds a third—depth or height. In plane geometry a circle is flat, but in solid geometry it becomes a sphere. If you deny the validity of solid geometry, if you think that plane geometry is the only way to look at a circle, your circles will always be flat. You won't appreciate the peculiar qualities of the sphere. It is true, you *could* look at all geometric figures from the vantage point of plane geometry alone, but you would miss the third dimension. When you cut yourself off from part of reality your judgments are defective.

Now, with man, you *could* consider him merely from the standpoint of matter, but you wouldn't really understand him. You'd be mystified by some of the things he does. Metaphorically speaking, he'd be flat. We've already noticed that morality and aesthetics seem "ontologically peculiar" to some people. Human thought is just as peculiar. If you wish to understand all these peculiar traits in man, you'll have to leave the reductive position of materialism and posit another dimension to completely explain man.

What evidence do I have to show that thought is ontologically peculiar, like morality and aesthetics?

1. I have the difficulty of naturalism in affirming its own position concerning reason. Often, the difficulties of one theory can become evidence for another theory and this is true for naturalism and theism. When the naturalist tries to affirm his worldview, he can't do it without self-contradiction. Any worldview must explain not only the universe in general but also itself in particular. Remember the dog who said, "Dogs don't talk"? Well, the naturalist is in the same boat, because he starts out thinking and then utters a worldview which

makes all thinking suspect. His worldview says everything—including mind—is physical, natural, material. Yet he must use this physical mind to affirm, and prove, his metaphysic.

But how could a physical brain prove the superiority of its thoughts over another physical brain? If the mind is totally physical, then it somehow "secretes" thought as the liver secretes bile or the heart pumps blood. But how can you prove one secretion superior to another in truth-content? Your mind secretes naturalism, mine secretes theism, but which one is the correct secretion? Does not the phrase "correct secretion" sound out of place? How could a secretion be correct or incorrect? Furthermore, why have men secreted such strange things through the years: materialism, pantheism, theism, rationalism, deism? What causes the secretion to change? Sunspots? Cosmic rays? Why, all of a sudden, is the contemporary secretion—naturalism—the true one? To try to explain truth in terms of a secretion seems a bit strange.

The puzzle clears up if you simply assert the existence of another dimension where thinking—even thinking naturalism—is something that transcends neurology. Thus the very difficulty naturalism has in affirming and proving itself becomes a piece of evidence for a supernatural worldview. If a dog must talk to affirm "dogs don't talk," it proves that dogs can talk after all.

2. Another piece of evidence for the ontological peculiarity of thinking is the strange dualism that exists in our language between words that refer to things and words that refer to ideas.[7] Our language betrays the fact that we instinctively sense a difference between consciousness and mere bodily behavior. Make a list of words that describe material things: thick, thin, dense, hard, solid, slick, sticky, fast, slow. Then make a list of words that describe ideas: cogent, witty, persuasive, incisive, intelligible, plausible, contradictory.

Now, try to modify material things with words that describe ideas and vice versa and just see what strange combinations you get. Consider the following questions: How fast is the theory of communism? What color is the theory of evolution? Is the motion of a pendulum witty, clear, or cogent? Does naturalism proceed in a northerly or a southerly direction? How dense is the Fallacy of Composition? How slick is deduction? Did you hear about the two cars that contradicted each other? Why do these questions sound strange? Because ideas like

7. See Brand Blanshard, *The Nature of Thought* (London: George Allen and Unwin, 1939), p. 336.

evolution, communism, and naturalism don't have density, color, or velocity. But if all reality is material, why shouldn't they have material qualities? Why does our language habitually polarize around two centers: thoughts and things?[8]

3. A third piece of evidence for the ontological peculiarity of thought is man's capacity for conceptual thought. There is no need for the theist to affirm that *all* thinking transcends physical neurology, for man obviously has a physical brain and it is obviously involved in the total activity of thinking. However, there is a special type of thinking, formation of concepts, which can't be explained by neural mechanisms. Students of the subject generally agree that *man's power of conceptual thought is the key to all the observed behavioral differences between him and the animals.* There is cogent evidence that conceptual thought requires something immaterial for it to operate.[9]

When the mind forms a concept there is nothing in the world of particular empirical objects to which the concept applies in a direct relation. If you see a horse you usually don't say, "There goes horseness" or "There goes a mammal." You probably refer to the object by its species, horse, and then perhaps by a proper name, like Dobbin. The names we use for things fall into (1) the particular or individual and (2) the conceptual or abstract. Proper nouns we use to refer to specific, identifiable individuals. But if you look carefully at all languages you spot a number of terms that have no specific reference to individual objects, terms like mankind, animal, plant, quadruped, mammal, carnivore, vertebrate. These names or designators don't refer to an individual entity but to the traits of a class. We call them "universals." One of the oldest problems in philosophy is: "What is the status of universals?"

Suppose I ask you to point to the specific referent for the word "mammal." If you point to a cow that would be incorrect, because the cow shares this quality with the tiger and the whale. More accurately you would say, "There is one example of a mammal." But by saying this you indicate that the word "mammal" refers to a whole class of animals who share a certain trait. A tiger, for instance, is simultaneously a mammal, quadruped, carnivore, and vertebrate, but we seldom mention all of these concepts when we talk of the in-

---

8. This is one reason why Karl Marx's use of the Hegelian dialectic is a distortion of the original scheme. Hegel was an idealist, and in a system of idealism two things can really "contradict" each other and form a synthesis. But Marx asserted that all is matter. In case of contradiction, then, it must be two material particles that are contradicting each other—very strange!

9. See Adler, *Difference of Man*, pp. 220-22; also footnote 42 for ch. 12, pp. 340-47.

dividual tiger. The only thing that can give meaning to the word "mammal" is our concept, our understanding of the general class of animals that suckle their young. If the mind didn't have concepts with which to recognize classes or kinds as such, we would never use common or general names to designate the class that an individual belongs to. The mammal as such doesn't exist in the world, but the concept certainly exists for the mind.

Thus, there must be something in the mind, a concept-building mechanism, by which the mind is able to look at several instances of a class and then abstract the essence of that class. True, the mind must look at the particulars in the world to abstract the essence of the group, but the concept, once abstracted, doesn't have a referent in the world the same way that a single perception of the particular does. Its true referent is in the mind.

Now, if concepts are only in the mind, they're ontologically peculiar; they really don't exist in the empirical world. We can now complete the argument by stating it in the form of a categorical syllogism:

1. All concepts are universal.
2. No physical thing is universal (i.e., all physical things are particular).
3. Therefore, concepts are not physical.

This syllogism is valid because it meets all the requirements of the categorical syllogism (three terms, a distributed middle, etc.). If the premises can be proved, the conclusion is sound. Our reasoning so far has established premise one: concepts must be universal in their intention or else they wouldn't enable us to understand, as we do, what it is to be a mammal or a quadruped.

The second premise is proved by the observations of common sense. No one would claim that the dog at his feet is the universal dogness; he would say the dog is an instance of its class. Individual or particular things are always material, and, conversely, material things are always individual. Since both premises are empirical generalizations, you could destroy either with a single negative instance. But none has yet been found. Adler remarks: "No one has ever produced an existent object of common experience or of scientific knowledge that is at once physical or material in its mode of existence and also universal in character (i.e., a class of things rather than an individual thing)."[10]

If this argument is sound it shows that our concepts are immaterial. You can't explain the power of conceptual thought by reference to a

10. Ibid., p. 222.

physical brain, for that would mean that a concept is material and hence particular. This explains why the naturalist has difficulty affirming his worldview with a purely physical brain, since naturalism is a giant concept that transcends millions of individual percepts. It also explains why our language polarizes around two primary entities: thoughts and things.

I admit, Agnos, that this argument is rather abstract and involved, and I know that the prime objection you may want to level against it will come from the empirical study of the brain. You may argue: when the physical brain is damaged it affects even the operation of conceptual thought. This proves that the brain is involved in conceptual thought just as it is involved in perceptual thought. If the brain is injured in certain ways or if certain drugs are given to the individual, conceptual thinking can be distorted. Doesn't this prove that *all* thinking is merely physical?[11]

Not necessarily. Proving that the physical brain is *involved* in conceptual thought isn't the same as proving that the physical brain is the *complete* cause of conceptual thought. Many complex phenomena have two kinds of causes: (1) a necessary cause, and (2) a sufficient cause. The necessary cause is all the conditions that must be present for the effect to occur. The sufficient cause is the condition that suffices to produce the effect, the true cause of the effect, if you please. The necessary cause is the conditions *without which the effect will not occur*, but which, by themselves, can't cause the effect (i.e., if not-a, then not-b). The sufficient cause, however, is the condition *with which the effect will occur* (if a, then b).

For example, if you ask, "Why is the light burning?" you probably wouldn't be satisfied with the answer, "Because we have wires coming from a source of electricity connected to an incandescent bulb." These are all necessary conditions for the bulb to burn, but what you really want to know is: "Who turned the light on?" Your explanation of the burning light is incomplete until someone gives you this sufficient cause. Wires and bulbs by themselves don't make a light burn.

Now, the physical brain is a necessary cause of conceptual thought, but not the sufficient cause. This explains why drugs can distort conceptual thinking just as cutting the wires puts out the light. By cutting the wires to the bulb you don't prove that a person couldn't be the sufficient cause of the light burning, that is, *if* the wires were in good condition. Likewise, you don't really disprove the immateriality of con-

---

11. The hypothesis which says that the mind is totally equivalent to the physical brain is called the "Identity Hypothesis." It is a logical corollary to naturalism or materialism.

ceptual thought by showing that brain disorders affect it. And that you don't disprove its immateriality in this way is what you would expect if the physical brain is indeed a necessary cause, but not the sufficient cause of conceptual thought.

By the way, isn't there a contradiction slumbering beneath this objection? You say chemicals can distort right thinking, but yet you say the brain is just an electro-chemical organism. Aren't all chemical reactions equally necessary? If some chemicals distort thinking, how could chemicals guarantee any truthful thinking? This is another form of the very problem we had in saying that one secretion can be superior to another in truth-content.

4. Another line of evidence for the ontological peculiarity of human thought is the human memory. The study of memory mechanisms is still in its infancy, and thus any conclusions must necessarily be tentative. Yet even in the infant stage there is some very interesting material about memory that fits with our thesis.

Memory researchers point out, for instance, that you exist in two states at the same time when you are recalling a past experience. You can be on the table talking with the doctor examining you and at the same time back in the context of a remembered event. Your brain operates like a high-fidelity tape recorder; it has an amazingly truthful reproduction of reality. It records not only past experiences but also the very feelings associated inextricably with them. When you recall the past experience you sometimes re-experience the feelings.

Research on memory indicates that the cortex is the locus of memory but that it doesn't act exactly like a computer's memory banks, in which each bit of information is stored in a single electronic cell. Memory seems to be "diffused" throughout the brain rather than concentrated in one particular section. Surgeons can remove large portions of the brain, but this doesn't destory a proportionate amount of memory. This suggests that every specific memory is, as it were, cross-filed all over the brain.

Another interesting fact is that nerve cells don't divide, and thus after a certain stage of development we have only a limited number of cells in which to store memory. Nerve cells that die from the age of (roughly) 25 onward aren't replaced. Yet our intellectual capacity can keep on increasing and incorporating new learning. The contraction of the physical brain does not produce a corresponding contraction in knowledge.

The permanence and longevity of memory is amazing. A very old person can forget something you told him five minutes ago and yet remember something that happened 80 years ago. If memory were purely physical it would take an unusual chemical to explain this longevity. In the past researchers thought that protein could be the specific chemical that stores memory but this seems unlikely because nearly all the protein in the brain is renewed every three weeks. A chemical with this high turnover could hardly serve as the long-term receptacle of information. More recently some have suggested that DNA is the storage molecule for memory.

Much of this evidence fits with our hypothesis that, even though the physical brain is a necessary cause for human thinking, it isn't the sufficient cause. If there were a crude one-to-one relationship between the brain cells and the intellect how could you explain (1) the fact that removal of the brain does not destroy a proportionate section of the memory, or (2) the fact that after age 25 cells decrease in number but the intellect grows in complexity?[12]

All of the evidence thus far—the self-contradiction of naturalism, the psycho-physical dualism in our language, conceptual thought, and the mysterious behavior of memory—all of it converges to make a powerful case for the transcendence of man. But transcendence in science and philosophy is simply the counterpart of the supernatural in theology, and if you must invoke the supernatural to explain man then naturalism has an inadequate anthropology. Like plane geometry, naturalism leaves man flat.

Perhaps the reason that empirical science has missed the transcendent in man is that scientists are always looking *with* the mind *at* the world. If you look at only the world for too long you tend to forget the unique features of the instrument you are looking with. Emerson said that if the stars came out only once every century we would make elaborate preparations for the sublime spectacle, but since they appear every night we take them for granted.

The same is true of mind. We take it for granted because we know it immediately and intuitively. We tend to think that atoms, molecules, and electrons are the more primal reality, and we speak of the mind as being "merely subjective." The mind, however, is that of which we are the *most* certain. As Carl G. Jung argued:

> How on earth do people know that the only reality is the physical atom, when this cannot be proved to exist at all except by means of the psyche? If there is anything which can be described as

12. See W. Penfield, "Memory Mechanisms," *A.M.A. Archives of Neurology and Psychiatry*, 67 (1952): 178-98; Denis Alexander, *Beyond Science* (New York: A. J. Holman Company, 1972), pp. 36ff.

primary, it must be the psyche, certainly not in any circumstances, the atom, which, like everything else in our experience, is only directly given as a model or picture.[13]

There was a scientist in the last century who said that he didn't believe in the soul because he couldn't find it in his test tube. It never occurred to him that he might be looking in the wrong place with the wrong instrument. David Hume denied the soul and said that the self is only a collection of fleeting images. He said, to use an analogy, that the mind is just like a string of pearls without the string, i.e., without the self to bind together the fleeting succession of sensations. But how can you have a collection without a collector? If the mind were just a string of pearls, which pearl was it that made the judgment, "The mind is just a string of pearls"? How did the pearl that made this observation acquire the ability to transcend and observe the whole collection of pearls? The self, therefore, would have to be transcendent to affirm that it wasn't transcendent!

Agnos, you may not like people talking about the soul, or the spirit, Geist, anima, personality, reason, mind, or whatever word they use, but these words are just designators for a necessary model we use to understand human behavior. Models help you understand what an object is and how it works. Man is a highly complex creature, and analyzing his behavior has preoccupied the genius of men from prehistory. All through history concepts like spirit and flesh, or mind and soul, were means of grasping some of the mystery. If you now say that we must drop the idea of soul, then you must have a new model to take its place that does equal justice to the complexity, the ontological peculiarity, we've been discussing. I don't think you can suggest a model that will improve on the soul. All you can do is suggest a synonym for it.

One of the most interesting stories in European intellectual history is that of how psychology dropped the word "soul" because of its association with theology. But what did they put in its place? The Greek word for soul—psyche! I can't find a psyche in my test tube. Why then do psychologists believe in it? They are just as guilty as theologians of postulating unseen entities to explain man's behavior. Look at the concepts Sigmund Freud used: Id, Ego, Superego, Dream Censor, Oedipus Complex. Can you find them in a test tube? A dedicated materialist could ask Freud: "What precise neurological conditions obtain in the brain when one has an Oedipus Complex?" What could Freud answer? He could only say that it is a model, a

13. Cited in Joseph Wood Krutch, *The Measure of Man* (New York: Grosset and Dunlap, 1968), p. 122.

device to understand behavior. You never see the model directly, just as you never see the wind. You believe in it indirectly because it explains the things you do see. [14]

Unbelievers often complain that you can't talk about God except in symbolic, metaphorical, or analogical terms. True, but isn't this also true of mind? Did Freud want us to understand that there is a literal Dream Censor guarding the door from the Id to the Ego? Hardly. But the word "censor" is a very handy, helpful, colorful term for whatever is there, and it describes very well what that something does. Freud was right to use it if it represented the reality effectively.

Denis Alexander is very helpful on this matter of proposing models to explain behavior. In his *Beyond Science* he points out that science never gives you the "real truth" about the world but rather a model which tries to conceptualize observed phenomena, much as a map symbolizes the earth. A map *represents* reality but it isn't reality, nor does it *cause* the reality it represents. A good map closely represents the earth, but no map is perfect. Sometimes the thing you're trying to describe is so complex (e.g., man) that several maps may be necessary to give a complete representation. To give an accurate account of a simple thing like the earth you need maps for altitude, rainfall, vegetation, geology and so on. If you try to put all that information on one map it becomes so confusing you can't read it. When the entity is complex your analysis of it must be made one facet at a time. [15]

With man the phenomenon is so complex you need a separate map from biochemistry, anatomy, anthropology, sociology, history, and, if I make my case in this chapter, from theology. The fact that my behavior can be studied in terms of biochemistry alone doesn't prove that man is merely chemistry, any more than a map can prove that the earth is merely vegetation.

D. THE REALITY OF FREEDOM.

The argument from the transcendence of man wouldn't be complete without a defense of freedom. No truth seems to be more readily accepted by the common sense of mankind than the freedom of the will. When you deny it you render a huge section of experience utterly meaningless. The reality of freedom lies deeper than arguments.

14. It seems to be no accident that in many world languages the word for "spirit" and "wind" is the same. Both are unseen, yet both have demonstrable behavioral effects. In a conversation with a friend, Ludwig Binswanger, Freud is reported to have said: "Yes, the spirit is everything. . . . Mankind has always known that it possesses spirit; I had to show it that there are also instincts." Cited in Leslie, *Jesus and Logotherapy*, p. 22.

15. Alexander, *Beyond Science* (Holman, 1977).

(1) Man blames himself and feels guilty when he does wrong because he believes he could have chosen the better action over the worse. (2) A court of law judges a man most severely when it holds him to have freely committed the crime with which he is charged. (3) Most world religions and moral codes have a Law of Karma, a principle of retribution whereby it is believed that "your sins find you out" or that "you reap what you sow." If you denied freedom, you would bring the business of the world to a standstill. You would have to reconstruct a large part of human language. Surely something that supports such a large part of our experience is not an illusion.

Yet, those who insist on viewing man as a totally material entity must deny freedom. They say man is governed by the law of cause-and-effect just as surely as a billiard ball. It always strikes me as strange to hear a determinist affirm his determinism. If the theory is true, it means that I'm fated to believe what I believe regardless of arguments used on me. Perhaps the determinist would do better to shake me and see if the rearrangement of molecules in my brain could make me a determinist. But no, he argues with me! Why?

A good question: Why do we argue? Argument implies to me that my determinist opponent assumes I'm free to choose his position, but his determinism denies this. E. J. Carnell writes: "If a person challenges moral freedom, he asks his hearer to evaluate his arguments in moral freedom; and thus his objection, like a critic's objection to the law of contradiction, destroys itself."[16]

Determinists complain that the belief in freedom destroys the causal basis of science. This isn't true, because we affirm a different kind of cause, a cause that operates in the spiritual realm. Freedom doesn't mean that a man may not inherit conditions and tendencies from his past. These don't cancel freedom, they only condition and qualify it. In freedom, man stands above nature and her mechanisms just as he does in his conceptual thinking. Just as the self that can know phenomena isn't one of the phenomena it knows, so also the will that can initiate action isn't itself caused in the same way everything else is caused. Those who believe in freedom aren't saying that an action is totally *uncaused*; they are simply affirming that it is *self-caused*, i.e., caused by the self and not by material reality.

If this distinction between two types of causes is wrong, then I must confess I simply can't make any sense at all out of the way human beings act. So much of our behavior is ludicrous if we're not free. Why should you resent the stab of the assassin more than the kick of a mule? Why resent the assault of the mugger more than the snow fall-

16. *Christian Commitment: An Apologetic* (Grand Rapids: Eerdmans, 1948), p. 115.

ing on your head? Why be grateful to someone for helping you? He couldn't help it. Remember, the duty of a theory is to explain.

Psychotherapy presents another line of evidence for freedom of the will. Most doctors know that many physical illnesses can be greatly modified by the patient's attitude. This "will to get better" is hard to locate, but its reality is indisputable. If man were a totally material entity it would seem that all of his problems could be solved by medicines, drugs, or surgery. These things play only a small part, however, in the management of mental illness. In recent decades we've seen the rise of several new schools of psychology, dedicated to the proposition that freedom and its corollary, moral responsibility, are prime requisites for mental health. Three of these schools are: Reality Therapy, Logotherapy, and Transactional Analysis.

Along with conceptual thought, freedom is what chiefly distinguishes man from the animals. A number of books have appeared lately emphasizing man's link with the animals: *The Naked Ape*, *The Human Zoo*, *The Human Animal*. Most of these studies overlook the big difference between instinct and reason, not to mention the philosophical implications of the difference. Darwin couldn't grasp this distinction and tried to bring the entire life of the mind under purely biological principles such as "the survival of the fittest." The mischief wrought by Social Darwinism in our century is too well known to document here. The sad thing is, the mischief could have been avoided if people had just understood the distinction between reason in humans and instinct in animals.

Man's nature comes primarily from the institutions he creates. Animals don't create institutions. Their instinctive patterns of behavior are "species-predictable," that is, their behavior is handed down from generation to generation by the mechanism of biological inheritance. Even those cute little actions that most resemble human behavior—like the warning cries of animals or the dance of the bees to indicate the location of honey—are all passed on by heredity. In human societies, however, most characteristic human behavior is transmitted by education, not heredity. Humans learn most of the forms of social life by a *free conscious initiation*, using the medium of language. To ignore this crucial difference is to blind yourself to the whole of human history.

Another way you could make this point is to observe that *there is no gene for morality*. If there were, you would find more consistency and predictability in human actions and in human moral codes. We noticed earlier that the difference in moral codes is used against the Moral Argument, but, really, if man is free and his ethical actions are not species-predictable, this variation in moral codes is exactly what you'd expect.

It has been well said that to confuse reason in man with instinct in animals is the "Ratomorphic Fallacy," attributing to man only those faculties characteristic of rats. It isn't a harmless fallacy; it led to the ovens of Auschwitz.

The Ratomorphic Fallacy is committed currently by Professor B. F. Skinner, the most famous American psychologist alive today. Skinner believes that if the world is to be saved from all its problems we must go "beyond freedom and dignity" to a utopia where proper conditioning will finally have worked all the evil out of us. Skinner asserts that "the hypothesis that man is not free is essential to the application of the scientific method to the study of human behavior."[17] The reason is obvious: anything, like the will, which hops around and can't be pinned down can't be studied by science. Funny, but Skinner doesn't so much refute the existence of free will as claim that whatever physical science can't study doesn't exist. What my method finds intractable simply doesn't exist, he says.

Sir Arthur Eddington once used a famous analogy which applies to Skinner's attitude. Eddington was one who felt keenly the limitations of science. He told of a fisherman who concluded from his fishing experiences with a certain net that "no creature of the sea is less than two inches long." Some people demurred, arguing that many sea creatures are under two inches and they just slip through the holes in the net. But the ichthyologist was unmoved: "What my net can't catch ain't fish," he pontificated, and then he scornfully accused his detractors of having prescientific, medieval, metaphysical prejudices.

Skinner is like the fisherman with the special net. Since Skinner, using only the empirical scientific method, can't "catch" or "grasp" such qualitative phenomena as freedom, dignity, morality, aesthetics, conceptual thought, mind, he concludes they don't exist. But, they just slipped through his net. They have been slipping through the materialist's net from Democritus to Skinner.

E. CONCLUSION.

I can't understand man, Agnos, without invoking the transcendent, the supernatural, the immaterial. I feel that the Anthropological Argument is the strongest strand in our rope, the brightest cross-light

---

17. *Science and Human Behavior* (New York: Macmillan, 1953), p. 447. For a fictional description of his behaviorist utopia, see Skinner's *Walden Two* (New York: Macmillan, 1948). For a non-fictional presentation of the same viewpoint, see Skinner's *Beyond Freedom and Dignity* (New York: Knopf, 1971).

on our stage. If man isn't unique, then as Chesterton said, "One of the animals just went off its head." I realize we must be cautious when we use unseen entities to explain the empirical, but if you have to do it to make sense of the data, you have to do it. St. Augustine once confessed: "The manner in which the spirit is united to the body cannot be understood by man, but it is the essence of man."[18] Even with theism man remains a puzzle, but to me the puzzle is augmented geometrically if theism is false.

Suggestions for Further Reading

Arthur Balfour, *Theism and Humanism* (New York: Doran, 1915).

William E. Hocking, *The Self, Its Body, and Freedom* (New Haven: Yale University Press, 1928).

Immanuel Kant, *Critique of Judgement*, trans. J. H. Bernard, 2nd ed. rev. (New York: Macmillan and Co., 1914).

C. S. Lewis, *The Case for Christianity* (New York: Macmillan and Co., 1947).

James G. Machen, *The Christian View of Man* (London: Banner of Truth Trust, 1965).

James Orr, *God's Image in Man* (Grand Rapids: Eerdmans, 1948).

H. P. Owen, *The Moral Argument for Christian Theism* (London: George Allen and Unwin, 1965).

Jordan Scher, ed., *Theories of the Mind* (New York: Free Press of Glencoe, 1962).

A. E. Taylor, "The Vindication of Religion," *Essays Catholic and Critical* (New York: Macmillan and Co., 1950).

Leonard Verduin, *Somewhat Less Than God: The Biblical View of Man* (Grand Rapids: Eerdmans, 1970).

John Wisdom, *Problems of Mind and Matter* (New York: Cambridge University Press, 1963).

Don Wolstan, *The Biblical Meaning of Man* (New York: Bruce, 1967).

18. *City of God*, xxi. 10.

NATURALISM, THE
PHILOSOPHICAL SMUGGLER

We end this philosophical section of our study, Agnos, by taking a last brief glance at naturalism. In the previous two chapters I argued that naturalism is a weak explanation for the contingency and design of the universe and for the nature of man. In this chapter I wish to summarize my case by dramatizing the fragility and the axiological poverty of naturalism.[1]

For about a century many thinkers have been calling Western culture a "cut-flower" civilization because of its detachment from the historical roots of Christian theism. You could also call it a "smuggler's civilization," since it continues to nourish itself on values derived from another worldview. I insist that naturalism also smuggles in values and can't subsist without them. I say that scientific humanism has no adequate metaphysical framework in which one can discover or embrace the True, the Good, and the Beautiful.

A. SMUGGLING IN EPISTEMOLOGY.

Naturalistic smuggling is evident, first of all, in the realm of epistemology, the study of knowledge. The naturalistic view of mind is so deficient that you wonder how a scholar in any field can keep on searching for truth with such a humble instrument as the human brain. The naturalist smuggles in a high regard for the operation of the mind, a regard that fits more comfortably with the synthetic-metaphysical approach of Plato and Augustine than with the

1. Portions of this chapter appeared in *Christianity Today*, XV:20 (July 2, 1971), 12-14.

analytical-empirical approach of Hume and Russell. A naturalist starts out thinking and then ends up by undermining all thought. He must use his mind to prove his philosophy, but then his philosophy affirms that all reasoning is mere cerebration by a physical brain. If reasoning is just an electro-chemical operation in the material brain, then why should a naturalist ask anyone to accept his thoughts as "true"?

Normally you advance ideas and philosophies because you believe they are true. But when a naturalist says "Naturalism is true," all that this can mean is that certain motions take place in his brain—he "thinks naturalism," an event that stands on the same footing as any other bodily event, like digestion or breathing. Now, it is pointless to ask if an event in my body is true or false. My blood pressure and temperature aren't true. Statements, assertions, or propositions about them may be true, but they are just events, waiting to be interpreted by some mind. They certainly don't interpret themselves. Hence, if thinking is only a bodily event, like temperature, it is meaningless to say "My idea is true." You can only say that your idea exists or occurs.

Yet the naturalist doesn't seem to labor under the humility and scepticism that this analysis implies. He claims to tell us truths about the entire universe, from the most bashful electron to the most remote quasar. He seems to assume that his own cerebration is exempt from the reduction he applies to thinking in general. His reduction is true, though all other reasoning is mere somatic secretion. But you can't have it that way; you can't have your mind and reduce it too. If the reduction to physical categories applies everywhere, it applies also to the mind or brain doing the reducing. That which reduces everything reduces itself also.

Charles Darwin, who contributed much to naturalism's diminutive view of mind, felt the force of this objection, especially as it touched on his theory of evolution. One could well ask: "If the mind, like all else in nature, is still evolving, how can we be sure that its present structure and operation guarantee any truth?" For example, did the Law of Contradiction, which is necessary for truth, evolve like the rest of the body? How can we be sure that there's not some new mental law, now struggling to be born, a law which will enable us to get even closer to the truth about reality? Would this new law confirm or contradict evolution and naturalism? Darwin confessed:

> With me the horrid doubt always arises whether the convictions of man's mind, which has been developed from the mind of the lower animals, are of any value or at all trustworthy. Would

anyone trust in the convictions of a monkey's mind, if there are
any convictions in such a mind?[2]

Naturalism must also smuggle in a sham objectivity and a mental
transcendence that "mere nature" doesn't contain. When the scientist
studies something, for instance, he demonstrates that he transcends
nature and matter. If he were nothing but a bundle of mindless
reflexes, as Skinner says, it would be extremely difficult for him to investigate, say, the behavior of a dog. The dog would be just another
bundle of unintelligent reflexes; both scientist and dog would merely
secrete that pointless stuff we call thinking. No study would occur
either way, just cerebration. If you said the man could investigate the
dog, that would only mean, in naturalistic terms, "his behavior
studies the behavior of the dog."

But mere behavior can't study anything. Behavior can't observe,
evaluate, criticize, interpret, and synthesize. Only a self-conscious
reason with powers of observation, selection, memory, evaluation,
comparison, interpretation, and synthesis can study an animal's
behavior. The mind must stand *above* a process to say that it can impart meaning to a process. One unconscious process can't evaluate
another unconscious process. Only that which transcends a process
can evaluate that process.

If man's mind isn't exceptional, I wonder why his secretions are
published and those of the dog are not? And why has the secretion of
this century been elevated above all others? Naturalism hasn't always
dominated man's thinking; human beings have also espoused
idealism, religion, pantheism, deism, and materialism. Why is the
secretion of this century true and the previous ones false? Will the next
century produce a new secretion? Will it be true or false?

The naturalist compounds the difficulty just discussed if he believes
in determinism—and logically he should. If all things, including our
thoughts, are mechanically determined, then objective science is impossible, for the scientist *automatically* selects the data he evaluates.
Einstein functioned merely as an automatic machine in formulating
the theory of relativity, as did Newton in devising the law of gravity.
Darwin was driven by brute force in devising the theory of evolution.
No scientist should be congratulated for his brilliant thinking, for he
just secreted what was inevitable—his work just oozed out of the
brain, so to speak. For all we know, these complex systems of thought
may have been caused by something like red beans or ulcers of the
duodenum. What a draft on credulity!

2. *Life and Letters of Charles Darwin*, ed. Frances Darwin (New York: Johnson Reprint
[reprint]), I, p. 285.

Freedom, objectivity, transcendence—none of these ingredients crucial to a viable epistemology is inherent in naturalism. Someone must have smuggled them in.

B. SMUGGLING IN AXIOLOGY.

Naturalistic smuggling is even more evident in axiology, the realm of values, not only in aesthetics, but especially in ethics. You remember, Agnos, how that the naturalist couldn't define God out of nature until he said that nature is impersonal and non-axiological (ch. 5)? Sooner or later, that thought will come home to haunt him, because if nature has no values or personal traits it's difficult to see how there can be any real values at all.

Naturalists claim they use only the scientific method; they exclude any other kind of truth. Yet when you come to ethics, you can't establish the *ought* from the *is*. Naturalism must posit an empirical theory of value but the trouble with such a theory is that values never come through the senses. Lies, wars, murders, and rapes are just as natural as plants and animals. Nothing comes through the senses with a bright red tag reading, "I am valuable." Science can't establish values; it can never verify empirically an ethical obligation. Tragic it is, that science, which can do so much, can never prove what it ought to do.

You can prove, for example, that human beings need to love and be loved in order to survive and live a full and happy life. But what you can never prove in a million experiments is the proposition: "I should love my fellow human being." To prove the survival benefits of love isn't remarkable; my wristwatch needs oil, my car needs gasoline, my lawn needs fertilizer, my neighbor needs love. These are all factual, descriptive statements, but where do I look for the imperative: *I am obligated* to oil my watch, gas my car, fertilize my lawn, and love my neighbor? The imperative isn't in nature, unless someone smuggled it in.

I'm not saying, Agnos, that naturalists don't have good moral lives. They often do, sometimes better than many Christians. What I'm saying is that there's no metaphysical buttress for their ethics. Their ought has no bite, no punch to it. They might as well say, "I should, because it is absurd!" Many humanists have a high-voltage ethical system but no source of electricity for it. If there's no Person who supports the moral realm, then ethical subjectivism is really true, and you should never condemn anyone for doing anything. But naturalists keep condemning bad behavior, just as they keep arguing and using their minds.

Let me illustrate this axiological poverty by reference to three thinkers: Hume, Russell, and Dewey.

David Hume was one of the greatest sceptics that ever lived. He jerked the rug out from under just about everything, including himself. Yet in one passage Hume said: "Be a philosopher, but in the midst of all your philosophy, be still a man." After all his iconoclasm, the jolly Scot seemed to be warning: "Be not sceptical overmuch." Now, this sounds noble and melodic, but if Hume's general philosophy is true I can't possibly carry out this piece of advice. What is a man? A nominalist like Hume says there's no "essence" to any class of particular things. The term "man" is strictly meaningless to a consistent nominalist and thus I couldn't be a man if I wanted to. Remember: a consistent empiricism destroys all normative propositions. Hume had to smuggle in a normative proposition to tell us to be men.

Bertrand Russell was a Logical Positivist most of his career and therefore felt that ethical judgments are meaningless, mere expressions of a person's feelings (this is called "Emotivism"). The statement, "genocide is evil," has no more meaning than, "I like cherry pie." Yet when it came time to write his autobiography, Russell spelled out the values that had governed his life:

> I have lived in the pursuit of a vision, both personal and social. Personal: to care for what is noble, for what is beautiful, for what is gentle; to allow moments of insight to give wisdom to more mundane times. Social: to see in imagination the society that is to be created, where individuals grow freely, and where hate and greed and envy die because there is nothing to nourish them. These things I believe, and the world, for all its horrors, has left me unshaken.[3]

This sounds beautiful but if you apply Russell's empiricism and positivism consistently you have no imperative to undergird these sentiments. There is no "vision" possible for empiricism. Words like "noble," "beautiful," and "gentle" are meaningless, as are words like "envy," "hate," and "greed." If determinism is true there is no society of the future to be created; society will be only what material components allow it to be. Also, the world has no "horrors," only physical events. A consistent naturalist or empiricist should avoid all such anthropomorphic thinking about the universe.

---

3. *Autobiography of Bertrand Russell* (New York: Simon and Schuster, 1969), Vol. III, p. 330. It is true that Russell eventually became dissatisfied with the ethical corollary of Logical Positivism but that does not change the point made here, because even when he was a champion of Emotivism he espoused a high quality morality.

John Dewey wrote a great deal about the good life that science could bring to mankind, but he never really told us how to detect the "good life." His pragmatism and instrumentalism taught that nothing is valuable in itself. A genuine value differs from a false value only because of its consequences. Yet in one work Dewey claims that there are wrong ideals, a claim which implies that there are right ideals. He says, for example, that without aesthetic enjoyment (art) man would become a race of economic monsters.[4] But why not choose economic monstrosity? Dewey never gave an answer to that question. Most of the time he seemed to assume that the old values are self-evident and need no special proof.

It takes a long time for the axiological poverty of naturalism to become evident, even to the most astute thinker. The old values taken from theism are like fruit cut from a living tree. Freshly cut, they are still infused with something of the original life of the tree. You can even preserve them for a time on the ice of habit, discipline, and moral education, but eventually they lose their flavor. The cut flower finally withers in your hand.

Occasionally some thinkers come along who realize the hypocrisy of smuggling values and try to expose the whole business. Three such men were Jack London, Friedrich Nietzsche, and Albert Camus. London put into the mouth of Wolf Larsen the brutal truth about a purely natural ethic:

> One man cannot wrong another man. He can only wrong himself. As I see it, I do wrong always when I consider the interest of others. Don't you see? How can two particles of yeast wrong each other by striving to devour each other? It is their inborn heritage to strive to devour, and to strive not to be devoured. When they depart from this they sin.[5]

Friedrich Nietzsche felt it his duty to cut the umbilical cord that centuries had forged between theism and morality. He scorned venomously all those who felt that the demise of Christian theism left the ethic of altruism unaffected. The English, he said, give up God and then do penance by becoming moral fanatics:

> When one gives up the Christian faith, one pulls the right to Christian morality out from under one's feet. This morality is by no means self-evident: this point has to be exhibited again and again, despite the English flatheads. Christianity is a system, a *whole* view of things thought out together. By breaking one main

4. *Reconstruction in Philosophy* (New York: Holt, Rinehart, and Winston, 1920), p. 127.

5. *The Sea Wolf* (New York: Macmillan, 1931), p. 79.

concept out of it, the faith in God, one breaks the whole. . . .It stands or falls with faith in God.[6]

Most of his career Albert Camus was agitated by the same problem:

The coexistence of a philosophy of negation and a positive morality illustrates the great problem that is painfully disturbing the whole epoch. In a word, it is a problem of civilization, and it is essential for us to know whether man, without the help either of the eternal or of rationalistic thought, can unaided create his own values.[7]

A problem of civilization! How very true—can man unaided create his own values? I say no, and I predict that human civilization won't last long if a majority of human beings honestly and consistently try to live a "naturalistic morality." If my moral experience is the response of a transcendent creature to a Creator-God who fashioned me in his own free, moral image, then I can live the altruistic ethic consistently. But if man is just a "bag of seawater," or "an accident in a backwater," or "a disease of agglutinated dust," as members of the smart set sometimes define him, then I really don't understand axiology or man at all.

In a word, Agnos, naturalism doesn't explain, but frustrates my desire to understand *knowledge, morality,* and *aesthetics.* By failing to explain these vital areas of my experience it remains, in my judgment, a worldview inferior to theism.

6. *Die Götzendämmerung,* §5.

7. Cited in Henry Grosshans, *The Search for Modern Europe* (New York: Houghton Mifflin, 1970), p. 421.

WHY HISTORY?

We have reached a crucial turning point in our discussion, Agnos. From now on the argument changes complexion. Up to now the evidence has been inferential; for the rest of the journey the arguments are more direct. The remainder of our study is devoted to elucidating the historical or revelational argument for the Christian God.

Before we plunge into history it would be well to pause and ask: What have we proved so far? What would one be if he stopped here? I personally would be a theist, but I must confess that the evidence so far is not exactly overpowering. Because of contingency, design, and man's nature, I'd think that theism is a more satisfactory hypothesis than naturalism. But I'd be less than honest if I said I was totally satisfied with our case thus far. I find some shortcomings in natural theology, the attempt to prove God from nature without any appeal to revelation.

A. THE LIMITATIONS OF NATURAL THEOLOGY.

1. Natural theology can never prove an infinite God because it starts with a finite nature. If the finite world supplies the evidence (the premises), then you can never infer an infinite cause. You must have infinity in the premises to get infinity in the conclusion. The only argument that has infinity in the premises is the Cosmological Argument, but, as we saw earlier, this argument in isolation proves only that there is a necessary something to account for contingent being. This something needn't be personal, intelligent, or moral. Further,

1. Parts of this chapter appeared with the same title in *Christianity Today*, XVI:21 (July 28, 1972), 6-8.

there is no definite way to prove that the being implied by the Design Argument is the same being as that implied by the Cosmological Argument.

Of course, I could reply that this objection applies to all thinking which involves postulation. No empirical hypothesis is ever deductively certain. A defense lawyer could argue to the jury: "You must have murder in the premises to reach murder in the conclusion," but the jury would probably be unimpressed if the circumstantial evidence was very incriminating. Proofs for any matter of fact are never deductive, but that doesn't mean they are utterly worthless. Somewhere between being totally worthless and being deductively certain the theistic proofs stand.

I could answer the objection this way but it sounds a bit hollow. I've always had the feeling that certitude is an essential property of any religious commitment and "highly probable" isn't the same as "certain." That pushes me to an interesting question: If deduction is the most certain form of knowledge, why didn't God make himself known in this way? This question has dogged philosophical theology for centuries.

One possible answer is that only through induction could God reveal himself in the world of fact. Another is that only through induction is the will involved, for only in induction does man get excited and breathe heavily. Induction has an existential sting to it that deduction doesn't have. Only with induction do you have the venture of faith, which, presumably, God wants man to make.

2. Natural theology can never establish the existence of the God most people consider the highest conception of God ever proposed, the Yahweh of the Hebrew-Christian revelation. There is no way to get the 100 per cent Yahweh from natural theology. With all our lights clicked on you still won't see the living God of the Bible on the stage without that extra cross-light called revelation. Reason without revelation always comes up with a deity different from Yahweh, as you can easily see by comparing the God of the Bible with the God of Aristotle, Spinoza, or Tom Paine. The God of the Bible is severely personal; he becomes jealous and angry; he repents and changes his mind; he has juice and daring that no clinical deity established by reason could ever have.

The Biblical God is unique. We must reject the current myth that all religions teach essentially the same thing. The religions of man disagree sharply on this very fundamental point: the nature of God. The gods of the East are totally infinite; they encompass all of being. This is pantheism, or more correctly, as Francis Schaeffer observes, pan-everything-ism. The gods of the West, such as those of Greece and Rome, tended to be personal but very limited. The God of the Bible, both Old and New Testament, combines these two features; he is the infinite-yet-personal God.[2]

The fact that the theistic proofs can't prove the Biblical God doesn't mean that we can't anticipate *some* features of Yahweh from material already introduced in evidence. We can anticipate something about the character of God by using elements drawn from our own moral and spiritual experiences because we are made in his image. Once fully revealed, Yahweh doesn't frustrate, though he may modify and enlarge, what we've already learned about the true, the good, and the beautiful from our own experience.

3. Natural theology seems inadequate when you realize that the God we seek is a personal God. If we stop here the most we have is a viable hypothesis about God. I'm sure that God is very impressed at this point. "Thanks a lot," he says, "you're so nice to let me have the status of a hypothesis!" God seems to be speaking to us through Psalm 2:4—"He who sits in the heavens laughs; the Lord has them in derision."

Agnos, what if you had lost your wife in a big house and were searching frantically for her? What if you found little clues that let you know she was probably in the house: shoes, stockings, lipstick, hairpins, threads of hair? Would you rest satisfied with this inferential data? Or would you keep searching until you found her in the flesh? Once you had found her, would you be so crazy as to go back and prefer the inferential evidence? So also is it with one who has only coherence proof for God; he longs to press on to correspondence proof. Once you've found the person you were searching for, whether wife or God, you would exclaim like Job: "I had heard of thee by the hearing of the ear, but now my eye sees thee" (Job 42:5).

Of course, the rules for finding God are different from those for finding anything else in the world, whether person or non-person. In finding most things you must memorize a set of rules for finding X and then follow them. But God is an X so different from the usual X's that the rules are never the same. He is personal and that implies an element of freedom or whim. He can stay just a jump ahead of you if he wishes. He can hide himself if he desires. He doesn't knock about the streets. Never can you say of God, as of a tree or an automobile, "See, there he is!" I wish you could, but I know you can't.

2. Francis Schaeffer, *The God Who Is There* (Chicago: InterVarsity Press, 1968), p. 94.

4. All of this, finally, suggests that natural theology gives man a weak foundation for a dynamic religion. You really can't pray to a hypothesis; there is something indecent about worshipping a postulate; a theory can't forgive you. A God known only by inference is an inadequate God for a viable religious life. Karl Barth once said, "Apart from Christ I would be an atheist." That is a bit strong for me, but I can say that apart from Christ I wouldn't be a missionary theist. The gods of Aristotle, Spinoza, and Paine neither desire nor deserve worship. Pascal said of natural theology:

> The metaphysical proofs of the existence of God are so remote from men's methods of reasoning and so involved that they produce little impact; and even if they did help some people, the effect would only last for a few moments while they were actually watching the demonstration, but an hour later they would be afraid that they had made a mistake.[3]

One could even say that an excessive preoccupation with the theistic proofs actually inhibits the religious life. Philosophical reasoning accentuates the thinking ego and sometimes turns it away from other people, away even from God himself. There is a story of the man who spent so much time proving the existence of God that he forgot to say his prayers! When this happens, the God proved by philosophy becomes an idol. As Kierkegaard insisted, purely rational apprehension of God doesn't change the philosopher making the apprehension. You may be the greatest logician in the world and still be spiritually empty. True belief in God transforms the whole person, not just the intellect. To believe in God without transformation is mockery, not belief. "Even the demons believe—and shudder" (James 2:19). Knowledge of God by theistic proofs can make a man proud and haughty, just the opposite effect of what true knowledge of God would have.

Therefore, dear Agnos, we cannot, we dare not, stop with the arguments for God given thus far. Whether those arguments have made you a theist, a deist, or just a curious agnostic, you must have all kinds of questions about this God: What is his nature? Does he care for me? What does he want of me? What will he do with me in the future? Has he ever spoken directly to anyone? Christians feel that most of your questions will be answered if you press on and examine the Hebrew-Christian revelation.

B. HISTORY AS A MEDIUM OF REVELATION.

It is extremely important to note that nowhere in the Bible do you

3. *Pensées*, #381.

find a formal, systematic proof of the existence of God. Why? Why is there no *Summa* à la Thomas from a Biblical writer on the existence of God? Because to Jews and early Christians the direct experience of God in history was much weightier than any mere argument from inference. To prove the historical Yahweh would be as ridiculous as to prove the existence of the wife sitting on your lap.[4]

Agnos, if you have an aversion to history you must correct it (it *is* a defect, you know) before you can fairly evaluate Christianity, because our faith teaches that God revealed himself supremely in historical events. He started history by an act of creation, he governs it by his providence, he entered it in various miraculous ways, he dwelt in a historical person, Jesus Christ, and he'll terminate it at the final judgment. Chronologically, you could develop the scheme of divine redemption by a series of revelatory events: Creation, Exodus, Exile, Crucifixion, Resurrection, Second Coming. Unlike Buddhism or Hinduism the Christian faith takes history very seriously. Christians feel that history is not an absurdity to be endured, nor an eternal cycle to be escaped, nor an illusion to be dispelled.

But you ask: Why use such a weak reed for divine revelation? Why did God disclose himself in past events? Why should the Almighty compel me to rummage through happenings of thousands of years ago to find him? Why must the sovereign Lord of the Universe play hide-and-seek with me, his putative creature, who supposedly radiates his image? If this Infinite Person really exists, he must be the most important entity in the cosmos. Why can't he make himself contemporary? Would an earthly father hide from his offspring? Why couldn't God reveal himself directly to every human being (say) on his seventh birthday, at high noon? Then if anyone refused to believe he would be blameworthy. But as it is, one is not to blame for refusing to believe in a God who plays hide-and-seek.

So the objection runs. But what specifically is the problem with God revealing himself in history? The critic affirms that history isn't immediate; it is removed, removed from the person God is trying to reach, especially if the revelatory event happened thousands of years ago. Being removed, history is therefore contingent, uncertain. You can never be absolutely sure that something happened exactly as the story has come down to you. You are at the mercy of the eyewitnesses; you get the event secondhand. If the story is 2000 years old, like the Resurrection, you really have a problem. Why would God shower

4. There are a few scriptural references that seem to use natural theology, e.g., Rom. 1:20; Ps. 19:1; Acts 17:27; Job 12:7-12. These verses, however, are not direct, formal proofs for God but more like asides, incidental to the main argument of the passage.

signs and wonders on the first generation of Christians and leave the sixtieth generation with only a collection of books documenting those original miracles?

The critic insists that any religion coming from God wouldn't be limited to a specific time and place (called "the scandal of particularity") but would consist of a corpus of general ideas accessible to the solitary rational thinker in every time and place. We have a bit of verse that embodies this complaint: "How odd/of God/ to choose/ the Jews." Only a religion which is rooted in something universal in all humans can be the true religion.[5] Sometimes the critic comes close to saying religion should be deductive, not realizing that this would denude it of any factual content.

Let me defend history as a discipline. No one should claim that history is a physical science, for it isn't. But this doesn't mean that it isn't knowledge, unless you have a remarkably narrow definition of knowledge. Many thinkers have amused themselves with cute little definitions of history like "a lie agreed upon" or "a bag of tricks we play on dead men," but practicing historians seldom take such definitions seriously. Those who practice the craft say that history yields positive knowledge. One of the greatest, Jacques Barzun, says, "Large parts of man's history are thoroughly well known and beyond dispute. . . . Taken all in all, history is genuine knowledge, and we should be lost without it."[6]

It is wrong to say that the farther away from an event we go the less certain it becomes. Any historian knows that just the opposite can be true. The farther away we get the more perspective we have on the event and thus the more accurate becomes our assessment of it. Also, the farther away you get the more data you gather (artifacts, documents, coins, etc.) to firm up your account of what really happened. George Lichtheim writes:

> The closer we are to an epoch, the more difficult it is to comprehend its essential details; we know at once too much and too little. While innumerable details elude us, enough information is available to make us wonder whether our principle of selection is not arbitrary and irrelevant. With periods lying in the remoter past this difficulty is lessened; we know . . . what gave them their

5. Even a Christian thinker like Kierkegaard felt that the contingent nature of history is a problem. He said that all Biblical studies result only in approximations and approximations are "incommensurable with an infinite personal interest in an eternal happiness" (*Concluding Unscientific Postscript* [Princeton, N.J.: Princeton University Press, 1941], p. 26).

6. Jacques Barzun and Henry F. Graff, *The Modern Researcher* (New York: Harcourt, Brace, and World, 1970), pp. 163-64.

particular character; what it was, vulgarly speaking, that made them tick. Our immediate ancestors are at once more familiar and less comprehensible.[7]

If you admit, Agnos, that history supplies us with genuine knowledge, I can give you several reasons which may help to explain why God chose to reveal himself in this way.

1. Man is a historical creature. He acquires his specific human behavior patterns through institutions founded in history. Very little of his human behavior is passed on by heredity. Since religion is one of his most unique possessions it fits with the general nature of his learning to have religion, like everything else, taught through institutions founded in history. And, since all human institutions use language, both oral and written, it isn't unreasonable that God would use the same medium. It is a relevant fact that most of the great world religions were founded by specific historical individuals: Moses, Zoroaster, Buddha, Christ, Mohammed.

2. If God is a person, it makes a great deal of sense for his revelation to occur in historical events. You can see this point if you think of how a person reveals himself more in *words* and *deeds* than in merely being seen. A rock can be seen, with no initiative on its part, but a person must *say* or *do* something deliberately for us to really know what is "on his mind." To a taciturn person we sometimes exclaim: "Say something; do something!" The same is true of God; revelation is an experience brought about deliberately by the subject (God) so that the object (Man) can gain knowledge of him. As St. Paul wrote to the Corinthians: "What person knows a man's thoughts except the spirit of the man which is in him? So also no one comprehends the thoughts of God except the Spirit of God" (I Cor. 2:11, 12).

Now the Bible is crammed with the wonderful acts of God that reveal his character. In this it differs from the other sacred books of world religions. Most of them read like textbooks on philosophy, or theosophy, or mythology, or cosmology, or religious psychology. But the Bible reads like a textbook of history. There is a prologue in heaven and an aftermath in heaven, but in between it is mostly a narrative of the acts of God in time and space.

3. When God reveals himself in history he at least places his self-disclosure in a realm of objective, empirical fact. Logical Positivists have always complained that statements about God are meaningless because there is no empirical situation to which you can appeal to

7. *Marxism: An Historical and Critical Study* (New York: Praeger, 1961).

check them. They don't make a difference in the real world. This criticism of the Positivists isn't true of some of the theistic arguments and it certainly isn't true of the historical argument. If Biblical history is accurate then God has spoken forcefully in the history of Israel, in the history of the Christian church, and especially in the person of Jesus Christ.

As long as God remains a theory, a postulate, or a hypothesis man may ask, "Why does he hide?" But when he breaks into history and works miracles then unbelief becomes reprehensible, as Christ claimed (John 15:24). Scripture pictures God as the true and living God, not like the idols, which are false and dead. Yahweh makes a difference in history. "The lion has roared; who will not fear? The Lord God has spoken; who can but prophesy?" (Amos 3:8). "Is not my word like fire, says the Lord, and like a hammer which breaks the rock in pieces?" (Jer. 23:29).[8]

4. Christians don't believe that God placed all of his self-disclosure in the past. True, the crucial events are in the past, but even they are preserved in an institution, the Christian church. Furthermore, Christians believe that with the new birth the Holy Spirit of God dwells in every obedient child of God, and this indwelling is certainly a form of contemporary self-disclosure (John 3:5; Acts 5:32). "Whoever confesses that Jesus is the Son of God, God abides in him, and he in God" (I John 4:15). When Christ gave the Great Commission he promised: "Lo, I am with you always, to the close of the age" (Matt. 28:20). The external witness of Scripture and history joins with the internal witness of the Spirit to give certainty to the Christian.

5. Finally, I feel that history is a method of revelation that fits well with the nature of faith, at least as I have used it in this study. I fashioned this idea once while reading Pascal, who was disturbed by the problem we're discussing. Pascal reasoned that if God had wanted to overpower the most stubborn unbeliever he could have revealed himself so clearly that the truth of his existence would have been inescapable.

> It is not in this manner that he chose to appear in the gentleness of his coming; because since so many men had become unworthy of his clemency, he wished them to suffer the privation of the good that they did not want. It would not have been right therefore for him to appear in a way that was plainly divine and

8. Bernard Ramm weaves this theme all through his excellent study, *The God Who Makes a Difference* (Waco, Tex.: Word Books, 1972).

absolutely bound to convince all mankind; but it was not right either that he should come in a manner so hidden that he could not be recognized by those who sought him sincerely. He chose to make himself perfectly knowable to them; and thus, wishing to appear openly to those who seek him with all their heart, and hidden from those who flee him with all their heart, he tempered the knowledge of himself, with the result that he has given signs of himself which are visible to those who seek him, and not to those who do not seek him.[9]

My thesis is that history is an ideal way for God to "temper" the knowledge of himself so that he is partly revealed and partly concealed. If sin has distorted man's thinking—a fundamental Christian tenet—then man would naturally complain that God has hidden himself. But the person who truly seeks God will rejoice at what is revealed, however partial. The person fleeing God will use the partial to justify his unbelief.

How does history reveal God? Well, to give the classic case, if a man could perform miracles, teach a high ethical code, and embody that code in his own person for a period of time, rise from the dead, and then ascend into heaven, I personally would conclude that he was divine or at least had divine power. That is why Christians can say with conviction: Jesus Christ reveals God.

But there's the rub—Christ revealed God to the eyewitnesses of his own time. They were the only ones who directly observed all these things. As soon as you get to the second generation, you get to the partial revelation; you must accept the testimony of eyewitnesses. In this way history partly conceals God, especially from those past the first generation. If Christ would only return to each new generation and arrange his affairs so that every human being could observe these marvelous events for himself, then God's revelation in Christ would be much easier to confirm. The task of the apologist would be much easier.

But then, that is where sin comes in again. Maybe it would be wrong, yes, even indecent, for God to expose the evidence for the faith so frankly. Maybe it would be like casting pearls before swine. Maybe God tucked the evidence back into history so the diligent seeker would find it but the unbeliever would fail to find it because of his prejudice.

We can see this point better if we consider the paradoxical nature of history. People "back there" make history, true, but the practicing historian makes just about as much history as the original participants in the drama. History is *objective* in the sense that the events happened outside the minds of us all and are thus amenable to the in-

9. *Pensées*, #309.

vestigation of all. Yet at the same time history, in a sense, is *subjective*, because the events are not immediately accessible to all—except the eyewitnesses. What happened "back there" must be reconstructed by the practicing historian "right now." You can't go and personally observe the resurrection of Jesus, but this doesn't make the event totally inaccessible to your investigation. Events in the first century are removed, but not totally removed. In a sense, as in a law court, you "see" the event through the eyes of competent witnesses. Perhaps we should say history is "remotely objective."

History and faith, therefore, are closely akin because both demand the attitude of trust before you can use them at all. We believe in order to understand. The layman must trust the work of the historian; the historian must trust his witnesses and his documents; even the witnesses must have first trusted their own senses. This trust, like any kind of faith, isn't credulity or gullibility; there are sufficient reasons to put stock in it, but it still doesn't reach the level of rational certitude. History is like man, in Alexander Pope's words,

> With too much knowledge for the skeptic side,
> With too much weakness for the stoic's pride,
> He hangs between . . .

By being a kind of centaur, partly objective and partly subjective, history avoids the two extremes we discussed in chapter three, rationalism and mysticism.

History avoids *rationalism*, because you must have some faith when you assent to a historical proposition. Unless someone develops a time machine, there'll always be some uncertainty about an event in history. Nowhere in history (or in most of life, for that matter) do you escape the necessity of believing and trusting in others—a condition that fairly enrages a compulsive rationalist. If you insist on believing only what you can directly experience, then history will be the first sacred cow to perish from your scepticism. You'd have to live in the specious, eternal present, because even your own memory wouldn't be immediate enough!

History avoids *mysticism*, on the other hand, because it insists that the historical event isn't totally subjective. An event actually occurred back there, and thus it isn't locked up in anyone's mind. Having occurred objectively, it is from then on available to all inquiring minds. Furthermore, your apprehension of an event can be verbalized and described; it isn't ineffable, for you can tell others of the event and invite them to examine it. Those who complain that religion should be universally known to all men overlook the fact that a historical event, by being objective, is potentially a universal truth. All you have to do to make it universal is spread the news—hence the Christian emphasis on preaching the good news of the gospel of Jesus Christ.

Rationalism overlooks the subjective element in faith and history; mysticism overlooks the objective element. These two extremes seem to promise certainty, the one by inescapable deductive operations, the other by perfect personal contact. Both dislike the distance, the partial contact, affirmed by the moderate position of faith and history. Yet this is precisely the strength of the moderate position: it has enough rationalism to keep subjectivism from degenerating into sheer superstition, yet enough mysticism to keep objectivism from evaporating into the air of intellectualism. History and faith go hand in hand, because together they combine the best elements of rationalism and mysticism. They create a subtle balance between knowledge and hope, a beneficent tension between reason and will, analysis and choice, head and heart, logic and axiologic.

Just as faith is a state of conviction midway between certainty and credulity, so history is a mode of revelation midway between (1) total disclosure of God and (2) total concealment of God. Those who seek God with a pure heart and an open mind will find him in history, I believe, for his revelation there is adequate. But for those who have already made up their minds that they won't believe, history is unconvincing; they gleefully point to its uncertainty, its contingency, its lack of demonstration. Very well, God lets them remain in their unbelief, for if history were totally demonstrative, their intellectual acceptance of Christian theism would have no impact on their wills. As Pascal concluded: "There is light enough for those who desire only to see and darkness enough for those of a contrary disposition."

Jesus had a disciple who distrusted history: Thomas "the Twin." When Thomas heard the other disciples testify, "We have seen the Lord," he said, "Unless I see in his hands the print of the nails, and place my finger in the mark of the nails, and place my hand in his side, I will not believe." A week later the risen Lord appeared to Thomas and granted his request: "Put your finger here, and see my hands; and put out your hand, and place it in my side; do not be faithless, but believing." Thomas responded: "My Lord and my God!" The final words of Jesus sum up my point very well: "Have you believed because you have seen me? Blessed are those who have not seen and yet believe" (John 20:24-29).

C. CONCLUSION.

Jean Jacques Rousseau once wrote to a friend: "Is it simple, is it natural, that God should have gone and found Moses in order to speak to Jean Jacques Rousseau?"[10] Well, Agnos, I admit it isn't simple, but I wonder if we have the right to assume that truth is always simple or that God governs his universe on a plan that we would regard as simple? If I've opened your mind to the possibility of God revealing himself in history then read on—we are now ready to argue from Biblical history.

Suggestions for Further Reading

James Connolly, *Human History and the Word of God* (New York: Macmillan, 1965).

H. G. Wood, *Christianity and the Nature of History* (New York: Cambridge University Press, 1938).

G. Ernest Wright, *God Who Acts* (Naperville, IL: Allenson, 1952).

10.   Cited in John Baillie, *A Reasoned Faith* (New York: Scribner, 1963), p. 164.

THE BIBLE AS HISTORY

The historical accuracy of the Bible, Agnos, is a crucial part of our case for Christianity. The great difference between the Christian faith and most other religions is the status of history. The Bible claims that God participated in actual history, that he revealed his mind and will to real people, not to mythical beings on Mt. Olympus or Mt. Parnassus.

If God worked in history and if the Bible is a record of that work, then we'd expect the Bible to be substantially accurate. We'd expect it to be truthful to the external reality surrounding the events of divine revelation. In this chapter we'll survey some of the evidence for the factual accuracy of the Bible.

A. THE BIBLE AND PHYSICAL FACT.

History takes place on earth and the earth has certain definite features: seas, rivers, mountains, valleys, plains. When the Bible mentions such features it is, as far as we can determine, accurate. It mentions many rivers: Nile, Jordan, Tigris, Euphrates, Jabbok, Arnon, Zered, Abana, Pharpar. It mentions many mountains: Hermon, Lebanon, Tabor, Nebo, Sinai, Carmel, Ebal, Gerizim. It mentions plains and valleys: Jezreel, Philistia, Aijalon, Shinar. In all such references the Bible never has a geographical feature out of place. In some cases, the Bible is the only ancient document that preserves the correct location of the geographical feature. The river Ulai, for instance, was unknown outside of the Old Testament (Dan. 8:2) until it was found in the Assyrian inscriptions of Ashurbanipal.

The Bible mentions hundreds of cities: Ur, Babylon, Nineveh,

Raamses, Jerusalem, Bethlehem, Hebron, Megiddo, Nazareth, Capernaum, Antioch, Ephesus, Athens, Corinth, Rome, and hundreds more. The Scripture has all of them, large and small, in the right location. Many, like Damascus and Jericho, have known continual occupation for about 8000 years. Others, like Ai and Lachish, had to be excavated, and archaeology shows that such cities were always occupied at the time the Bible says they were.[1]

Even local geological features are rendered accurately by the Bible. It's correct to speak of "bricks and bitumen" going into the Tower of Babel (Gen. 11:3), instead of stone, the material customarily used in towers of antiquity, because there is no stone in the alluvial plain of Babylon. It's correct to speak of "bitumen pits" in the Valley of Siddim (Gen. 14:10), since bitumen (asphalt) deposits have been found both in and around the Dead Sea. It's not at all fanciful to talk of "fire and brimstone" destroying Sodom and Gomorrah (Gen. 19:24), since sulphur, natural gas, volcanic and earthquake conditions all exist in the region south of the Dead Sea.

World famous Jewish archaeologist, Nelson Glueck, once gave the Bible a nice offhand compliment: he said it was so accurate in geographical and topographical matters that he carried a copy with him all the time, like a road map.

B. THE BIBLE AND SOCIAL FACT: OLD TESTAMENT.

A far greater test of accuracy, however, lies in the ability of the Bible to correctly represent social phenomena: politics, economics, historical events, social customs. In this realm also the Bible has an excellent track record.

1. The Patriarchal Period (Gen. 1–46) has been confirmed and illuminated by discoveries in the Near East such as the Code of Hammurabi and the Nuzi Tablets. Critics in the past century had a bad habit of writing off the whole period of Abraham, Isaac, and Jacob as mythical or only quasi-historical, but archaeology has shown it to be, in Albright's words, "essentially historical."

For example, the Code of Hammurabi shows that a woman who

---

1. One notable exception to this is the cities of the Philistine Plain. The Book of Genesis (chs. 20, 26) shows Abraham and Isaac having dealings with these people, whereas archaeology indicates that they didn't settle in the plain until c. 1200 B.C., several centuries after Abraham. Some harmonists suggest that the writer of Genesis was using "Philistia" as the name of the area because it was known by that title to later generations. See M. Burrows, *What Mean These Stones?, The Significance of Archaeology for Biblical Studies* (New Haven, Conn.: American Schools of Oriental Research, 1941), pp. 97, 277.

was childless could give a handmaid to her husband and claim the offspring, a privilege used by both Sarah and Rachel (Gen. 16:2; 30:4). The Nuzi tablets show that it was unlawful for a mistress to drive out her handmaid, a regulation which explains Abraham's apprehension when Sarah expelled Hagar and Ishmael (Gen. 21:11). In that region a childless couple could adopt someone to care for them and to inherit the estate when they died, a custom which explains Abraham's complaint to God that he would have to leave his estate to a non-relative, Eliezer of Damascus (Gen. 15:2). From recent discoveries we can understand why Isaac didn't revoke his oral blessing on Jacob even after he had discovered Jacob's fraud (Gen. 27:33). The Nuzi tablets show that an oral blessing was irrevocable and had legal sanction even in a court of law. A man's dying words were accepted as a legal will and testament, a practice which helps us understand Jacob's blessing on the twelve tribes when he died (Gen. 49:3-27). The Nuzi tablets, the Assyrian Code, and the Hittite Code all contain references to the practice of a man taking his brother's widow and raising children in the name of her dead husband (Deut. 25:5-10).

A very striking confirmation of Biblical accuracy concerns the mysterious *teraphim* that Rachel stole as she departed from her father, Laban (Gen. 31:33ff.). To explain Laban's frantic attempt to recover them, older commentators suggested that the images were made of gold. The Nuzi tablets cleared up the mystery when they showed that the teraphim were actually household deities that functioned as title deeds to a person's estate. Any daughter who possessed them could appear in court and claim the family property for her husband.

Wandering around the south end of the Dead Sea today you might wonder if anyone ever lived there, much less if five cities existed in that barren region during the time of the patriarchs, as the Old Testament indicates (Gen. 14:3). Archaeology shows that this region in c. 2500-2000 B.C. was fertile, prosperous, and well populated.

2. The Old Testament story of Israel in Egypt fits well with what we know of Egypt from external sources.

One of the most subtle confirmations of Biblical history we have is the undesigned correlation between the pharaoh "who did not know Joseph" (Exod. 1:8) and the rise of a new dynasty of native Egyptian pharaohs in the 16th century B.C. The Israelites had been invited into Egypt under the rule of the Hyksos, foreigners who gained control of Egypt from c. 1900 to 1730 B.C. When the Hyksos were expelled it naturally follows that the new native dynasty would enslave and oppress any similar Semitic group that had migrated into Egypt at the same time (Exod. 1:11).

Critics have often cast doubt on the possibility of a slave from Canaan such as Joseph being elevated to a high position in the government of Egypt. Inscriptions give many illustrations, however, of this sort of thing happening. They also tell us that the pharaoh often allowed families from Palestine to settle in the delta region. We have documents from c. 1350 B.C. indicating that it was normal for frontier officials to allow people from adjoining regions to come into Egypt in periods of famine.

Genesis 47:13-26 tells us that during the great famine the people of Egypt sold their livestock, their land, and finally themselves to the government in order to survive. That the government could have such complete political and economic power over the people is something we know to be true from the external sources. It was considered necessary for survival. When Joseph described his position to his brothers as "a father to Pharaoh, and lord of all his house and ruler over all the land of Egypt" (Gen. 45:8), he used the regular official titles found on many monuments.

Many Egyptian social customs are correctly represented in the Old Testament. Inscriptions mention the "chief of butlers" and "chief of the bakers" as well as the "overseer of the house" and "superintendent of granaries." We know that mummification of great men was a common custom, that magicians were plentiful at the court of pharaoh, that shepherds were held in contempt, that dreams were very important, that straw was used in brickmaking, and that the priests had their own allotments of grain and land from pharaoh.

3. Various aspects of Canaanite culture have been confirmed and illuminated by archaeology. One of the most subtle, defying all claims of forgery in the Bible, is the quality of workmanship found in the building of cities, walls and fortifications. Archaeology shows that just at the time Joshua and Israel entered Canaan, there was a noticeable deterioration in the walled fortifications of the cities, a fact that fits nicely with the influx of Hebrews from the desert. Canaanite city-states could construct buildings with a feudal organization using forced labor, whereas the Israelites were only loosely organized by tribes. Furthermore, you could hardly expect a people who had been wandering in the wilderness for 40 years to match the Canaanites in building techniques. By the time of King Saul, however, their construction ability had improved a great deal, as Albright discovered in his excavation of King Saul's highland castle at Gibeah. Excavations of buildings in Megiddo show that more improvements in technique

began to appear about the time of David and Solomon, a fact which coincides with the Biblical claim that those two monarchs imported Phoenician building materials and workmen (I Kings 5:1-12).

The Israelites were forbidden to boil a kid in its mother's milk (Exod. 23:19; 34:26), a prohibition which long puzzled commentators. The Ras Shamra tablets, from ancient Ugarit in Syria, show that boiling a kid in its mother's milk was a characteristic rite in Canaanite religion, used as a magical technique for producing early rains. Canaanite religious literature generally confirms the Old Testament references to Canaan's religion. This literature has all the gods we meet in the Old Testament: El, Baal and their sacred courtesans, Anath, Asherah, and Astarte. It has all the degrading cult practices: a sex-centered ritual, snake worship, human sacrifice, and many eunuch priests. We even have burial jars with the remains of children sacrificed to idols.

The Old Testament leaves the impression that the Philistines were a very powerful people in the period of conquest and the judges. The monuments of Ramses III of Egypt depict his battles with some Philistines who tried to land in the Nile delta. References to the Philistine "temple of Dagon" (I Chron. 10:10) are shown correct by the discovery of such a temple at Ugarit as well as two steles erected to Dagon. Excavations in the plain of Philistia have shown that the Philistines had iron weapons and chariots. This confirms the statement in Joshua 17:16-18 that the Canaanites had iron weapons while the Hebrews had none. Diggings all over the plain have turned up special jugs with a special spout used to separate the beer from the husks. The great number of these jugs suggests a heavy-drinking folk, a description which fits with the picture of the Philistines we get from the Book of Judges.

Many historical events in the remainder of the Old Testament have direct confirmation from external sources. To mention just a few: the invasion of Pharaoh Shishak into Palestine (I Kings 14:25, 26); the rebellion of King Mesha of Moab (II Kings 3:4, 5); Tiglath-Pileser III's destruction of Samaria and deportation of the people of the Northern Kingdom (II Kings 17:5, 6); the existence of Ahab and Jehu (I Kings 16–22; II Kings 9, 10); Hazael's usurpation of the Syrian throne (II Kings 8:7-15); Hezekiah's payment of tribute to Sennacherib (II Kings 18:14); Hezekiah's construction of a pool and conduit (II Chron. 32:2-4, 30); Sennacherib's campaigns in Judah (II Kings 18, 19; Isa. 36–38); Nebuchadnezzar's campaigns in Judah (II Kings 25:21, 22); the existence of Gedaliah, governor of Judah (II Kings 25:22); Jehoiachim's residence in Babylon (II Kings 25:27-30); Cyrus' policy of liberating captive peoples and rebuilding their religious sanctuaries

(Ezra 1:2, 3); the existence of Sanballat and Tobiah (Neh. 2:10, 19); the existence of a colony of Jews in Egypt after the conquest of Nebuchadnezzar (Jer. 41–44); and many, many more.

C. THE BIBLE AND SOCIAL FACT: NEW TESTAMENT.

When we come to the New Testament world, the first century Roman Empire, the socio-political situation becomes so complex that the accuracy of the Biblical writers is severely tested. For example, the political divisions of Asia Minor given in the New Testament agree amazingly with those given by the Roman geographer Pliny. Phrygia, Galatia, Lycaonia, Cilicia, Pamphylia, Pisidia, Asia, Mysia, Bithynia—all are recognized by Pliny and modern archaeologists as politically distinct divisions of the empire in that region.

The various sections of Palestine represented in the New Testament correspond exactly with the political situation of the first century and with no other. Judea, Samaria, Galilee, Trachonitis, Ituraea, Abilene, and Decapolis are all recognized as politically distinct at this period by such external sources as Pliny, Strabo, and Josephus, and these sources are confirmed by countless pieces of archaeological data like coins and inscriptions. This "crazy-quilt" situation would have made it extremely difficult for a forger to do his work undetected.

1.   The gospel records of the life of Christ breathe the atmosphere of first century Palestine as we know it from the external sources. We meet the correct types of people: Herod's family, Judeans, Galileans, Greeks, Romans, Samaritans, soldiers, tax collectors, farmers, fishermen, beggars, lepers. We meet the correct religious groups: Pharisees, Sadducees, Herodians, Zealots, rabbis, and the common people, the "quiet in the land." We hear the proper theological questions discussed: Should Jews give tribute to Caesar? Is there a resurrection? What is the greatest commandment? Can a man divorce his wife for any reason? We hear of the correct Jewish feasts: Passover, Tabernacles, Dedication. We find accurate references to Jewish purification rites, burial customs, wedding celebrations, synagogue procedures, laws of evidence in the Sanhedrin, sheepherding practices, and so forth.

2.   The gentile historian, Luke, deserves to be singled out as a special case when one discusses the accuracy of the New Testament. More than any other New Testament writer, Luke tried to set his record in the total context of imperial Roman history. He began his Gospel in the grand style of the great Greek historian, Thucydides:

> In the fifteenth year of the reign of Tiberius Caesar, Pontius
> Pilate being governor of Judea, and Herod being tetrarch of
> Galilee, and his brother Philip tetrarch of the region of Ituraea
> and Trachonitis, and Lysanias tetrarch of Abilene, in the high-
> priesthood of Annas and Caiaphas, the word of God came to
> John the son of Zechariah in the wilderness. (Luke 3:1, 2)

Only Luke among New Testament writers mentions Roman
emperors: Augustus, Tiberius, Claudius, and (though not by name)
Nero. He also mentions several Roman provincial governors:
Quirinius, Pilate, Sergius Paulus, Gallio, Felix, and Festus. He also
refers to three Herods (the Great, Antipas, Agrippa), Bernice, Drusilla,
Annas, Caiaphas, Ananias, and Gamaliel, the greatest Jewish rabbi of
that time. As F. F. Bruce remarks: "A writer who thus relates his story
to the wider context of world history is courting trouble if he is not
careful; he affords his critical readers so many opportunities for
testing his accuracy."[2]

Luke's accuracy has been confirmed so many times in the past two
centuries that it is safe to say that anytime there is a conflict between
him and an external source Luke should be given the benefit of the
doubt.

In support of Luke we know, for example, that there was a
Synagogue of the Freedmen in Jerusalem in the first century (Acts
6:9); that there was a dynasty of queens in Ethiopia at that time (Acts
8:27); that a Sergius Paulus ruled Cyprus at mid-century (Acts 13:7);
that the people of Lycaonia used their old native language (Acts
14:11); that Gallio was proconsul of Achaia while Paul was in Corinth (Acts 18:12); that there was a Synagogue of the Hebrews in Corinth (Acts 18:4-7); that the people of Athens loved idle discussion and
had altars to unknown gods (Acts 17:21, 23); that grain ships from
Alexandria, Egypt, sailed under the lee of Crete, stopped at Cauda
and Malta, and unloaded at Puteoli (Acts 27, 28).

Luke understood the complicated political terminology used in the
eastern parts of the Roman Empire. He knew that Sergius Paulus was
proconsul not procurator of Cyprus (Acts 13:7); that the Greek word
meris was used to denote a political district (Acts 16:12); that the city
of Ephesus called itself "Warden of the Temple of Artemis" (Acts
19:35); that Ephesian officials were called "Asiarchs" (Acts 19:31);
that the chief magistrates of Thessalonica were called "politarchs"
(Acts 17:6, 8); that the magistrates of Philippi were "praetors" at-

---

2. *The New Testament Documents: Are They Reliable?* (Grand Rapids: Eerdmans,
1965), p. 82.

tended by "lictors" (Acts 16:20, 35); that the Roman governor of Malta was called the "first man of the island," or, in Latin, *Meliten-sium primus* (Acts 28:7).

In Acts 14:8-14 Luke says that Paul healed a man in the city of Lystra in the province of Lycaonia. The people immediately tried to worship Paul and Barnabas, calling them Zeus and Hermes. We know from many dedicatory tablets to these two deities that they were the patrons of the city. But how do you explain the excitement of the priests of Zeus, whom Paul and Barnabas could hardly restrain from sacrificing in their honor? The answer comes when we note that, according to an old story, these two deities once visited Lystra in human form. When only two of the townspeople welcomed them, the angry gods turned the city into a lake and all the inhabitants into fish. Obviously, therefore, the people of Lystra didn't want to repeat the previous mistake of mistreating heavenly visitors.

In Acts 14:6 Luke says that Paul and Barnabas left Iconium and "fled to Lystra and Derbe, cities of Lycaonia." This implies that Lystra and Derbe were in the territory of Lycaonia and Iconium was not, an assertion which is contradicted by Cicero, another first century author. This conflict was often used to prove Luke untrustworthy. In 1910, Sir William Ramsey discovered a monument in Asia Minor which showed that Iconium was considered to be a Phrygian city, not a Lycaonian city, thus exonerating Luke from the charge. Ramsey said that discoveries like this changed his evaluation of the historical accuracy of Luke.[3]

3.   The epistles of Paul yield many parallels with external sources. His picture of the city of Corinth is very accurate, for the city was well-known in the Roman Empire as a center of vice and debauchery (I Cor. 6:9-11). "To corinthianize" was a synonym for sexual license. "Shambles" or market places, such as are mentioned in I Cor. 10:25, have been found at Corinth. Greek papyri of the time speak of a "table of Lord Serapis," which parallels Paul's reference to a "table of demons" (I Cor. 10:21).

Paul's mention of the ethnarch of King Aretas in Damascus (II Cor. 11:32) is confirmed by discoveries which show him to have reigned there c. A.D. 35-40. Many statements in Galatians and Romans resemble closely the formulae used in the adoption and emancipation of slaves in the first century. Paul's reference to a "middle wall of partition" (Eph. 2:14, AV) between Jew and Gentile may be literally ac-

---

3. *St. Paul the Traveler and the Roman Citizen* (Grand Rapids: Baker, 1962), pp. 7, 8.

curate, for such a barricade around the Temple has been found, with death warnings for violators.

4. The Book of Revelation touches on secular history at a number of points. For example, a coin from the time of Emperor Vespasian represents Rome as a woman seated on seven hills, the very symbol John uses (Rev. 17:9). The custom of using the letters of the alphabet as numbers was common and may shed light on the 666 of Revelation 13:18. On a wall at Pompeii, Italy, is scribbled, "I love a girl whose number is 545." Pliny the Elder *(Natural History,* IV.12.23) confirms the statement that the island of Patmos was used for banishment of undesirable persons (Rev. 1:9).

The city of Pergamum was a notable center of idolatry, with temples to Zeus, Athena, Apollo, and Asclepios, as well as a shrine for emperor worship. All of this well qualifies it for John's description, "where Satan's throne is" (Rev. 2:13). Laodicea had warm springs nearby, was a wealthy banking center, and was known for its eye-salve; these facts illuminate John's charges that the Christians there were lukewarm, poor, and blind (Rev. 3:15-17).

D. SOME STARTLING REVERSALS.

At a few critical junctures in Bible history discoveries from archaeology and secular history have dramatically reversed the negative critical opinion of Biblical accuracy. Let's look at five of these cases.

1. Higher critics used to ridicule the story in Genesis 14 of the rout of the Mesopotamian kings by Abraham and his small band. Julius Wellhausen said the account was "simply impossible." Specifically, they objected that: (1) the names of the kings were fictitious, (2) such extensive travel was unknown in Abraham's day, (3) there was no highway or line of cities along which the invading army could march, and (4) there was no motive for the invasion.

All four objections have been eliminated: (1) the names have been deemed authentic, (2) travel is known to have been that extensive, (3) the line of march has been established, and (4) a good motive— copper—has been found in the region between the Dead Sea and the Gulf of Aqaba. On point #3, Glueck and Albright established that there was a line of early and middle Bronze Age cities running along the border of the Arabian desert in Transjordan. This was undoubtedly the route of the invasion and in fact was later called "the King's Highway." Albright testified that this discovery began to change his

estimate of the Book of Genesis. He said that he "formerly considered
this extraordinary line of march as being the best proof of the essentially legendary character of the narrative."[4]

2. In the last century, one of the most "assured results" of higher
criticism in Old Testament studies was that Israel's religion went
through an evolutionary development from animism to polytheism to
monolatry to monotheism, the last stage coming, not in Moses' time,
but as late as the sixth century B.C. Thus, critics denied the antiquity
of the second commandment, "Thou shalt not make unto thee any
graven image" (Exod. 20:4, AV). They maintained that the Israelites
worshipped images of Yahweh in the time of Moses, just as the Canaanites worshipped images of their gods.

If this critical opinion were true, you'd expect to find images of
Yahweh in Palestine. We have images of many other gods: Baal,
Astarte, Mekal, Dagon. Yet after about 200 years of rather extensive
excavations in Palestine we still can't lay our hands on an image of
Yahweh. There is no reason why images of Yahweh should be more
perishable than (say) images of Dagon. Thus, archaeology, by its
silence, fails to support the critical theory at this point.

3. The Old Testament contains references to many obscure
peoples of ancient times, such as Hurrians, Horites, Hivites, Hittites. It
has over 40 references to the people called the Hittites (e.g., Josh. 1:4).
Despite these many references, scholars in the past doubted the very
existence or at least the importance of this nation. In 1906 Hugo
Winckler of Berlin uncovered Boghasköy in central Turkey, which
proved to be the capital of the old Hittite Empire. Hittite writings
were excavated and deciphered, opening up a new chapter in the
history of western Asia and confirming the numerous Biblical
references to this forgotten people.

4. Critics used to attack the Book of Daniel for its statement that
Belshazzar was the king of Babylon at the time of the fall of Babylon
(Dan. 5:30). The charge seemed valid because ancient historians like
Berossus (c. 250 B.C.) and Alexander Polyhistor asserted that
Nabonidus was the last king of Babylon.

Actually, all three sources (Daniel, Berossus, Alexander Polyhistor)
were telling the truth, in a sense, because Nabonidus, the real king,
had a bad case of wanderlust which took him for long periods into
Tema, Arabia, leaving Belshazzar, the crown prince, in control of

---

4. *The Archaeology of Palestine and the Bible* (New York: Revell, 1935), p. 142.

Babylon. Since Nabonidus was absent when Babylon fell, Daniel told the truth when he said Belshazzar was the ruler. This, by the way, explains Belshazzar's mysterious statement that whoever could read the handwriting on the wall would become *"third* ruler in the kingdom" (Dan. 5:7, 29).[5]

5. In New Testament studies, one of the most upsetting (to critics) discoveries of the twentieth century was the John Rylands Fragment of John. This small piece of papyrus was discovered in 1935 by C. H. Roberts, working in a pile of documents excavated several years earlier and sent to the John Rylands Library in England. The fragment contained only a few verses (John 18:31-33, 37, 38), but it was large enough to prove, after certain tests, that it came from the first half of the second century. Sir Frederic Kenyon, Director of the British Museum and specialist in New Testament manuscripts, said that the original manuscript circulated in Egypt (where the fragment came from) about A.D. 130-150. This means that the original Gospel of John was composed some time earlier than A.D. 130. This comes so close to the traditional date for John (c. A.D. 90-100) that, in Kenyon's words, "there is no longer any reason to question the validity of the tradition."[6]

If John was written at the close of the first century, much of the old critical position on the four gospels is destroyed forever. Many critics said the synoptics were written around A.D. 150 and some dated John as late as A.D. 240. As we shall see later, this discovery has an important bearing on our argument for Jesus Christ, because it eliminates the possibility of there having been a lengthy time period between the life of Christ and the writing of the gospels—a period the critics said was necessary for his claims to have evolved.

E. CONCLUSION.

All I've tried to establish in this chapter, Agnos, is that the Bible is a substantially reliable historical document. I've barely scratched the surface of the material data that support this claim. I hope you will continue to read in the field of Bible history and archaeology, especially from the "old masters" like Albright, Glueck, and Ramsey.

5. R. P. Dougherty, *Nabonidus and Belshazzar* (New Haven: Yale University Press, 1929). Nothing has been discovered, however, to help us solve another problem of the Book of Daniel. Daniel (5:31; 9:1; 11:1) has Darius the Mede conquering Babylon, while history and archaeology insist that it was Cyrus the Persian. It has been suggested that Darius was a general of Cyrus who led the actual capture of Babylon, but we really don't know for sure.

6. *The Bible and Modern Scholarship* (London: Murray, 1948), p. 21.

Most scholars in this field would concur with me when I say that it's
no longer proper to ridicule the Bible as an old folk tale full of myths
and legends that never really happened. Most scholars would agree
with Glueck, when he says, "It may be stated categorically that no archaeological discovery has ever controverted a Biblical reference.
Scores of archaeological finds have been made which confirm in clear
outline or in exact detail historical statements in the Bible."[7]

A good worldview will have a broad base of factual support. The
Bible has such a base. The popular phrase, "archaeology proves the
Bible," is an unfortunate one, because there is utterly no way that archaeology by itself could prove the Bible inspired or divine. What archaeology *does* show, however, is that in many, many cases of a factual nature the Scripture speaks accurately. And with that humble
result, Agnos, our argument can continue.

Suggestions for Further Reading

William F. Albright, *Archaeology and the Religion of Israel* (Baltimore: Johns
Hopkins Press, 1942); *From the Stone Age to Christianity* (New York:
Doubleday, 1957).

George A. Barton, *Archaeology and the Bible* (Philadelphia: American Sunday School Union, 1916).

C. W. Ceram, *Gods, Graves and Scholars* (New York: Knopf, 1951).

John Elder, *Prophets, Idols, and Diggers: Scientific Proof of Bible History*
(New York: Bobbs-Merrill, 1960).

Jack Finegan, *Light from the Ancient Past* (Princeton: Princeton University
Press, 1946).

Sir Charles Marston, *The Bible Comes Alive* (London: Eyre & Spottiswoode,
1937).

J. B. Pritchard, *Ancient Near Eastern Texts Relating to the Old Testament*
(Princeton: Princeton University Press, 1950).

George E. Wright, *Biblical Archaeology* (Philadelphia: Westminster Press,
1957).

7. *Rivers in the Desert* (New York: Farrar, Straus, and Cudahy, 1959), p. 31.

11

MIRACLES

If the Bible is an accurate historical record, Agnos, then you now
face the brunt of the historical argument for God: miracles. You're
now ready to confront the God who makes a difference, the God who
"hooks" the senses, the God who drives his existence home in the dimension of history, the realm of the empirical, the tangible, the concrete. In the next two chapters we'll look at the miracles of Christianity and in the four following chapters we'll examine *the* miracle, Jesus
Christ.

In stressing miracles, we don't add anything to the Bible itself.
Christian apologists didn't invent the emphasis on miracles; it is already in the Bible (John 20:20; Heb. 2:3, 4). We're not using a strategy
devised by Christians after the Bible had been written; miracles are an
inherent part of the scriptural witness. They are integral, not incidental, to God's revelation. They occur through the entire Bible, from the
Exodus to the church.

At a critical juncture in Israel's history God gave Moses special
signs to answer Pharaoh's demand, "Prove yourselves by working a
miracle" (Exod. 7:9). Christ made special appeal to his wonders to
authenticate his message. To his disciples he said, "Believe me for the
sake of the works" (John 14:11). To a crowd questioning his messiahship, he said, "The works that I do in my Father's name, they bear
witness to me" (John 10:25). To prove his messiahship to his cousin
John, he pointed to the fact that "the blind see, the lame walk, the
lepers are cleansed, the deaf hear, the dead are raised" (Luke 7:22,
AV). The strongest statement of all is in John 15:24, where Christ
said, "If I had not done among them the works which no one else did,
they would not have sin; but now they have seen and hated both me

137

and my Father." His miracles were so clear that an unbelieving eye-witness hated both him and God!

It wouldn't be wrong, therefore, to say that the truth of the Christian faith stands or falls with the historicity of its miracles. Those who deny the historicity of its miracles have no right to apply to themselves the term "Christian" in its historic meaning, any more than a Marxist has a right to call himself a Platonist.

A. DEFINITION OF A MIRACLE.

It is important that we properly define a miracle before our investigation begins. Those who define a miracle as a violation, interruption, transgression, or contradiction of natural law prejudge the question before the examination can even start. It is far more honest to define miracles so that their historical possibility is left an open question. That is, your definition shouldn't have any metaphysical implications. It is a curious species of logical knavery that defines something as impossible and then concludes from the definition that there is no evidence for it.

The safest general definition of a miracle is "an event initiated by God." The most general definition mustn't say that a miracle is an exception to law, because the Bible often treats a completely natural and everyday event as a miracle, such as the wind blowing in a favorable direction, or a battle ending in victory before sunset, or a rainstorm occurring at an auspicious time. Such events, though natural, were regarded as remarkable demonstrations of the power and love of God.

Usually, however, a Biblical miracle is an exception to natural law and it is this concept of miracle that has more apologetic value, because the exception is more of a wonder than the rule. When King Hezekiah asked Isaiah for a sign, the prophet gave him the choice of having the shadow on the sundial go forward ten steps or backward ten steps. Hezekiah replied:"It is an easy thing for the shadow to lengthen ten steps; rather let the shadow go back ten steps" (II Kings 20:10).

For apologetic purposes, therefore, I would define a miracle as "an event, occurring in history, which is so different from a well-known natural law that it arrests the attention of the spectator(s) and deserves to be considered a special intervention of a supernatural agent." Notice I haven't concluded that a miracle is necessarily a sign from God, only that it is so different from the regular order that it *might* be interpreted as a divine sign.

You may expand this definition in the interest of precision by saying that a miracle is a "non-repeatable counter-instance of a law of nature." If the event didn't run counter to natural law it wouldn't be considered a miracle at all, for a wonder must have a background of uniform activity to stand out as unique. By "non-repeatable" we don't mean that the miracle occurred only once in history, but that ordinary men can't duplicate it at will, as they could if it were a law of nature. If men could cause a counter-instance of an alleged law to occur regularly, we would then change the law the miracles were countering; the miracle would become regular and not unique, and the original law would have to be revised.

Therefore, miracles and laws are different, but it is wrong to define a miracle with words like "violate," "transgress," or "contradict." These words, as we shall see, conjure up a misleading analogy between nature's laws and the laws of society. Our definition is neutral; it identifies the event we are looking for while leaving open the possibility of its actual occurrence.

You might think that all we have to do now is present historical evidence for Biblical miracles. Actually we must wait until the next chapter for that. The attorney for the defense has all kinds of interesting motions to have the whole case thrown out of court before the trial even begins. We need, that is, to remove a host of objections before we look at Biblical miracles. Most of the objections fall into two major groups: (1) *philosophical* and (2) *historical.*

B. PHILOSOPHICAL OBJECTIONS.

The essence of most philosophical objections to miracles is the assumption that the universe is so structured that miracles are impossible by definition. The objections usually come from two major systems: naturalism and philosophical theism.

1. **Naturalism.** The objection to miracles from naturalism has a crude version and a subtle version. The crude version is essentially deductive, strange as it may sound for a naturalist to use *a priori* reasoning. It rules out miracles by an *a priori* metaphysical assumption and relieves the objector of the hard task of examining the alleged miracles in history. In short, it says: "There is no God, only nature, only matter, mechanically determined matter, ruled by uniform, unchanging, physical laws. Miracles are obviously impossible in such a cosmos."

I've stated it rather baldly to bring out the obvious bias in the position. Such a dogmatic statement needs a lot of proof before you can use it as an *a priori* club. Has the naturalist carefully surveyed the theistic arguments and ruled—beyond all doubt—that all of them are totally worthless? What arrogant person would say this? But this is what you must say to use naturalism as an *a priori* club against miracles. You seem to say: "I know what all is possible in this universe, and I know that non-repeatable counter-instances to natural laws are impossible."

Really? Do you know all that? As a matter of fact, many who have carefully and systematically examined the theistic proofs have come away from the experience actual believers, or at least reverent agnostics. You can't say that the proofs are totally worthless. In their total, cumulative effect they are rather impressive, one might say probable, certainly possible, maybe plausible. And the fact that you can't be certain that theistic proofs are worthless prevents you from viciously ruling out miracles.

This question reminds me of the man who asserted that "in theory a bumblebee can't fly." Why? Because his body violates some fundamental rules of aerodynamics (short wings, wrong body size, disproportionate weight, etc.). Now, that's fine, Agnos, but have you ever seen a bumblebee fly? I have, and I therefore strongly suspect any theory that says he can't. Similarly, if I look into history and find good evidence for miracles, I strongly suspect a worldview that says they are impossible. Especially if it makes this assertion *before* I'm even allowed to look at the historical evidence!

Suppose for the moment that there *was* strong evidence for a miracle. How would this objector react to it? He would probably classify it as a "random malfunction" of nature, a strange phenomenon he might best forget. But what if the miracle was so clear and the law it countered so well-established that this rationalization wouldn't satisfy his inquiring intellect? Couldn't this make the objector wonder if such events might not indeed be miracles and if a causative agent (God) might not really exist? Yes, this could happen and, as a matter of fact, has happened many times over the centuries.

The problem here is similar to the small child who was brainwashed by his criminal parents for several years to believe that "all cops are bad." The first good cop he met disturbed his conviction. He had the choice of either giving up his prejudice or explaining away the good cop. Every good cop he met placed more and more strain on his prejudice. Finally, he met so many good cops that the pressure of the evidence made him modify his conviction to: "Not all cops are bad."

The same is true with miracles. You can come to believe in miracles in a variety of ways: (1) you can allow the pressure of the evidence to change your rigid worldview so you can "see" them. (2) You can look at alleged miracles with a more flexible naturalistic worldview and let them change your "glasses." Or, (3) you may already believe in the agent who is able to cause miracles and accept them when you receive adequate testimony. In the history of the Hebrew-Christian religion people have accepted them by all three methods (though I admit that #1 is probably rare). But, in all cases, the data are the same: the historical evidence for miracles; *that* remains constant and must either be explained away or accepted.

But the naturalistic objection to miracles takes a subtler form than this. Instead of the dogmatic statement just analyzed, you more often will hear it like this: "Science is not friendly to miracles. A universe in which miracles occurred would be completely capricious, whimsical, unpredictable. It would destroy science, which must have uniform laws."[1] Stated this way, the objection is much harder to answer.

The core of this objection is really just a complaint, not an argument. The naturalist complains that miracles ruin the closed, mechanical character of the physical universe and thus frustrate scientific prediction. Note first the metaphysical assumptions that bristle beneath the surface: the objector blandly assumes that this *is* a closed universe, a mechanical universe, one where prediction would never be frustrated. The objector implies that the universe is, as it were, a perpetual virgin who has taken an oath of chastity to the scientist. The cosmos has promised never to "commit a miracle" because that would be metaphysical rape or perhaps philosophical fornication! The god of scientism turns out to be as jealous as Yahweh!

This objection rests on a fallacy we call "Misuse of Analogy," which is assuming without warrant that two things being compared are alike in every possible respect. There is an old rule in literary interpretation which says: "Don't make a metaphor walk on all fours." If, for instance, you called your child, "my little lamb," it would be ridiculous for someone to ask: "Then where is his wool?" The word "lamb" is obviously a metaphor suggesting that the child and the lamb are similar on some, but not all, points.

Now, in the question of miracles, the Misuse of Analogy occurs when the naturalist assumes that "laws of nature" are like laws of human society. Perhaps there has been no greater source of confusion in the history of linguistics than the use of the same word "law" to refer to both (1) the command of a sovereign authority and (2) the generalization of a Newton, a Darwin, or an Einstein. A law of society is a personal command with a moral orientation and a capacity for enforcement. None of these characteristics is applicable to the so-called laws of nature.

1. See, e.g., the remarks of several scientists interviewed by F. E. Trinklein, *The God of Science* (Grand Rapids: Eerdmans, 1971), pp. 78-93.

Scientists don't "pass" laws, they discover them. And often the law they discover is more of a choice among averages than something forced on the investigator. Furthermore, a scientific law is usually contingent; it can be modified or even completely rejected when a new model comes along. So, scientists are more like historians than legislators: *they describe how nature acts; they can't prescribe how nature must act.* Science, as science, has no right to presuppose a finite Führer of Determinism, an Emperor of Uniformity, who watches over the cosmos with his celestial machine gun.

The naturalist opposes miracles by appealing to the principle of the uniformity of nature, the first premise of every natural law. This principle allows you to say that an event which you have observed in only one time and space (i.e., Earth) can be predicated of many times and spaces. But the problem is this: there is no way to prove the principle of uniformity. The idea that the future will be like the past is just hope, expectation, "blind animal faith." A scientist merely assumes it on pragmatic grounds. But if the principle is grounded pragmatically and can't be proved by empirical methods to be in the nature of things, then you surely can't use it to brutally exclude the possibility of miracles. Verifications that are merely pragmatic leave open the possibility that situations will occur in which the principle doesn't hold.

For example, you may say, if you wish: (1) "I have never personally observed water becoming wine by just standing in stone jars." Fine, neither have I. You may even add: (2) "Furthermore, modern science has never observed it." Fine again, you're probably correct. But here's the rub: you have no right to press on and say: (3) "Therefore, water can never become wine by this method."

Your first two statements are historical, empirical, descriptive, inductive, and humble. Your third statement is normative, metaphysical, deductive, and arrogant. It is really bad form for you to pass from the empirical to the normative without admitting that in the process you cease to be a scientist and become a metaphysician. You can make this leap from (1) and (2) to (3) but don't call it science, because it is sheer metaphysics and what is more: it may be bad metaphysics.

But someone will ask: "Are you not arguing for a complete lack of order in the universe?" No, assuredly not. We Christians also believe in a cosmos, not a chaos. Our purpose is not to destroy order and uniformity but to show that there are different kinds of order than the mechanically physical. The question of miracles brings before us three possible pictures of the universe, two extremes and a *via media.*

First, the naturalist insists on an orderly universe, described exhaustively by science, closed, determined, with no miracles, no events that are counter-instances of law. Second, the naturalist accuses the Christian of believing in a universe of utter spontaneity and irregularity in which literally anything could happen, where everything would be a miracle. These two positions constitute a faulty dilemma; there is a third position between the horns that preserves both science and miracles.

The third position posits a universe that is usually orderly, not because it is dead, material, or mechanically determined, but because its creator wants it orderly most of the time. Order that stems from a personal creator would be a purposive or teleological order. Christians look at nature as the activity of Mind and thus there is no good reason why we can't consider even regular, repeated events as "willed" by the Creator.

This Mind imparts as much order and dependability to nature's behavior as any scientist could want, because purpose is just as opposed to chance as is mechanism. Even when miracles occur, therefore, they too are willed by the same Mind and hence don't at all constitute a "break" in the nexus of universal cause and effect. Henry Stob expresses it well:

> The "laws of nature" which we formulate are nothing but our transcripts of God's "customary ways." They are not prior to but after God; they record His habits. They "hold" because God is wont to travel the same way; but they do not bind Him. God is free to plant His steps precisely where He will, and sometimes He plants them on unaccustomed ways. He does this, we may be sure, to serve some holy purpose.[2]

The Christian, therefore, can boast, in a sense, of a "closed universe" also. God closes it. Whatever happens, law or miracle, is his will. Miracles don't break any genuine order if God wills everything. Now, as a matter of record, miracles *are* exceptional to us, but that is only because we can't see everything from the aspect of eternity, as God can.[3] If we knew everything about the total system of nature, as God does, then a miracle wouldn't appear as a break to us. It *is* a break to us now, because we are finite, and that is precisely its purpose: to arrest the attention of finite creatures. There are no miracles to God because omniscience couldn't possibly be startled. For God, there is no distinction between natural and supernatural because his intelligence is infinite. What is so defective, therefore, about the

---

2. "Miracles," *Basic Christian Doctrines*, ed. Carl F. H. Henry (New York: Holt, Rinehart, and Winston, 1962), p. 83.

3. Bett gives a good discussion of this in his *Reality of the Religious Life*, pp. 111ff.

naturalist's objection to miracles is that puny, finite man, behind his blinders of positivism, claims that *he* can close the universe and limit all possible events to physical, mechanical events.

Is there really any difference, Agnos, between what a miracle does to our scientific laws and what our own freedom of will does? You say every event has a cause—but so does the Christian. A miracle has a cause, just like an act of free will. It is a different kind of cause from that of physical events. Man can modify the regular action of nature by the energy of his will. He can, for example, make water flow uphill or throw a rock into the air against the law of gravity. An act of will that modifies a law of nature is, to me, just as inscrutable as God's will modifying nature in a miracle. Most of the speculative difficulties we meet when we inquire into the will are met again when we inquire into the miracle. This is why the most consistent naturalists, like B. F. Skinner, believe in neither free will nor miracles.[4]

Miracles, to sum up, don't disturb causation; they disturb materialistic determinism, as well they should, since it is a defective metaphysic. If you believe in free will, morality, aesthetics, or anything that transcends materialism, you already have the door partly open to miracles.

2. **Philosophical Theism.** Strangely enough, some theists try to close the door on miracles for the same reason as the naturalists; they want a totally determined universe. Even though such people believe in a Person powerful enough to work miracles, they still reject them. "God would never do it that way," they insist. "Miracles are embarrassing; it's easier to believe in God without them. They are cheap parlor tricks, performed by old deities, or, better, ascribed by ignorant people to the true deity." Max Born, a famous German physicist, argues:

> Something which is against natural laws seems to me rather out of the question because it would be a depressive idea about God. It would make God smaller than he must be assumed. When he stated that these laws hold, then they hold, and he wouldn't make exceptions. This is too human an idea. Humans do such things, but not God.[5]

Dr. Born resembles the deists of the Enlightenment, who claimed that God reveals himself perfectly through the order and harmony of

4. "Mr. Bernard Shaw speaks with hearty old-fashioned contempt for the idea of miracles, as if they were a sort of breach of faith on the part of nature; he seems strangely unconscious that miracles are only the final flowers of his own favourite tree, the doctrine of the omnipotence of will" (Chesterton, *Orthodoxy*, p. 128).

5. Cited in Trinklein, *God of Science*, p. 80.

the creation and needs no marvels to make himself known. The deist is really not unlike the naturalist—he values the order of the cosmos so much that he is perplexed by a disturbance of that order.

My chief question for the deist is this: How does he know God would never suspend one of his laws? Where did God say to Dr. Born that the laws of nature hold forever? The Bible nowhere says this; on the contrary, it records hundreds of miracles where God contravened nature's laws. Did Dr. Born have a private revelation? Or does he just have a personal preference for uniformity and order? What is the evidence that this preference defines what really happened in history or what God has truly done?

Ask yourself: How could God better make his presence known than by temporarily suspending or reversing the regular pattern of nature? Wouldn't it dazzle the mind and draw attention to the miracle-worker and to his message? How could God really reveal himself through an ordinary and repeatable event like the rising of the sun? Once you see nature acting in a regular way you tend to take it for granted. Natural law wouldn't convince you of God's presence nearly as well as a sudden suspension of law. Like the naturalist, the deist has a complaint and a preference to express, but he has no real objection to miracles, provided there is adequate historical evidence for them.

3. The third philosophical objection accuses the Christian position of circularity. Walter Kaufmann states it this way: "A miracle requires faith; to those who lack faith it is not a miracle. Appeal to miracles as evidence to prove beliefs is therefore circular."[6] Some say that miracle stories occur only among people who already have a spiritual preparation or an acceptance of the miraculous.

First, no Christian would argue simply, "Miracles prove the Christian faith." Our evidence comes from many sources, miracles being only one of them. We don't think that isolated, naked marvels would prove any kind of worldview.

Further, the circularity involved here is precisely the kind of circularity we noted in chapter four on proving a worldview. To see if certain data confirm a worldview you must put on the proper glasses (i.e., assume tentatively that the metaphysic is true) and then determine whether the glasses present a coherent picture of the data. I could just as easily argue that the naturalist can't prove his determinism by looking at regular laws because he already wants to believe in regularity! It would sound strange in a court of law for the district attorney to say to the defense counsel: "But you *want* your client

6. *Critique of Religion and Philosophy* (New York: Harper, 1958), p. 92.

to be innocent and that is why you can't see this incriminating evidence against him!"

It is unfair to insist on "scientific conditions" (whatever that may mean) in order to check on the reality of miracles. Some things can only be checked if you place yourself in a situation where the phenomenon could be experienced, *if it occurred*. If I predicted that the sun would rise tomorrow at exactly 6:00 A.M., you certainly couldn't confirm or deny the prediction by running off to a mine shaft a thousand feet deep at the appointed time. If a psychologist were obtaining data from drunkards, it would be ludicrous for him to taunt them during the investigation for always being drunk. The fact that revelatory theists may want miracles to occur, or expect them to occur, doesn't disprove their actual occurrence.

Besides, we have at least one case of a man who experienced a miracle and certainly wasn't in a favorable frame of mind—St. Paul. Before he met the risen Christ on the road to Damascus and lost his eyesight, Saul of Tarsus was "breathing threats and murder against the disciples of the Lord" says Luke. He "went to the high priest and asked him for letters to the synagogues at Damascus, so that if he found any belonging to the Way, men or women, he might bring them bound to Jerusalem" (Acts 9:1, 2).

C. HISTORICAL OBJECTIONS.

If a person stops making philosophical objections to miracles, like those above, he then admits that miracles are possible. The essence of a historical objection is usually the assertion that history is an improper medium for revelation or that there are insuperable difficulties involved in observing and/or reporting a miracle that actually happened.

1. The complaint is that miracles happened so long ago that they can't possibly be valid data for a contemporary worldview. This is usually coupled with the assertion that miracles always occur in ages when people are ignorant and don't know the laws of science. For example, Dr. Arthur B. Komar, Dean of the Belfer Graduate School of Science, Yeshiva University, New York, asks: "Why isn't there a density of miracles today proportional to the density of miracles reported thousands of years ago? Quite clearly because people are more critical today."[7]

Dr. Komar has a bad case of "chronological snobbery" if he thinks that all ages before our own were so credulous that they believed in

7. Cited in Trinklein, *God of Science*, p. 79.

marvels happening every day. An "age of science" is not always the opposite of an "age of ignorance." Those who live in the modern era have no monopoly on knowing how nature works in her macroscopic behavior. Most of Christ's miracles are exceptions to laws of nature so well-known that they would have been recognized as wonders in any part of the world at any time in history.

Joseph, for example, knew how babies got started in the womb. That's why he was tempted to put Mary away secretly when he found her pregnant during their betrothal; he thought she had committed fornication (Matt. 1:19). If Dr. Komar is correct, Joseph would have said when he found Mary pregnant: "Well, my, my, here we have history's first case of parthenogenesis. What a lucky chap am I!" Why didn't Joseph instantly attribute Mary's pregnancy to a visitation of the deity—so credulous were folks in those days? No, the Jews of first century Palestine weren't that ignorant; it took a special visit of an angel to explain the origin of the child in Mary's womb (Matt. 1:20, 21).

The same goes for most Biblical miracles. It doesn't take a Harvard or Oxford graduate to know that water won't become wine standing in stone jars, that men don't come back from the grave, that five loaves and two fishes won't feed five thousand people, that mud won't cure congenital blindness. The person making this objection needs to remember that the first century was the heart of the Pax Romana and that Palestine was close to the heart of the empire, not on the fringes. This was one of the most cultured, secular, affluent, educated, sceptical periods in human history before the modern era. It hardly qualifies as an "age of ignorance." If Christ had performed his miracles in the ninth or tenth century A.D. the objection might have a point.

The objector needs to remember also that the Jewish people had a history of going after strange gods and being punished for their disloyalty to Yahweh. They were thus very cautious about being led astray by false prophets and false miracle-workers (see Deut. 13:1-5). The fishermen, farmers, and tax collectors of Christ's own company could hardly be termed "credulous." You don't catch fish, raise crops, or collect taxes believing in marvels all the time. Most men have a basic "will to order" about them; they know that, macroscopically, nature is usually regular.

The second of Komar's complaints—that there is a density of miracles in Biblical history and few since that time—is easily answered by explaining the purpose of miracles. Biblical miracles occur in "revelatory clusters," that is, they aren't spread out in perfect proportion through the Bible. The two big clusters occur during (1) the Exodus from Egypt, and (2) the time of Christ and the foundation of the

church. These periods witnessed the two most important revelations
God ever gave—the Law and the Gospel. If miracles accompany and
attest to revelation, these clusters are exactly where we'd expect to
find them in Biblical history. There is a small cluster around the time
of Elijah and Elisha which doesn't correspond to any particular revelation, but that was a time when Yahweh was in conflict with the
idols of Canaan. We might call this a "booster cluster" of miracles,
since Yahweh was attempting to return his people to the Law given at
Sinai.

The fact that there have been few miracles since Biblical times
proves nothing in particular. Instead of complaining about miracles
being in clusters and in past times we should face the real issue: Is
there any historical evidence for them, regardless of *where* or *when*
they occurred?

2. Next, the objector may attack the very ability of any human to
observe and accurately describe *any* event. You may assert that
humans are all poor reporters. Experimental situations have been constructed where spectators all contradict each other after viewing a
staged event. The objector, therefore, takes refuge in historical
agnosticism; he doubts all of the past.

It doesn't take long to see that this doubt thrown on miracles also
destroys all human reporting. This objection will kill all history; it
will close all law courts; it will stop all newspapers. The objector
shouldn't even trust his own memory since it too isn't "immediate"
enough. It's one thing to prove that human testimony is not infallible;
it's another thing to prove it totally worthless. There is a middle
ground: human testimony is basically reliable provided certain pro-
cedural canons are observed. This middle ground has satisfied most
people for a long time.

Furthermore, the man making this objection is apt to contradict
himself. If he sets up an experimental situation and then shows that all
observers see the event differently, one must ask, how did he see it accurately? Why doesn't the same disability he attributes to the observer
affect him also? If all human observation is faulty, why shouldn't we
be sceptical of the proposition, "all human observation is faulty,"
since it was established by observation?

Any good lawyer will tell you that not only can human testimony
be reliable, but also that discrepancy among witnesses is often a good
sign of authenticity, since differences that don't result in outright contradiction can be harmonized and may demonstrate that each witness
remembered an individual portion of the event and reported his portion accurately. Memory research has shown that the individual re-

members only those sensory elements in an event to which he was paying attention. A person won't recall every single thing in the environment he confronts. When we reconstruct an event we need only combine the testimony of several witnesses to see the event in its fullness. This happens in court almost every day.[8]

3. If our hypothetical objector admits that history can provide us with truth, he may then attack the Biblical books themselves. He may allege that they contain errors in natural facts and therefore are unreliable when they attest to miracles.

I can't possibly answer this objection in detail. It must be answered in specifics. Where, for example, is there an error in the Bible? When one is pinpointed, we can go to work on it. Space prohibits a long argument for the historical accuracy of the entire Bible; that was the purpose of the previous chapter. I can only say in general that very learned men today just do not ridicule the Bible as an old collection of worthless folk tales. That may have been possible in the last century but not in this one. We have too much evidence showing that the Bible is basically accurate. There are still difficulties, to be sure, but these don't make a document worthless; if they did, we would have no dependable history. I can only ask, Agnos, that you read some good general accounts of Biblical history and archaeology before you generalize too much about the historical worth of the Bible. (See the works cited at the end of the previous chapter.)

4. Certainly the most serious attack ever launched against miracles was by David Hume in his famous "Essay on Miracles," published in 1776.[9] Hume defined a miracle as a violation of natural law and then proceeded to argue that since the laws of nature are established by the universal experience of man a miracle must be impossible by definition because it is contrary to that universal experience. Before a rational man accepted a miracle, he would probably say that his senses deceived him or that those who reported a miracle to him were either deceived themselves or were deceiving him.

This is a strong objection, because it rests on an obvious truth: we all tend to reinterpret strange events and seek for a natural explanation before we invoke the category of miracle.

First, in reply, I can't resist the temptation to point out that Hume (again!) has contradicted himself. Hume says miracles are impossible

---

8. For a good discussion of how practicing historians handle the problem of alleged contradictions in historical witnesses, see Barzun and Graff, *Modern Researcher*, pp. 146-73.

9. This essay is chapter 10 of Hume's larger work, *Essay on Human Understanding*.

because they violate "laws of nature," but according to his own sceptical empiricism and nominalism we have no impression of nature as a whole. Nature *in toto* is never a simple impression, like "red" or "slick." The same goes for the "order of nature" which miracles violate. And how could you have a concept of "violation" without the idea of order? Moreover, the notion of order implies time, which implies sequence, which implies that the self is continuous—which Hume denied. Further, you can't talk about the universal experience of all men without assuming the existence of other minds—which Hume denied. When he criticized the Design Argument Hume complained that we know very little about the entire universe; yet when he attacked miracles he spoke boldly of the all-pervasive order of natural law throughout the universe! Surely, Hume's attack on miracles sinks on the first principles of his own philosophy.

But, of course, this doesn't answer the objection. It just proves Hume inconsistent—or dishonest. The main objection still needs a reply. The basic flaw in the objection is that it begs the very question at issue when it asserts that miracles are "contrary to experience." Contrary to whose experience? If Hume answers, "my experience," that hardly matters for historical purposes. There may be many things in heaven and earth and history not dreamt of in Hume's experience.

If Hume asserts that miracles are contrary to *all* men's experiences he assumes the very thing to be proved. *If* a miracle occurred, it certainly wasn't contrary to the experience of the man observing it. If you can use experience to establish natural law, why can't you use it to establish a counter-instance to law? If Hume replies that the testimony of the *majority* must determine what happens in history, his reply is an untenable use of the democratic method. You don't determine history that way.

Actually, Hume has left the realm of history and jumped into metaphysics. He is affirming that all events must be repetitious, that *something cannot happen only once!* But this is a philosophical criterion, not a historical canon, and Hume's argument claims to be historical.[10]

If you applied Hume's criterion rigidly you would put out the eyes of science. Glorifying the regular and stigmatizing the unusual is certainly no path to learning progress. The story is related of a missionary who told his African friends that in his native land water became so hard in the winter you could walk across it and even drive a

---

10. Richard Whatley, Archbishop of Dublin, took the various criteria of Hume and showed that, if rigorously applied, they would make us doubt even the historicity of Napoleon Bonaparte. See his *Historical Doubts Relative to Napoleon Bonaparte*, published in 1819.

wagon across it. Since the natives had never seen ice they rolled on the ground laughing at such an incredible lie. The natives were wrong, of course, because ice does exist, but they were just applying Hume's criterion.

Hume's objection is considerably weakened when we realize, as stated earlier, that laws of nature aren't rigid prescriptions of how nature *must* act, but rather descriptions of how nature *does* act. If a new fact should contradict our hitherto uniform experience, instead of denying the fact, we would make our science broader and look for some new law or some new force to explain it. When Madame Curie got an unusual reading from pitchblende she did what most scientists would have done—she assumed that a new radioactive element existed in pitchblende. If she had been stubbornly dedicated to the proposition that there are only two radioactive elements, uranium and thorium, we wouldn't have radium today.

Now, God wants us to broaden our science when we investigate a miracle. He wants us to stop and note the unusual nature of the event and ask what new force must be presumed to account for it. He wants us to invoke the supernatural and the transcendent to explain it. He wants us to exclaim, like the magicians of Pharaoh: "This is the finger of God" (Exod. 8:19). Or like the 5000 people that Jesus fed: "This is indeed the prophet who is to come into the world!" (John 6:14).

I feel that if a naturalist doesn't accept a miracle, even when its historical evidence is persuasive, it is because he views it through his own metaphysic. Viewed this way, it appears only as a naked marvel, an isolated wonder. This is an unfair procedure. You can no more understand a miracle torn from its context than you can understand a comet detached from the solar system in which it moves.

If, for instance, you looked at some ordinary historical events in isolation you might ascribe to them an air of improbability that would vanish when viewed in context.[11] If I told you that the ruler of a certain nation on a certain day deliberately set fire to his capital city and burned up all its palaces and art works and then evacuated the city, you might find it hard to believe. But this is exactly what Czar Alexander I of Russia did in 1812 when Napoleon approached Moscow. Once you know the background of the event and the motives of the participants the improbability decreases. There are quite a few such unlikely events in history.[12]

---

11. But, then, a consistent empiricist can have no "context" about anything, can he? If the mind is just a series of fleeting impressions there can be no framework or context for regular experiences.

12. See the discussion of probability in Barzun and Graff, *Modern Researcher*, pp. 151-60.

As I've emphasized many times, Agnos, you don't do a worldview justice until you tentatively grant its truth to see if it presents a coherent picture of all the data. You can't give miracles a fair trial unless you view them in their total system. The miracles of Christ are meaningless if studied in isolation from Biblical prophecy about Christ, the claims Christ made, and the character and personality of Christ. It's not fair to look at data that might possibly shatter your glasses through the very glasses that would be shattered!

All Hume proved, therefore, is that no evidence can prove a miracle to an atheist or a deist. John Stuart Mill, who was certainly no friend to Christianity, saw this clearly in his *System of Logic* (II, 110). But is this really newsworthy? Hardly. A naturalist will interpret all data in terms of naturalism and reinterpret any data that seem to overthrow his naturalism. Could a naturalist give up his naturalism by confronting the miracles of the Hebrew-Christian religion? I believe so, but probably not if his worldview were very rigid. That's why I like reverent agnostics like you, Agnos. If you will keep on having a flexible worldview I think I can persuade you.

We're not finished with Hume. We'll return to him in the chapter on the Resurrection.

D. MISCELLANEOUS OBJECTIONS.

1. One favorite position today is to say that Christ was just a super faith healer, a skilled practitioner of psychotherapy.[13] Many of his cures do have a superficial resemblance to modern psychotherapy. This view has the virtue of accepting many of Christ's miracles and explaining them in a natural way, a way that can be duplicated and checked by modern psychology. In principle, any good psychotherapist could copy the cures of Christ. Most everyone would agree, however, that Christ was probably the most magnetic, charismatic psychotherapist in history.

The prime difficulty with this theory is it can't possibly explain all the miracles of Christ. It explains only those that have human psychology as a factor in the event. It can't even explain all the healing miracles; it has trouble with the healing of congenital blindness and leprosy, the restoration of amputated ears and withered limbs, and it is especially weak in explaining how Christ could raise people from the dead.

This view also fails to provide any explanation of Christ's nature miracles, such as stilling the storm, multiplying bread, and walking

---

13. John B. Noss, *Man's Religions* (New York: Macmillan, 1963), p. 599. Noss calls this view of Jesus "a minimum view" of his powers, to which much could be added.

on water. You need a subtheory to explain all the wonders left over from your main theory and the necessity of a subtheory always weakens the main theory. This subtheory would have to account for the fact that the gospels attribute nature miracles to Christ, when he, according to the main theory, performed only faith cures. The whole matter leaves Christ in a bad light for he interpreted his miracles in a far different way (see, e.g., Mark 2:9, 10; John 14:11).

2. Another favorite dodge today is to say that the very existence of several world religions with miracles disproves the miracles of Christianity. If they all happened they would confirm several contradictory religious systems.

There really aren't as many miracles in other religions as you might think. Islam has very few, as St. Thomas complained. Hinduism has some, but they hardly constitute the philosophical basis of the religion. In their original forms, Buddhism and Confucianism were so humanistic that a miracle would have been a scandal. Buddhism, Confucianism, and Taoism, all three, are more like social and psychological moral systems than they are religions. The miraculous is very weak in all three.

The fact is, only in the Hebrew-Christian religion do you find miracles put on a stand, offered as the decisive proof of the whole system. Especially is this true of the Resurrection. If Christ didn't rise from the dead, argued Paul, our faith is futile, we are still in our sins, those who died in Christ died without hope, and we are the most pitiful group in the world (I Cor. 15:12-19). Remove the linchpin of Christ's resurrection and the entire structure falls apart. Christianity is metaphysics in historical form; kill the historical event and you kill the religion.

Hasn't this objection missed the point? You don't prove the Biblical miracles false by just showing that the world's religions are full of miracles (though they aren't), any more than you prove all diamonds fake by proving that we have a few imitations. The logical procedure is to ask: Which group of miracles has the best evidence, both eyewitness and circumstantial?

E. THE PARABLE OF THE TRAFFIC LIGHTS.

The issue surrounding miracles is so vital, Agnos, that I will end this chapter with a parable to make my meaning clear.

Once upon a time there was a king who ruled over a small principality. He controlled all the traffic lights in his capital city from a single room in a castle high on a hill. One day, while admiring his city, he noticed an emergency developing down on Main Street: a truck loaded with dynamite was out of control because its brakes had failed. The king knew that if it collided with any cross traffic on the way down the hill many people would be killed. He instantly rushed to the big switchboard and pulled a special lever that turned all the traffic lights on Main Street green. The truck rolled safely to the bottom of the hill and no collision occurred with cross traffic. There was no explosion; no one was injured; many lives were saved. But a law was suspended for a brief time.

Meanwhile, a young man driving a delivery truck got caught by a red light at exactly the time the king turned all the lights on Main Street green. He was delayed so long that he couldn't make an important delivery on time. When he got back to the store the customer had already called and complained to the manager. He was angry.

"What happened? Why didn't you deliver the goods on time? You left in plenty of time."

"I couldn't get there on time. I was held up by a strange event—the traffic light stayed red about five minutes."

"That's ridiculous. The lights in this city never vary. They always stay the same color exactly one minute."

"But sir, I timed it myself after it passed the one minute mark. It stayed red over five minutes."

"Young man, you've been drinking or something. Everyone knows that traffic lights in this city don't stay the same color over one minute. The one-minute rule is a Natural Law in this city, an eternal feature of traffic lights. It's been checked thousands of times by thousands of people."

"But sir, I timed the light with my own watch. You can check my watch and you can give me a drunk test, if you wish, but I saw what I saw."

"Why would the red light run over one minute? Who or what would have caused this irregularity?"

"Furthermore," added the assistant manager, "even if there were someone to cause this variation, why would he do it? No one in his right mind would go around fouling up the regularity of traffic lights in the city. It would be downright criminal! It would confuse everyone and cause all kinds of problems."

"I don't know, but we can ask around and see if anyone else was stopped by the red lights for over one minute. It might have been a general phenomenon. We could also do some research and see if a person controls all the lights somewhere and if he had a purpose in making the lights behave this way."

"Baloney! Anyone else who would say such a thing is as crazy as you are. Or else he's trying to deceive you."

"You mean you're not even going to check around and see if my story could possibly be corroborated?"

"No. A story like that is impossible by definition. I *know* it never happened!"

Here, dear Agnos, we have the prejudice of the naturalist and the deist in bleak review. One denies the God who works miracles, the other admits the God but denies the purpose of miracles. Both assume something metaphysical: both assume they know the town perfectly. The one stops there (naturalism); the other also assumes that there is a king who runs the town and that he knows the king's mind (deism).

Well, if I were king of that town I would stop the lights anyway and save all those lives and let the sceptics complain. As a matter of fact, when the whole matter came to court a few weeks later, the delivery boy was able to collect a large group of witnesses who testified that they too were held up by an unusually long red traffic light. This leads us to the next chapter, the historical testimony for miracles.

Suggestions for Further Reading

D. S. Cairns, *The Faith that Rebels* (New York: Cambridge University Press, 1929).

Carnell, *Introduction to Christian Apologetics*, chs. 14, 15.

C. S. Lewis, *Miracles* (New York: Macmillan, 1947).

Ramm, *Protestant Christian Evidences*, chs. 2, 4, 5.

Alan Richardson, *The Miracle-Stories of the Gospels* (London: SCM Press, 1942).

Trueblood, *Philosophy of Religion*, ch. 15.

THE CASE FOR
CHRISTIAN MIRACLES

If my reasoning in the previous chapter is sound, Agnos, no honest person would reject the miracles of Christianity until he showed that they lack adequate historical evidence. So far, none of the objections, philosophical or historical, relieves him of this duty. We've already noted in chapter ten that there is a good deal of evidence from archaeology and other disciplines confirming the substantial historical accuracy of the New Testament. In this chapter we look more closely at the miracles of Christ to show their superiority to other miracles in history.

A. THE MIRACLES OF JESUS CHRIST.

When space is limited it suffices to focus only on the miracles of Jesus Christ. We may forget for the moment the remainder of Biblical miracles. If Christ worked his miracles and if he arose from the dead then he is the divine Son of God (Rom. 1:4); and since he confirmed the Old Testament retrospectively (Luke 24:44), and the New Testament prospectively (John 14:26), he, in his divine person, ties the entire Bible together into one neat apologetic package. If we can break through the naturalist's defenses at this juncture his entire front will collapse. If the miracles and the resurrection of Christ are established then the whole Biblical revelation falls into your lap, because Jesus Christ is the Son of the same God who spoke and acted from Genesis to Revelation. What, then, are the features of his miracles that commend them to rational men?

1. The number of Christ's miracles is adequate. The four gospels, Matthew, Mark, Luke, and John, record 35 miracles in all (or 38 depending on how you count them). Most of these miracles appear in two or three gospels. The most public miracle of all, the feeding of the 5000, appears in all four. In addition, each gospel indicates that Christ performed many more miracles than the writer selected to record (see, e.g., Matt. 4:23; Mark 6:56; Luke 6:19; John 20:30). If a man performed only one or two wonders under selective conditions with carefully chosen observers we would probably not consider this enough to qualify him as a messenger from God.

2. Christ performed his miracles with great ease, without ceremony and ostentation. With many false prophets and miracle-workers there is an obvious strain to perform a wonder. Much ceremony and hand-waving must occur to produce the effect. In most of the miracles of Christ, however, there is an immediate effect following a simple word or gesture. It is noteworthy that a word very frequently used to denote his miracles simply means *works* (Greek: *erga)*, as if miracles were a natural and necessary outgrowth of his life. "The works that I do in my Father's name, they bear witness to me" (John 10:25).

3. Christ's miracles have unusual publicity. Paul told Festus that the facts of Christ's career weren't "done in a corner" (Acts 26:26). Actually they *were* done in a corner of sorts, one of the best-known corners of the globe, the eastern Mediterranean, the hearth of several great civilizations for three millennia. Palestine was right on the world's crossroads; it would have been difficult for God to select a more public area in which to stage an incarnation. If Christ's career had taken place in Iceland or Ireland or on the fringes of the Roman Empire we'd have a problem with publicity. But there is no problem with Palestine.

Even inside Palestine we find that Jesus never hid his light under a bushel. He performed wonders in the very thick of things, in crowded cities, at busy street corners, at lakesides, around market places, while discoursing with multitudes, in and around the Jerusalem temple, surrounded by crowds as large as four and five thousand. He didn't perform miracles in one place or in a special staging area where his followers could control the event in any way. His miracles could literally happen anywhere. (See, e.g., the following passages which speak of "great multitudes" and "entire cities" witnessing the miracles: Matt. 15:30, 31; 19:1, 2; Mark 1:32-34; 6:53-56; Luke 6:17-19.)

By contrast, the miracles of Mohammed, few as they are, almost all occurred in private. The Prophet tells us how Gabriel made night visits to him, how the Koran was delivered to him from heaven in fragments until the whole was complete—but who was there to prove or disprove his testimony? Neither could friend confirm nor foe deny the report.

4. Christ's miracles have the necessary variety we would expect of a divine agent. If one claims divinity I would expect him to demonstrate the power and control a creator has over his creation (Heb. 1:3; John 1:3; Col. 1:16). I would demand a variety of wonders to demonstrate the role of creator. Pseudo-saviors sometimes show a limited power over a part of reality (e.g., psychotherapy), but Christ displayed power over all aspects of the creation.

a. He often exhibited powers of knowledge and insight, as when he divined the evil thoughts of enemies (Mark 2:8), or when he knew of Nathanael under the fig tree (John 1:48), or when he told the Samaritan woman about her previous marital life (John 4:17, 18).

b. In seventeen recorded miracles Christ showed complete control over a great variety of physical conditions—palsy, leprosy, fever, blindness, deafness, mutism, blood hemorrhaging, lameness, withered limbs, paralysis, dropsy, and amputated ears.

c. Most importantly, Christ showed power over the greatest enemy of all, death. He raised at least three people from the dead: the daughter of Jairus in Capernaum (Matt. 9:18-26), the widow's son at Nain (Luke 7:11-15), and his friend, Lazarus of Bethany (John 11). The first had just died, the second was already on the bier, and the third had lain in the tomb four days.

d. Christ also had power over nature. He could stop a storm, make a fig tree dry up, create over one hundred gallons of wine, cause fish to swim into a net, walk on water, and make food increase in volume. Nature, mind, body—none of these could resist his power. There have been many alleged miracle-workers in history but none have approached Christ in this comprehensive control over the whole of creation.[1]

5. Christ's miracles have consistency. I mean that the quality of power we're describing was maintained during a ministry of over

1. Of Christ's 35 recorded miracles, 17 are bodily cures, 9 are miracles over nature, 6 are cures of demoniacs, and 3 are resurrections. For an official list see any good Bible handbook or dictionary, e.g., Halley's *Bible Handbook* (Grand Rapids: Zondervan, 21st edition, 1957), pp. 416, 417. A complete list of all Biblical miracles is printed in the back of some Nelson RSV Bibles.

three years and over a sufficiently wide spatial area. Jesus performed wonders at such varied times and places that you can't ascribe any naturalistic explanation to them that depends on space or time. The power never varied or waned. Every place he went and every time he worked a miracle it was consistently the same power. He performed them in Galilee, Samaria, and Judea, in Capernaum, Jerusalem, Jericho, Cana, and Nain. He performed them in summer, winter, spring, fall, morning, noon, and night. Occasionally he even worked them in non-Jewish areas (Mark 7:24-30) and on behalf of gentiles (John 4:46-53) so that none could say only his compatriots believed in him.

6. Christ performed miracles for an altruistic reason. Most of his miracles were helpful, benevolent, restorative, curative, therapeutic. He seldom used his wonders in his own interest. Nowhere in the gospels do we see Jesus tempted to use his awesome power to destroy his enemies or to punish violators of God's will. When Peter tried to prevent his arrest in the Garden of Gethsemane by striking off Malchus' ear, Jesus corrected him: "Put your sword back into its place; . . . Do you think that I cannot appeal to my Father, and he will at once send me more than twelve legions of angels?" (Matt. 26:52, 53). When James and John wanted to destroy a Samaritan village by fire, Jesus rebuked them (Luke 9:54). In the Temptation, he refused Satan's suggestion that he make bread out of stones and assuage his hunger (Matt. 4:4).

When a miracle occurs one can ask: Did it come from God or the devil? Miracles point to the supernatural but there are two divisions of the supernatural: the divine and the satanic. A miracle by itself doesn't prove the truth of a doctrine or the divine mission of the one performing it. What it proves is his right to be heard; we know he is either from heaven or hell. The Bible implies in several places that false prophets can work miracles (e.g., Deut. 13:1-3; II Thess. 2:9; Rev. 13:13, 14).

Now, Jesus gives us an additional standard when he warns us against false prophets: "You will know them by their fruits" (Matt. 7:16). The fruits of Christ's miracles are always admirable. "He goes through life like a kind of embodied beneficence, creating health and happiness."[2] His wonders show him to be the enemy of disease, the enemy of bodily imperfection and suffering, the controller of nature, and the opponent of Satan and his servants. No other set of miracles in history can match the altruism of Christ's miracles. After studying

2. Andrew Fairbairn, *The Philosophy of the Christian Religion* (New York: Macmillan, 1902), p. 336.

them, we can understand how hurt Jesus was when the Jews sought to stone him: "I have shown you many good works from the Father; for which of these do you stone me?" (John 10:32).

Moreover, the benevolent character of Christ's miracles fits the tenor of his ethical teachings. We expect such merciful and helpful acts from the one who taught us that mercy is a prime moral obligation. If a brutal man like Nero or Hitler were to work miracles for three years it would distress me; if a saintly man like St. Francis couldn't perform them it might arouse pity in me. But notice how natural it is for one who claimed so much, who taught such high ethical principles, to have at the same time such power. If God be defined as the Person who unites perfectly both power and goodness, then the miracles of Jesus Christ surely show him to be divine.

7. Christ's miracles are sober, restrained, and conservative. They are chaste, reasonable, and dignified. They are never grotesque, childish, amateurish, or selfish; they never have the quality of the magician's tent. There are no card tricks, no flying carpets, no Aladdin's lamps, no genies appearing out of bottles. One might say that his works are miraculous but not marvelous. They don't move in the region of the weird or the uncanny; they don't strike us with fear like black magic or witchcraft. His miracles are, as it were, aligned with natural processes. They show things happening that really do happen in nature (e.g., the creation of wine). Perhaps Christ made them happen faster or made them occur in a different way. Unlike mythical miracles, Christ's wonders don't reflect a morbid, fanciful, childish temper. In the Middle Ages, for example, we're told that a certain saint hung his coat on a sunbeam. The miracles of Christ are prosaic compared to this.

You can see this point better if you contrast Christ's miracles with some of those attributed to him by apocryphal gospels written later than the first century, when the pious imagination of some Christians had gone to work on the life of Christ. In these works we're told that Christ as a boy made a snail shell on the Sea of Galilee suddenly grow to the size of Mount Tabor and then as suddenly shrink back to its original form; that he impressed his friends by having six birds recite the Old Testament in six different languages; that he would fashion birds of clay and make them fly; that he would, in a fit of rage, transform his friends into stones and animals.[3]

---

3. See Wilbur M. Smith, *The Supernaturalness of Christ: Can We Still Believe in It?* (Boston: Wilde, 1941; Grand Rapids: Baker), pp. 115, 116; F. F. Bruce, *Jesus and Christian Origins Outside the New Testament* (Grand Rapids: Eerdmans, 1974), pp. 86f.

Nothing so puerile occurs in the canonical miracles of the four gospels. I judge the New Testament miracles to be canonical not only because they occur in the canonical gospels, but also because they fit together in accordance with this rule of sobriety.

8. Finally, Christ's miracles have sufficient testimony from competent witnesses who saw them at the time they were performed, and from circumstantial data both during and after the time they were performed.

a. We have the testimony of those who were beneficiaries of the miracles, especially of those who were cured of their infirmities. In some cases the person healed went everywhere telling about the miracle, even after Christ cautioned him against doing so (Mark 1:45). In other cases, Christ enjoined the man to tell of his healing, as in the case of the Gadarene demoniac (Mark 5:19). For other notable cases, see the healing of the blind man in John 9, the Samaritan leper (Luke 17:11-19), the infirm man of Jerusalem (John 5:11), and the feeding of the crowds of 4000 and 5000 (Matt. 15:38; John 6:14).

b. We have the testimony of observers who weren't beneficiaries but spectators of the miracles. Several passages in the gospels speak of the wonder and amazement experienced by the crowds that saw the miracles (Matt. 15:30, 31; Mark 2:12; Luke 4:36; 9:43). Typical responses were: "We never saw anything like this!" "Surely this is the prophet who is to come into the world." "When the Christ comes will he do more signs than this man has done?"

c. We even have the testimony of the disobedient and the sceptical, though it is often indirect. John tells us that many of the Jewish leaders believed in Jesus but for fear of the others wouldn't confess him (John 12:42). The Jerusalem scribes obliquely testified to Christ's power of exorcism by charging that "he is possessed by Beelzebub, and by the prince of demons he casts out the demons" (Mark 3:22).

d. The circumstantial evidence for Christ's miracles lies in the complex way the miracles are interlocked with the entire gospel narrative. In a historical narrative any single fact is part of a general web of truth; rip out one fact and you disturb the entire web. Conversely, if you want to forge a story, you must create an entire web of falsehood to support a single untrue claim. An old proverb says that "a liar must have a long memory." When someone tells a lie, we sometimes say: "Tell another one to prop that one up!" Recall also the line: "Oh, what a tangled web we weave, when first we practice to deceive."

Now, the simple fact is, if you go around ripping the miracles out of the gospels, leaving only the "natural" material, you make a shambles of the whole account. So much of the life of Christ is built around the miracles that if you destroy a miracle, you also destroy its prelude and its aftermath. You violate the rule of coherence.

For example, some of the longest discourses in John came after a notable miracle (chs. 5, 6). If the miracle didn't occur then the entire discourse was also fabricated. When the Pharisees charged Christ with casting out demons by Beelzebub, surely something unusual must have occurred for them to have suggested such a drastic counter-hypothesis! When John the Baptist's disciples came asking if he was the true Messiah, Christ told them to look at his miracles (Luke 7:22). If the miracles didn't occur, the whole story is left limping. If you deny that Jesus raised Lazarus, you can't explain why the Jewish rulers, from that moment on, set in motion the plan for his death.[4] Literally dozens of such examples could be given from the gospels. If one denies the miraculous element in the life of Christ, he should deny the whole record; he should become an agnostic and admit that we know little or nothing about Jesus of Nazareth.

Another facet of the circumstantial evidence for Christ's miracles is to be found in the rest of the New Testament. Even if you date the gospels late (you shouldn't), we still have evidence from Acts and the epistles about Christ's miracles (Acts 2:22; Rom. 1:4). Christ commissioned his apostles to work miracles to authenticate their mission (Matt. 10:1, 8; Mark 3:14; Luke 9:2) and we find them doing so (Acts 2:43; Gal. 3:5; Heb. 2: 3, 4). Paul told the Corinthians that "signs and wonders and mighty works" were the "signs of a true apostle" (II Cor. 12:12). It isn't very likely that Christ expected his ambassadors to furnish the kind of proof that he had failed to furnish himself.

Finally, there is the argument from silence, which is never conclusive, but always needs to be thrown on the scales. There is no contrary evidence from the first century concerning the miracles of Christ. One can usually find an exposé of alleged miracle-workers; if not an exposé, then an explanation of their wonders. But none exists for Christ's miracles, except in the Jewish Talmud, where his miracles are attributed to magic or the use of secret charms that he stole from the Temple. Some of the later opponents of the faith (Celsus, Hierocles, Julian the Apostate) admitted that Christ worked miracles during his ministry.

---

4. The example of Lazarus is so striking that even the French sceptic, Ernst Renan, in his *Vie de Jésus*, had to admit that "something" occurred at the raising of Lazarus, either a miracle or something taken for a miracle.

B. A CRITIQUE OF THE MYTH HYPOTHESIS.

This is a good spot, Agnos, to analyze the Myth Hypothesis concerning Christ and Christian origins. We will encounter it several times in later chapters. We should discuss it, not because it is the consensus of most Bible scholars (it isn't), but because it is still the favorite hypothesis of the sophomoric unbeliever. There are several versions of the·theory but they all have a family resemblance.

The official Communist position is that Jesus Christ is just a myth, a creation of Christians. Most people won't go that far, but many still think that much of his life, especially the miraculous element, was added later by the church. This idea was very popular in the last century, though the evidence for it even then was very weak. There are several lines of evidence that militate against the Myth Hypothesis.

1. The theory requires a process of evolution in the picture of Christ that simply couldn't have occurred in the time span allowed for it. As long as critics thought that the New Testament was written in the second and third centuries, instead of the first, this view could be held with some justification. Most critics in the last century dated the synoptic gospels well into the second century, while some dated John as late as A.D. 240. These dates have been exploded by archaeological discoveries, notably the John Rylands Fragment of John, mentioned earlier. In 1955, William F. Albright wrote:

> We can already say emphatically that there is no longer any solid basis for dating any book of the New Testament after about A.D. 80, two full generations before the date between 130 and 150 given by the more radical New Testament critics of today.[5]

If the New Testament was all written in the first century, there isn't enough time for this evolution from the humble prophet of Galilee who made no claims and performed no miracles to the theological Christ who did both. Granted that "pious imagination" has distorted the truth about other religious leaders, this proves absolutely nothing about Christ if the time span won't allow it. Already in Paul's epistles we have the full-blown theological Christ proclaimed, and Paul's epistles were written (roughly) between A.D. 51 and 62. The simple prophet of the critics appears nowhere in the New Testament. If imaginative Christians transformed the simple Jesus into the theological Christ, then they did it in the second decade after his death and they did it right under the noses of hundreds of original eyewitnesses, both

5. *Recent Discoveries in Biblical Lands* (New York: Funk and Wagnalls, 1955), p. 136.

friends and enemies, who knew better. Why did none of the eyewitnesses come forward to contradict this fraudulent picture?

2. If Christians evolved the miracle stories, why do we have no miracles assigned to John the Baptist? If the masses tended to imagine miracles where there were none, and if they tended to attribute miracles to all their prophets and saintly heroes, why no miracles for John? His prototype, Elijah, had performed such wonders.

3. Furthermore, if the church imagined the miracles of Christ, why didn't they ascribe a single miracle to him prior to his public ministry, which began at age 30? If the entire narrative is to be assigned to creative fancy, why this lacuna? Why not invent stories about Christ in his childhood and adolescence? Why not some wonderful tales of his love life? Fancy and imagination don't control themselves so conveniently.

4. Another feature of the gospel narrative that is incongruous with the Myth Hypothesis is that the writers often record their own short-comings, their weakness, ignorance, superficiality, naivete. They don't seem to have been anxious to protect their own reputations. Jesus rebuked them for pride, insensitivity, and ignorance (e.g., Mark 8:33; 10:14; Matt. 15:16). The gospels record without apology the argument that broke out over who would be the greatest in the coming kingdom (Mark 9:33-37). The mother of James and John requested chief positions for her two sons (Matt. 20:20, 21). All four gospels relate the cowardly denial of Peter, "the rock," the chief apostle who later evangelized the Jews (Gal. 2:8). All four writers relate how the entire apostolic band forsook Christ at his trial and left his burial to women and to outsiders—Joseph and Nicodemus.

All of this has the "ring of truth" to it. Men don't usually invent stories that discredit them, that make them appear foolish, treacherous, and cowardly. Nor do groups usually invent such stories of their founders and leaders. When you find these elements in a story they create a strong presumption for its credibility.

5. The same disarming candor occurs in the gospel picture of Jesus. If the miraculous aspects of his life were invented, why didn't the inventors make the picture more consistent? Why tell of the human weaknesses of Jesus in the same book which asserts his miraculous power? A forger tends to construct a picture that is "logical," that lacks jarring inconsistencies. Why, then, didn't the Jewish Christians evolve a political Messiah? That's what most of them wanted anyway.

Why invent a Messiah who died as a criminal on a cross of the hated Romans? Why construct something that later became such a scandal (I Cor. 1:23)? If there was an unconscious attempt on the part of the church to "glorify Jesus," then I can only say they had a strange conception of glory.

6. Why, if the Myth Hypothesis is true, do we find no material in the gospels on those burning problems that later engrossed the church? If the gospels reflect church thinking, why, for example, do we find no statement from Christ on equality between Jew and gentile? Why no discussion of circumcision? Why no references to the Jew-gentile debate? Why do the gospels contain no snatches of hymnody, prayers, and brief confessions of faith? If the church gave Jesus the title, "Son of Man," then why is the title used in the gospels but seldom in the rest of the New Testament? Also, if the church originated Jesus' messianic claims, why did it picture him as reluctant to accept the title (Matt. 16:20)?

7. Finally, no Myth Hypothesis can explain why the apostles and early Christians suffered and died spreading a message they had invented themselves. We have no record of any Christian, even under the most trying circumstances, renouncing Christ because the miraculous element in the gospel story was fake. Persecution began as soon as the church was born and didn't abate until three centuries later. How did Christians sustain this colossal forgery against the inquiring minds of thousands of new converts each year?

No, Agnos, the evidence combines to make us agree with Peter when he said, "We did not follow cleverly devised myths when we made known to you the power and coming of our Lord Jesus Christ, but we were eyewitnesses of his majesty" (II Peter 1:16). Someone has well said that if the apostles or the church invented the picture of Jesus Christ, then perhaps we should worship *them*, because the person they fabricated is still worthy of worship.

C. THE DANGER OF MIRACLOLATRY.

It sounds strange, Agnos, but at the end of this chapter we should issue a warning about arguing from miracles. An exaggerated emphasis on the wonderful and the miraculous can become a defect, as Paul warned the Corinthians (I Cor. 14:5). Even Jesus complained to a suppliant: "Unless you see signs and wonders you will not believe" (John 4:48). His rebuke to the Pharisees was even sterner: "An evil and adulterous generation seeks for a sign, but no sign shall be given to it except the sign of Jonah" (Matt. 16:4).

These passages shouldn't be interpreted to mean that Jesus placed no emphasis at all on his miracles, because we have too many passages that say he did. But they do show that Jesus refused to play the role of miracle-monger, ready to perform wonders at the drop of a hat. He refused to work signs at the devil's behest (Matt. 4:3, 4), or when the people of his own city, Nazareth, were so sceptical it would have done no good (Mark 6:5). Miracles were a vital part of his message, but only a part. You could say that miracles were a *necessary* cause for believing him divine, but not the *sufficient* cause. This seems to be exactly what Jesus asserted in John 10:37: "If I am not doing the works of my Father, then do not believe me."

When the seventy disciples returned from their missionary journey, thrilled at their ability to exorcise demons, Jesus cautioned them: "Do not rejoice in this, that the spirits are subject to you; but rejoice that your names are written in heaven" (Luke 10:20). He wanted to train his evangelists to beware of the wonder-loving mentality that considered the miracle an *end* in itself, rather than the *means* to an end. Miraclolatry (worship of miracles) can be as dangerous as Bibliolatry (worship of the Bible) or ecclesiolatry (worship of the church). All three forms of idolatry mistake the impersonal sign pointing to Christ for Christ himself.

Miracles alone usually won't convert a man, though they may be the opening wedge. The Samaritan woman was so impressed with Christ's supernatural knowledge of her marital life that she convinced many of her friends to believe in him. "He told me everything I ever did." Other people in Sychar, however, needed a fuller testimony. After Jesus stayed in the town for two days, John tells us: "Many more became believers because of what they heard from his own lips. They told the woman, 'It is no longer because of what you said that we believe, for we have heard him ourselves; and we know that this is in truth the Saviour of the world' " (John 4:40-42, NEB).

I repeat: miracles primarily give the miracle-worker the right to be heard. If the evidence of the last two chapters is persuasive, there is no good reason why a rational man can't assent to the miracles of Jesus Christ. Now we're ready to hear him. And he truly has something to say!

Suggestions for Further Reading

F. F. Bruce, *The New Testament Documents: Are They Reliable?*, 5th ed. (Grand Rapids: Eerdmans, 1960).

Floyd V. Filson, *One Lord One Faith* (Philadelphia: Westminster, 1943).

Anton Fridrichsen, *The Problem of Miracle in Primitive Christianity* (Minneapolis: Augsburg, 1972).

13

THE CLAIMS OF JESUS CHRIST

I just admitted, Agnos, that miracles alone would probably not convert a man to Christianity. Modern day sceptics aren't any different from people of Jesus' day, who, even after witnessing many miracles, asked: "By what authority are you doing these things, and who gave you this authority?" (Matt. 21:23). Miracles force you to make a decision about the *person* performing the miracle. If Christ had never made a claim about his person, many people would still be asking: "For goodness sake, whom do you represent—God or the devil?"

As a matter of fact, however, Christ *did* make claims about his person, very explicit claims. His claims make him unique among religious leaders of the world. There is a false theory going around that many people in history have made such claims to deity. This is simply not true. Apart from Jesus Christ, such claims are rare, so rare that they usually suffice to prove the person demented. Moses didn't claim to be Yahweh; Socrates didn't claim to be Zeus; Zoroaster didn't claim to be Ahura Mazda; Mohammed didn't claim to be Allah; Buddha didn't claim to be Brahma. Only Christ claimed to be one with the God who sent him (John 10:30). Familiarity has dulled our ears to the wonder of his claims.

The claims of Christ are so varied and often so subtle that we must divide our analysis of them into three parts: (1) direct claims, (2) indirect claims, and (3) circumstantial evidence for the claims.

A. THE DIRECT CLAIMS.

1. **The first thing you should notice about Christ is that his claims usually center around his person, not his teaching.** Quite frankly, he

was always talking about himself! Other religious teachers are oblique; they hide behind the message. They say, "That is the truth, the way, as I can divine it" (Buddha) or "This is the truth, as God has showed it to me" (Mohammed). They say, "The truth is what counts; love the abstract truth; I am nothing."

Christ, however, said, "*I* am the way, and the truth, and the life; no one comes to the Father, but by *me*" (John 14:6). Instead of suggesting answers to life's problems, Christ claimed to be the answer. "Come to *me*, all who labor and are heavy laden, and *I* will give you rest" (Matt. 11:28). He didn't offer the guidance of an abstract code or a philosophy to help men in the uncertainties of life—he offered himself. "Lo, *I* am with you always, to the close of the age" (Matt. 28:20).

This unusual self-consciousness is subtly revealed in the famous "I-Sayings" of Jesus which fill the gospels. Those who read the gospels in translation miss this feature, because it isn't easy to translate into English. The Greek pronoun, *ego* ("I"), is usually not inserted in the Greek sentence except for special emphasis, because the pronoun is already implied in the form of the verb. The best translation we can give *ego* in English is the italicized "I." Leafing through a Greek concordance you can see how often Jesus used this sovereign *ego* in his many claims.

This strong emphasis on the person of Christ makes his claims inseparable from his total teaching. Many people want to separate the teachings of Christ, which they like, from the audacious claims, which they dislike. In an address on Christmas Day, 1931, the great Indian leader, Mahatma Gandhi, told a London audience:

> I may say that I have never been interested in an historical Jesus. I should not care if it was proved by some one that the man called Jesus never lived, and that what was narrated in the Gospels was a figment of the writer's imagination. For then the Sermon on the Mount would still be true for me.

Obviously, Gandhi hadn't read the Sermon on the Mount very well, for Jesus said that we must accept *him* as well as his teaching. He didn't simply say, for example, "Blessed are you if you are persecuted," he said, "if you are persecuted *on my account*" (Matt. 5:11). He didn't simply say, "Deny yourself," he added, "and take up your cross and *follow me*" (Matt. 16:24). He didn't simply say, "Lose your life," he said, "Lose your life *for my sake*" (Mark 8:35). These phrases, "on my account," "for my sake," and "follow me," change the meaning of his sayings dramatically. You can't "abstract" Jesus the person from his sayings and leave them the same, as Gandhi and others thought.

His claims show that Jesus wasn't the ordinary type of teacher. Ordinary teachings can be separated from the teacher and their truth or falsity doesn't depend on the person doing the teaching. For example, the Pythagorean Theorem would be just as true if discovered by Euclid. A hundred French philosophers could have uttered, *Cogito ergo sum*, and it would still be true; the fact that Descartes said it doesn't keep it from being a general truth. But the sayings of Jesus are different; they aren't just "wise sayings" that would be true detached from his person. They are true only if he was true.

Before the great Buddha died, his disciples asked him how they could best remember him. He answered: "It doesn't matter whether you remember me or not; remember my teachings. Remember the way, the truth. Practice that way and illumination and release will be yours." Buddha felt you could understand his truth without knowing anything about the man who discovered it. Contrast this with Jesus Christ who left the earth commanding his disciples to evangelize the world in his name, leaving them a special memorial meal by which to remember him, promising to be with them until the end of the age.

2. Jesus claimed a unique relationship with God. He wasn't merely *a* Son of God, one among many, but *the* Son of God, the unique, unparalleled Son. This is seen, first of all, in his use of the word, "Father." Christ referred to God as his Father over 100 times in the gospels, but it was always "my Father," "the Father," or "your Father." Only once did he use the phrase, "our Father," and that was while instructing the disciples how to pray (Matt. 6:9). One case where he could easily have used "our Father" and seemed to deliberately avoid it is John 20:17, where he told Mary Magdalene, "I am ascending to my Father and your Father."

This special relationship with God is further indicated by his use of the Aramaic word, *Abba* (Mark 14:36). *Abba* is a very personal, intimate word for God, which translates roughly, "Daddy" or "Papa." Actually, any English translation is inadequate. Judaism had never used this word for God before, as far as we know. It was doubtless considered quasi-blasphemous to become so familiar with the Almighty. But Jesus used it, and St. Paul recommended it later to Christians (Rom. 8:15; Gal. 4:6).[1]

Perhaps the most remarkable statement Jesus ever made about his relation to the Father is found in Matthew 11:27 (see also Luke 10:22): "All things have been delivered to me by my Father; and no one knows the Son except the Father, and no one knows the Father ex-

1. For a thorough discussion of the significance of *Abba*, see J. Jeremias, *The Central Message of the New Testament* (New York: Scribner, 1965), pp. 29ff.

cept the Son and any one to whom the Son chooses to reveal him."
Here Jesus clearly claims "unshared sonship" with God. He then (v.
28) invites the weary to come to him and receive rest, to take his yoke
and learn of him. No saying of Jesus has caused the critics more concern than this one. Jewish scholar, C. G. Montefiore, expressed the
hope that scholars would prove the falsity of this saying, because, if
proved genuine, it would encourage orthodox Christianity! [2]

Jesus claimed to be so close to God that he could commit the Father
to a certain course of action. In John 14:23, he said, "If a man loves
me, he will keep my word, and my Father will love him, and we will
come to him and make our home with him." Christ claimed to be the
perfect agent, the perfect representative, the perfect deputy for God.
To see him was to see God (John 14:9); to hear him was to hear God
(John 14:24); to confess him was to confess God (Matt. 10:32); to reject him was to reject God (Luke 10:16); to honor him was to honor
God (John 5:23).

Jesus claimed to speak the very words of God. After the Sermon on
the Mount he said that whoever practices his teaching is like a man
who builds his house on a rock, while a man who fails to practice his
teaching is like a man who builds his house on the sand (Matt.
7:24-28; Luke 6:47-49). He complimented Mary for listening to his
words and chided Martha for being distracted from them by
housework (Luke 10:41). He placed his own words on a par with the
eternal words of God when he said, "Heaven and earth will pass
away, but my words will not pass away" (Mark 13:31).

The most explicit direct claim Christ made occurs in the Gospel of
John, chapter eight. Three times he subtly used the phrase, *ego eimi*
("I am"), claiming to be the I AM, the great incommunicable name
of Yahweh. "You will die in your sins unless you believe that I AM"
(v. 24). "When you have lifted up the Son of man, then you will know
that I AM" (v. 28). When Jesus claimed that "your father Abraham
rejoiced that he was to see my day; he saw it and was glad," the Jews
replied, "You are not yet fifty years old, and have you seen
Abraham?" Jesus said: "Truly, truly, I say to you, before Abraham
was, I AM" (vv. 56-58). You can check various Old Testament
passages (e.g., Exod. 3:14; Deut. 32:39; Isa. 43:10) to see that Jesus
was claiming to be one with Yahweh. The Jews knew exactly what he
meant; that's why they tried to stone him on the spot (v. 59). Stoning
was the proper punishment commanded in the Law for blasphemy
(Lev. 24:16).

2. See A. M. Hunter, *The Work and Words of Jesus*, rev. ed. (Philadelphia: Westminster
Press, 1973), p. 106.

3. Jesus claimed that his coming and his mission were unique, crucial, and final in God's plan. He began his ministry in Galilee with the stunning announcement, "The time is fulfilled, and the kingdom of God is at hand; repent, and believe in the gospel" (Mark 1:15). He told his listeners that a new epoch in God's dealings with men had dawned. "The law and the prophets were until John; since then the good news of the kingdom of God is preached" (Luke 16:16). He connected his miracles with the coming of the kingdom: "If it is by the finger of God that I cast out demons, then the kingdom of God has come upon you" (Luke 11:20). His new message was the "new wine" that would burst the "old wineskins" of Judaism (Matt. 9:17).

Jesus constantly dramatized the significance of his ministry for world history. "Zero hour" had dawned for the Jewish people; the ancient covenant nation had arrived at the redemptive crossroads. "Blessed are the eyes which see what you see! For I tell you that many prophets and kings desired to see what you see, and did not see it, and to hear what you hear, and did not hear it" (Luke 10:23). He was greater than anything that had ever gone before, greater than Solomon (Matt. 12:42; Luke 11:31), greater than Jonah (Matt. 12:41), greater even than the Temple (Matt. 12:6).

Because he was the final revelation of God, those who rejected him were especially reprehensible. This comes out very strongly in the Parable of the Wicked Tenants (Mark 12:1-9). A man planted a vineyard and let it out to tenants who then killed or mistreated all the agents he sent back. Finally, the owner decided to send his "beloved son," saying, "They will respect my son." When the tenants saw the son coming, they said, "This is the heir; come, let us kill him, and the inheritance will be ours." When they killed the son, the owner came and destroyed them and gave the vineyard to others. Obviously, Jesus equated himself with the "beloved son" in the parable, the final, unique, perfect representative of the owner, God. The Jews understood the parable, too, for they tried to arrest him.

Jesus claimed to be the last of a long line of prophets God had sent to Israel, all of whom they had persecuted and killed (Matt. 23:29-31). He said the Jews' rejection of him, the final word of God, would bring upon "this generation" the blood of all God's previous messengers, "from the blood of innocent Abel to the blood of Zechariah" (Matt. 23:35, 36). He predicted the destruction of his beloved Jerusalem by the Roman armies and said it was because "you did not know the time of your visitation" (Luke 19:44).

His greatest claim concerning his mission was that he was bringing in the new covenant. Jeremiah had prophesied that God would someday make a new covenant with Israel (Jer. 31:31) and Jesus boldly connected his death with the inauguration of that new covenant. When he gave the cup at the Last Supper, he said, "Drink of it, all of you; for this is my blood of the covenant, which is poured out for many for the forgiveness of sins" (Matt. 26:27, 28). The Hebrew concept of "covenant" *(berith)* is stronger than our English word implies. It means a reciprocal relationship in which God takes the initiative to enter history with a gracious purpose and create a new order of relations between himself and men. Christ therefore claimed to be taking the same initiative in covenant-making that Yahweh had taken with the patriarchs and at Sinai.

At his trial before the Jewish Sanhedrin, the high priest Caiaphas brought the matter of Christ's claims to a head. He made the key issue in the trial revolve around the question, "Who are you?" rather than "What have you done?" When the court failed to produce any incriminating evidence against Jesus, Caiaphas said, "I adjure you by the living God, tell us if you are the Christ, the Son of God" (Matt. 26:63). Jesus answered, "You have said so" (Matthew and Luke) or simply, "I am" (Mark). In his complete answer Jesus claimed three things: (1) he was the Son of the blessed, (2) he was the one who would sit at the right hand of power, and (3) he was the Son of Man who would come on the clouds of heaven (Matt. 26:64; Mark 14:62; Luke 22:69). All three affirmations are clearly messianic and their cumulative effect is jarring. The phrase, "at the right hand of power," is a peculiar Hebrew expression for the immediate presence of deity. Caiaphas couldn't mistake the meaning of this claim; he rent his garments, an action prohibited by the Law (Lev. 21:10).

Evidence from the gospels suggests emphatically that Jesus didn't make a strong *public* claim to be the Jewish Messiah (Greek: *Christ)* until he stood before the Sanhedrin. He had allowed the claim to be discussed in private (Matt. 16:16; John 4:26), but had cautioned people not to publicize it (Matt. 16:20). He seemed to prefer the less dangerous, more ambiguous term, "Son of Man," by which to refer to himself. The term "Messiah" was so broad and misleading that he didn't want to use it until his hand was forced. Certainly he was the Messiah—in his definition of the term. Instead of asking, "Did he claim to be the Messiah?" we should ask: "What kind of Messiah did he claim to be?"[3]

Once he was before the Sanhedrin, however, Jesus did not shrink from claiming to be the Christ, the Son of God, and the Son of Man. He allowed himself to be condemned to death on a cross for the claim;

3. See chapter vi of C. H. Dodd, *The Founder of Christianity* (New York: Macmillan, 1970), pp. 99ff.

surely that should be proof enough that he believed himself to be the Messiah.

B. THE INDIRECT CLAIMS.

You can claim to be something indirectly. For example, if a man said, "I am commander-in-chief of all the armed forces of the United States of America," that would be claiming to be president, since according to the constitution only the president can say that. In like manner, Jesus Christ claimed to be able to do certain things that only God can do. For example,

1. Jesus claimed to forgive sins, which, if you will but reflect upon it, is an extraordinary assertion. All men feel free to forgive sins against themselves, but Jesus asserted the right to forgive sins against God! When a paralytic was brought to him for healing, he first said to the man, "My son, your sins are forgiven." Some of the scribes immediately thought to themselves, "Why does this man speak thus? It is blasphemy! Who can forgive sins but God alone?" (Mark 2:5-7). This reaction of the Jewish leaders was quite normal; how could a spiritually sensitive Hebrew be anything but scandalized by this claim to forgive sins, a power that even the Messiah wouldn't possess?

Realizing their hostility, Jesus said, "Why do you question thus in your hearts? Which is easier, to say to the paralytic, 'Your sins are forgiven,' or to say, 'Rise, take up your pallet and walk'?" Of course, it's easier to say, "Your sins are forgiven"—that's internal, metaphysical and impossible to verify. Yet Jesus went ahead and performed an objective, external cure, for the very purpose of showing that the power to forgive invisible sins and the power to heal visible paralysis come from the same source. "But that you may know that the Son of man has authority on earth to forgive sins"—he said to the paralytic—"I say to you, rise, take up your pallet and go home." An imposter would more likely have claimed to forgive sins; that couldn't be checked.

On another occasion, Jesus forgave the sins of a woman who anointed his feet with a flask of costly ointment in the home of Simon the Pharisee. When Simon had some critical thoughts about the act, Jesus rebuked him and said, "I tell you, her sins, which are many, are forgiven, for she loved much; but he who is forgiven little, loves little" Luke 7:47).

2. Jesus claimed to be sinless. This claim fits logically with the claim to forgive sins. We wouldn't expect a sinful person to claim the right to forgive sins; we would expect it only of God. The claim to sinlessness fits also with the claim that his blood would be shed for the remission of sins (Matt. 26:28) and that remission of sins would be preached in his name to all nations (Luke 24:47).

We have no record of Jesus ever making confession of sins or worrying about his own shortcomings. He commended the publican for his confession of sins (Luke 18:14), but never confessed sins himself. On the contrary, he challenged his enemies to find sin in him. After calling them liars and children of the devil, he asked boldly, "Which of you convicts me of sin? If I tell the truth, why do you not believe me?" (John 8:46). In the same discourse, he asserted, "I always do what is pleasing to him" (John 8:29). By identifying himself with the Suffering Servant of Isaiah 53 Jesus subtly claimed to be the one who had "done no violence" and of whom it was said, "There was no deceit in his mouth" (Isa. 53:9).

Sin is a congenital condition with all men. If Christ said he was free from it, we have a strong indirect claim to divinity.

3. Jesus claimed that he would judge the world at the end of time. "For as the Father has life in himself, so he has granted the Son also to have life in himself, and has given him authority to execute judgment, because he is the Son of man" (John 5:26, 27). Christ said he would stand before all the nations at the Final Judgment and separate the righteous from the wicked as a shepherd separates the sheep from the goats. He would then send them into either everlasting life or everlasting punishment, depending on how they had treated his brethren (Matt. 25:31-46; see also Matt. 16:27).

To me, Agnos, this claim strikes the deepest in the soul. Anyone who can claim to stand and judge the whole human race, who can peer into the past and untangle all the twisted motives, all the mysterious wellsprings of human conduct, and render a just judgment—such a one would have to be divine.

4. Jesus claimed to supersede the Old Covenant. He claimed to replace Moses and the Law, and since God himself had instituted that Law it would take the full authority of God to replace it. Six times in the Sermon on the Mount he used the formula, "You have heard that it was said . . . but I say to you" (Matt. 5:21, 27, 31, 33, 38, 43). This formula reminds you of the "Thus saith the Lord!" of the Old Testament prophets. Notice Jesus didn't just set himself against the opinion of another rabbi, as Jewish rabbis were wont to do, for then he would have had to confirm his assertion with Old Testament references. Instead, Jesus set his own ego against and above the authority of Moses himself—"I say unto you."

Several of Jesus' assertions of authority are prefaced with the word, *amen*, which is translated "verily" or "truly" or "I tell you most solemnly." *Amen* is thus used about 60 times in the gospels, all in the sayings of Jesus. The word renders his assertions full of immediate certainty and authority.

Note the authority clearly implied in the discussion of marriage and divorce (Matt. 19:1-9; Mark 10:1-12). When the Pharisees heard Jesus condemn easy divorce, they asked, "Why then did Moses allow it?" Jesus answered, "For your hardness of heart Moses allowed you to divorce your wives, but from the beginning it was not so." He declared the Mosaic permission of divorce to be an unfortunate infringement of God's original purpose in creating the sexes. He claimed to know the purpose of marriage "from the beginning"!

Note the authority subtly asserted when Jesus healed on the Sabbath and defended his disciples working on the Sabbath (Mark 2:23-28; Luke 6:1-11). "The sabbath was made for man," he said, "not man for the sabbath; so the Son of man is Lord even of the sabbath." He claimed to know the original intent and basic purpose of the Sabbath. On a similar occasion in John 5:17 he said, "My father is working still, and I am working."

When he asserted that "Whatever goes into a man from outside cannot defile him. . . . What comes out of a man is what defiles a man" (Mark 7:18), he abrogated the law that made certain foods unclean.

5. Jesus claimed to fulfill the Old Testament prophecies concerning the Messiah. Early in his ministry, Jesus was asked to read in the synagogue of his home town, Nazareth. He picked an obvious messianic passage to read (Isa. 61:1, 2) and then said, "Today this scripture has been fulfilled in your hearing" (Luke 4:21). In other words, "Folks, Isaiah was talking about me. I am the one prophesied in this passage!" No wonder they tried to throw him down the local hill.

At his arrest in the Garden of Gethsemane he told Peter and the others that all this was occurring "that the scriptures of the prophets might be fulfilled" (Matt. 26:56). After his resurrection, he told the two men on the road to Emmaus, "O foolish men, and slow of heart to believe all that the prophets have spoken! Was it not necessary that the Christ should suffer these things and enter into his glory?" (Luke 24:25, 26).[4]

---

4. For a thorough examination of the numerous allusions in the sayings of Christ to the great messianic chapter, Isaiah 53, see Vincent Taylor, *Jesus and His Sacrifice* (New York: Macmillan, 1937), pp. 82-249.

6. Jesus claimed to know and predict the future history of mankind. He prophesied that he would be mistreated and killed by the Jewish authorities (Mark 8:31), that he would rise again on the third day (Matt. 16:21), that his kingdom would grow slowly like a grain of mustard seed or like yeast in a batch of dough (Matt. 13:31-33), that his disciples would be persecuted just as he was (John 15:20), that the Holy Spirit, the Comforter, would come to them after he had returned to the Father (John 14:28, 29), that the blood of all previously rejected prophets would fall on the present generation (Matt. 23:35), that Jerusalem would be destroyed by foreign armies (Luke 21:20), that the woman who anointed his feet would be remembered wherever the gospel was preached (Matt. 26:13), that he would after his death be reunited with his disciples and drink again of the cup he offered them at the Last Supper (Mark 14:25), that Jerusalem would be trodden down until the times of the gentiles had been fulfilled (Luke 21:24). In sum, Jesus predicted in outline the spiritual history of the race, from his first advent to the second. All of these predictions, by the way, have come to pass.

7. Jesus claimed to be omnipresent, an attribute only God can possess (see Ps. 139:7-12). "Where two or three are gathered in my name," he said, "there am I in the midst of them" (Matt. 18:20). When he ascended he promised them, "Lo, I am with you always, to the close of the age" (Matt. 28:20).

8. Jesus claimed man's highest loyalty. He demanded from his followers total, uncompromising devotion to him and his cause. He seemed to go out of his way to warn the crowds of his stringent demands for discipleship. One time, when the crowd got too large, he turned on them and said, "If any one comes to me and does not hate his own father and mother and wife and children and brothers and sisters, yes, and even his own life, he cannot be my disciple" (Luke 14:26). When a man asked to go bury his father before following him, Jesus answered, "Follow me, and leave the dead to bury their own dead" (Matt. 8:22).

Jesus often compared discipleship to "bearing a cross" (Mark 8:34). We can't appreciate this metaphor today since we don't use crucifixion for execution. But in Jesus' day the Romans used crucifixion as a swift way of dealing with rebels such as Spartacus and Judas the Galilean. A convicted criminal was made to carry his own cross to the site of crucifixion. By using this metaphor, Jesus was saying, in effect, "Loyalty to me must be so strong that you will risk the Roman cross to be my disciple." No absolute monarch, no totalitarian dictator ever demanded more of his followers.

9. Jesus claimed to be the defeater of the great adversary, Satan. When the seventy disciples returned from the limited commission elated with their power over demons, Jesus said, "I saw Satan fall like lightning from heaven" (Luke 10:18). He predicted that the "gates of hell" would never prevail against his church (Matt. 16:18, AV). He predicted that when he was crucified the "ruler of this world" would be cast out (John 12:31) and that when the Spirit came the devil would be judged (John 16:11).

10. Finally, Jesus claimed to bestow life and to be the author of life. Life has always been a mystery to man. It's hard to define and even harder to create. Nineteen centuries before modern science ever claimed to create life, Jesus of Nazareth boldly asserted, "As the Father raises the dead and gives them life, so also the Son gives life to whom he will" (John 5:21). He claimed to be the "bread of life" (John 6:48), the "resurrection and the life" (John 11:25) and "the way, and the truth, and the life" (John 14:6). A cursory glance at the Old Testament will show that the Jews considered God alone to be the fountain of life (e.g., Deut. 30:15; Job 12:10; Ps. 36:9; 66:9).

Any man who goes around claiming to be sinless, to forgive sins, to judge the world, to replace Moses and the Law, to fulfill the Old Testament, to know the future, to be omnipresent, to merit man's highest loyalty, to defeat Satan, and to bestow life—surely such a man has staked a strong claim to divinity. These ten claims are indirect, but their implication is clear, and anyone who misses the implication would miss the sun on a clear day.

C. CIRCUMSTANTIAL EVIDENCE FOR CHRIST'S CLAIM.

So far, we've examined the verbal claims of Christ, direct and indirect. We can now strengthen our case by considering the circumstantial, or non-verbal, evidence for Christ's claims to divinity. When a man tries to forge a story, it is the circumstantial features that test his creative powers. In a story, you can say that a man is strong-willed, you can even have him assert his strong will, but the good fiction writer must bring out the strong will in the small things, in gestures, mannerisms, small talk, and action. Now, Jesus not only claimed to be divine, both directly and indirectly, he also illustrated his claim with this type of circumstantial data.

1. Jesus always talked and acted like a God. Even if we had no verbal claims at all, we would still be impressed by a man who storms into the Temple and chases the moneychangers with their animal menagerie out of God's house (Mark 11:15-18), who exorcises demons in his own name instead of the name of someone higher, as exorcists usually do (Mark 5:8), who chooses twelve apostles to correspond to the twelve tribes of the Jewish old covenant (Mark 2:14), who deliberately rides into Jerusalem on a donkey as was predicted of the Messiah (Matt. 21:4, 5; Zech. 9:9), who ignores the Jewish authorities and their customs, who heals on the Sabbath and defends his disciples working on the Sabbath.

Especially unusual was the *manner* of Jesus' teaching. Matthew tells us that "he taught them as one who had authority, and not as their scribes" (Matt. 7:29). Socrates taught people by dialogue; he tried, like a midwife, to draw out of the student's mind the thoughts necessary for a good discussion. Every partner in the discussion had the duty of collaborating in the philosophical process. But Jesus didn't *discuss* so much as *proclaim*. He taught as if he "knew it all" before the discussion began, and this is what you would expect if he were divine. None of his opponents or his disciples could add much to the discussion by putting stimulating questions to him.[5]

Jesus' manner of teaching is full of references to unseen facts and invisible realities beyond the reach of normal human knowledge. He seemed to have a peephole to the transcendent, a "window on the Beyond." Little children are brought to him and he facilely observes that "in heaven their angels always behold the face of my Father who is in heaven" (Matt. 18:10). He notes that every sparrow is observed by God (Luke 12:6, 7). In arguing with the Sadducees about the Resurrection, he casually observes that "when they rise from the dead, they neither marry nor are given in marriage, but are like the angels in heaven" (Mark 12:25).

Perhaps the most stunning type of circumstantial evidence we have is the fact that Jesus received worship from various people and never forbade them. A leper and a Canaanite woman kneel and worship him (Matt. 8:2; 15:25); the man born blind falls down to worship him (John 9:38); the disciples worship him after he calms a storm on the Sea of Galilee (Matt. 14:33); Thomas the Doubter falls before the risen Lord and exclaims, "My Lord and my God!" (John 20:28). We have no record of Jesus ever rebuking any of these people for worshipping him. Contrast this with Peter who rebuked Cornelius for such worship

5. See Martin Dibelius, *The Sermon on the Mount* (New York: Charles Scribner's Sons, 1940), pp. 37, 38.

(Acts 10:25, 26) and the Angel of Revelation, who wouldn't allow John to worship him (Rev. 19:10). Surely one who accepts worship is behaving like a God.

2. If Jesus didn't make all the claims we've mentioned one is at a loss to explain various things recorded in the gospels. Why, for instance, did the Jews try to stone him for blasphemy? This was the punishment prescribed by the Law for such an offense (Lev. 24:16). Why was he tried for blasphemy before the Jewish Sanhedrin?[6] Why did the high priest rend his garment at the trial? Such action was prohibited by the Law (Lev. 10:6; 21:10). Why was Caiaphas so alarmed at the political consequences of Christ's miracles and his teachings (John 11:47-53)? Why was Pilate also alarmed by his claim to be the Son of God (John 19:7, 8)? Why did the demons cry out against him when they recognized him (Mark 1:24)? What drove the Pharisees and Sadducees into an unnatural alliance to eliminate him? Why did people mock him on the cross by saying, "He trusts in God; let God deliver him now, if he desires him; for he said, 'I am the Son of God' " (Matt. 27:43)?

Finally, why did the Christian community think it necessary to break away from historic Judaism if Jesus never claimed to be divine? If people could have interpreted Jesus merely as another Hebrew prophet there would have been no need for a break. Jesus would have taken his place alongside Moses, Elijah, and Jeremiah. No one in the church ever declared, "Yahweh is One and Jesus is his prophet." Jesus was more than a prophet; he claimed to be more, and Christians considered him to be more. The Christian church is a mighty tribute to that fact.

3. The final type of circumstantial evidence we have is the systematic coherence that prevails in the claims of Jesus Christ. A forger or deceiver would have had difficulty creating such an organic unity from the varied, spontaneous sayings we have in the gospels. All his claims fit together and form a systematic whole; they imply each other, and this gives the entire corpus a striking verisimilitude. If, for example, a man forgives sins it fits with the assertion of sinlessness. If he replaces Moses, he can act as he wishes on the Sabbath and modify any of the old Jewish customs. If he is God's final word of revelation he can truly tell us how marriage was supposed to be from the begin-

---

6. We have the testimony of the Jewish historian Josephus that Jesus died at the hands of both the Jews and the Romans. "And when Pilate, at the suggestion of the principal men amongst us, had condemned him to the cross, those that loved him at the first did not forsake him" (*Antiquities*, XVIII. 63ff.).

ning. If he is the world's Savior and Judge then he can rightfully demand our complete loyalty. If he is the Lord of nature it doesn't surprise us that he stills storms and multiplies bread.

What forger could have planned the following undesigned coincidence? We never find Christ following his own command, *if* that command can't be carried out by a divine being. Whenever possible, Christ carried out his own commands, but in two cases he didn't: (1) he commanded men to be humble yet he himself made audacious claims; (2) he praised the publican for confessing sins yet he himself never confessed sins and judged sin mercilessly in all others. Why did Christ not follow his own commands in respect to humility and confession? Simply because he couldn't! To say, "I am nothing," when you're divine would be a lie. To confess sins when you're sinless would be a lie.

Now, isn't it interesting that *we find Christ not doing those very things that a God can not do?* This undesigned coincidence is one of the strongest pieces of circumstantial evidence for the authenticity of his claims. Someone has well said, "If Christ wasn't God then he deserves an Oscar!"

D. YOUR RESPONSE TO THE CLAIMS OF CHRIST.

So here we have the claims of Christ spread out on the table, Agnos. Now, you can take only three positions in response to them: you can say either (1) he never made the claims, or (2) he made them and they were false, or (3) he made them and they were true. I will now try to eliminate choices one and two.

1. Jesus never made the claims. This is the easiest thing for a person to say who wants to accept Jesus as a great moral teacher but not as God. It gets Jesus off the hook and lays all the blame on his credulous, hero-worshipping disciples, who invented all the claims after Jesus was dead.

The trouble with this theory is it just won't wash in the twentieth century. We have too much documentary evidence showing that Jesus really made all those unusual claims. This theory was easy to assert in the last century when critics claimed (without good evidence) that most of the New Testament was composed after the first century. But discoveries like the John Rylands Fragment of John pushed the date of the Fourth Gospel back to the close of the first century, and this dating of John automatically pushes the other three gospels into the latter half of the first century.

Now, if the synoptic gospels were composed within about three decades of the death of Christ you need to explain carefully how it happens that they show Jesus making these claims if he really didn't. Why didn't the eyewitnesses rise up and contest this false picture? The apostles had to report the truth about Jesus accurately if for no other reason than many of his enemies were still alive and could have exposed such a false portrait of the Nazarene. In the first sermon on Christ, Peter noted that the men of Israel were well aware of his miracles ("as you yourselves also know," Acts 2:22). Later he emphasized the Resurrection and said, "We are witnesses of these things" (v. 32). He appealed to the general knowledge of Jesus which the inhabitants of Jerusalem had. This general knowledge, belonging as it did to both Jesus' disciples and his enemies, kept the gospel picture of Christ true to the historical person.

Whatever date you assign to the gospels, you are still left with a gap of at least thirty years between the life of Jesus and the earliest written records representing the content of apostolic preaching. If the old liberal theory is true, then the church rather suddenly, in three decades, transformed the humble Galilean prophet, who worked no miracles and made no claims, into the theological Christ, who worked miracles and made incredible claims.

But you can easily destroy this theory with the epistles of Paul, all of which were written between c. A.D. 51 and 62. The earliest of them, First and Second Thessalonians, already have the theological Christ fully developed, saving mankind from sins, rising from the dead, and coming at the end of time in judgment (I Thess. 1:9, 10). Now, it would be ludicrous to assert that Paul developed this complex Christology just before he wrote to the Thessalonians. He obviously had been preaching it for several years, and this drives the "Christ of the Church" back into the 40's and perhaps into the late 30's. But Christ died around 30 or 31; Paul was probably converted around 36 or 37. This leaves no time at all for the development of Pauline Christology. For the liberal theory to be true there would have to be a break—a rather large break—in the tradition. But there is none. I repeat: this theory could only be held at a time when it was thought that the New Testament was composed very late.

Why would the early Christians want to falsify the claims of Christ in the first place? Most of them were Jews who had inherited the strong monotheism of the Old Testament, and this would have kept them from attributing deity to a mere man without strong evidence. How, furthermore, could a Jew, working with his own imagination, come up with a Messiah who was sinless, who suffered rather than conquered, who built an ethical not a political kingdom, a redeemer who brought in the new covenant by his execution as a criminal on a Roman cross?

Critics usually say that only the miracles and the claims were fabricated; the moral teachings they attribute to Jesus himself. But this is a tenuous distinction. Since Jesus didn't write a single line, we must assume that he succeeded in conveying his moral teachings to his listeners. But isn't it inconsistent to believe that this part of the record represents solid factual reporting, and that the rest is sheer fancy? If the claims and the miracles are legendary, why not scrap the whole story?

Actually, there is no good reason, as Birger Gerhardsson so ably argues, to doubt that the entire story was faithfully transmitted to Jesus' followers. Since Jesus taught like a typical rabbi, his instruction was a combination of text and interpretation and he probably required his disciples to memorize large portions of his teaching. Disciples of rabbis were committed to accurate transmission rather than alteration or fanciful interpretation of the master's words. To suppose that "weak memory" (which the Jews didn't have!) or "pious imagination" (which remains to be proved) distorted the authentic words of Christ in two or three decades is quite a strain on the credulity.[7]

Sorry, Agnos, but this avenue of escape is closed to you. Jesus *made* all those preposterous claims. You are driven to alternative number two.

2. Jesus made the claims, but they were false. If you take this position you must choose between two sub-options:

a. Jesus was a liar.

b. Jesus was mentally disturbed.

You may not like these choices, but you have to take one or the other. If Christ made the claims and they were false, he either *knew* they were false—in which case he was a liar—or he *thought* they were true—in which case he was a lunatic.[8]

a. Was Jesus a liar? The question sounds so repulsive that to ask it is to answer it. One instinctively asks: How could the author of the Sermon on the Mount and the Parable of the Good Samaritan be a base deceiver? How could the founder of the most moral religion in history be a liar? Does pure water come from a foul stream? Can beautiful

7. Birger Gerhardsson, *Memory and Manuscript* (Lund, Sweden: Gleerup, 1961).

8. Actually, the fact that both these alternatives were suggested by his contemporaries shows that the issue hasn't changed much in 2000 years. See Mark 3:22, where they accused him of being in league with Beelzebub; John 8:48, where they accused him of having a demon; John 7:47, where they categorized him as a deceiver.

sayings come from a moral pervert? You might as well affirm that Hitler composed the *Divine Comedy* or Jack the Ripper wrote *The Imitation of Christ*. Hear the testimony of Lecky:

> The character of Jesus has not only been the highest pattern of virtue, but the strongest incentive to its practice, and has exerted so deep an influence, that it may be truly said that the simple record of three short years of active life has done more to regenerate and to soften mankind, than all the disquisitions of philosophers and all the exhortations of moralists.[9]

Jesus took pains to convince people that the devil is a liar and that those who lie are his children (John 8:44-47). Would he then do exactly what he had condemned others for doing? Why would he lie? What was his motive? Money? Fame? Power? He got none of these. Why would he lie all through his career and then suddenly die for his own lie? Liars are usually very self-serving; they lie to benefit themselves, not to harm themselves. To say that Christ lied all during his ministry and then martyred himself because he refused to renounce that lie is a very strange hypothesis.

b. Was Jesus a lunatic? Once again the question sounds repulsive. Normally the greater a man is, the less likely he is to make such grandiose claims. God is God, and a great man knows he is not God and the greater he is the better he knows it. Outside of Christ, the only man who ever makes such a claim is a low form of lunatic, a very small man, a self-centered monomaniac. Most of us feel deeply our own finitude and fallibility and, if we're honest and intelligent, this militates strongly against claims to deity. The case for Jesus' honesty is good, but was he also intelligent?

You can make a very strong case for the intelligence of Jesus Christ. He possessed, for example, that rare ability to compare several things at once. "Consider the lilies of the field, how they grow; they toil not, neither do they spin: and yet I say unto you, That even Solomon in all his glory was not arrayed like one of these" (Matt. 6:28, 29, AV). This ability to compare three things at once, on three planes—flowers, kings, ordinary people—is a subtle power few possess. It involves the ability to abstract, to conceptualize, to construct an analogy, and to see how three different things are alike. If you read carefully the sayings of Christ you will see this rare gift in action.

Christ's intelligence is further illustrated by his excellent knowledge of the Old Testament. He knew it well enough to confound the

9. W. H. Lecky, *History of European Morals from Augustus to Charlemagne*, 2nd ed. (London: Longmans, Green, 1869), II, 88.

Pharisees over a messianic prophecy (Matt. 22:41-46). His special insight into various passages became apparent when he confuted the Sadducees on the question of the Resurrection (Matt. 22:23-33). One of the scribes present on this occasion was so impressed with his refutation of the Sadducees that he asked him about the Great Commandment and agreed with his answer (Mark 12:28, 32). After several such answers, Matthew tells us that no one wanted to ask him any more questions that day (Matt. 22:46).

So many of Christ's moral teachings are the soul of common sense and reasonableness. Take his advice on fasting: don't do it when you're happy (Luke 5:34); or on prayer: don't waste empty phrases on God because he knows what you need before you ask (Matt. 6:7, 8); or on keeping the Sabbath: if you can take an animal to water on the Sabbath, why can't you heal a man (Luke 13:15)? A man of such practical common sense would not likely suffer from the peculiar intoxication of self-deification.

If a mere man thinks he's God that's about as mixed up as you can get. If Christ was that mixed up, how could he have exhibited such a broad, humane spirit as pervades the precepts he uttered? He didn't present an unbalanced, one-sided view of human nature. He was free of libertinism and of asceticism. In short, Jesus lacked the simplicity and narrow-mindedness of the ordinary madman. He possessed the subtlety of the true prophet.

Finally, if Christ was deluded about his relation to God, how did it come about that his general doctrine of God as personal Father to all men has become, by common consent, the highest conception of God in religious history? How could he be so wonderfully wise about God's nature and so strangely confused about his own relation to God?

No, Agnos, the lunatic hypothesis just doesn't explain the mystery of Jesus Christ. Unless you can suggest another alternative, or give some better evidence for the liar-lunatic alternatives, you're driven to number three:

3. Jesus made the claims and they were true. This is the conviction of every Christian. Making claims, of course, doesn't mean that they are true. What I am arguing here is only that, granted the hypothesis, "Jesus made the claims and they were true," we can clear up all the puzzles we get into with any other hypothesis. In the next two chapters we'll give evidence for the truth of his claims from (1) his character and (2) his resurrection.

One thing for sure: Jesus himself made forever impossible the ridiculous theory that he was a good moral man or a great religious teacher but not the Son of God he claimed to be. Unbelievers have never gotten over the contradiction between (1) his moral person and teachings and (2) his egomania, a characteristic we can't deny if he was really not divine. If Jesus made all the claims and they were false, then he was certainly *not* a great moral teacher. He was either the world's biggest liar or the world's most pitiful religious fanatic, deceiver or deceived. Let's not hear any more of this silly claptrap that "I can accept Jesus as a great moral teacher but not as the Son of God." You either accept him as the Son of God or else you have a strange taste in moral teachers!

If Jesus wasn't God in the flesh then he deserves an Oscar, because he certainly acted and talked like a God. If not Jesus, then the Christian community deserves an Oscar, because it wrote a beautiful description of the most impressive personality in history.

14

THE CHARACTER OF JESUS CHRIST

You're now in the Holy of Holies, Agnos, the innermost part of the sanctuary, the character of Jesus Christ. We've already passed through the outer court of the Temple, the miracles and claims of Jesus, and we're now ready to look at the most precious treasure of all. If you've followed our argument up to now you could say, "Well, Jesus, when it comes to wonders and claims, you're certainly no slouch. But wonders can be tricks and claims can be false. How do I know that you're not just the greatest religious con man in history? One thing you lack yet—a godly character."

True, wonders and claims only heighten our anticipation to press on and look at the person, Jesus Christ. Few men in history have dared to assert that they revealed the very mind of God and that obedience to them is the only true foundation for life. When someone preaches like that to us, when he demands perfection of us, we logically ask: "What about you? Do *you* practice what you preach? Do *you* have a godly character?"

Before you can answer the question, "Did Jesus have a godly character?" you need to answer the question, "What is God like?" We seem to be reasoning in a circle when we say that Jesus reveals God, because the assertion implies we know what God is like even before we see Jesus and we then check for the family resemblance. This is really not the way it happens. "If we were honest," says Leonard Griffith accurately, "we should reverse the order and realize that all we know about God with any certainty we have learned from Jesus. Christianity does not look from God to Jesus; rather it looks from

Jesus to God; and it is a real question whether, apart from Jesus, we should be able to form any clear picture of God at all."[1]

Without getting into this briar patch of what we can know about God before revelation, let me just say that most people nowadays would agree that if God existed he would be more than human in things like (1) power, (2) intelligence, and (3) goodness. If the theistic arguments we've covered have any merit at all, we can believe that God has power and intelligence. His goodness may be suspect because of the problem of evil, but we'll try to reduce that problem later (ch. 17).

Now, if God were to become man, we'd expect that man to exhibit the same general trinity: power, intelligence, goodness.[2] We've already mentioned the intelligence of Jesus and his miracles show his power. But what of his goodness? That's the theme of this chapter. As usual, we begin our investigation of the data with a thesis: *the divine humanity of Jesus Christ.* It's not wrong, as argued earlier, to start your examination with a theory, since all thinkers do so. It's especially helpful when the data are complex, as they are with the claims, deeds, and sayings of Jesus. My thesis says that if you'll start with the assumption of the divine humanity of Jesus, this hypothesis will unlock all the mysteries of his person. The facts of his life will support your presupposition; they won't support any other theory. Any other hypothesis will leave large blocs of data suppressed, ignored, or contradicted.

We say, in sum, that you can't explain Christ without invoking the transcendent once again, as we've done so often in this study. Christ is redolent with the "aroma of eternity." He enters and exits trailing clouds of glory. First, let's look at his relation to the perennial problem of sin.

A. JESUS CHRIST AND SIN.

If you don't like the old theological term, "sin," Agnos, just substitute a synonym of your own: misconduct, wickedness, evil, or just plain cussedness. Call it what you will, it's an endemic human problem. "All have sinned and fall short of the glory of God" (Rom. 3:23). Unless you're an ethical nihilist you've probably agonized many times over the cause and the cure of sin in your own person. Did

---

1. *Barriers to Christian Belief* (London: Hodder and Stoughton, 1961), p. 92.

2. Ramm uses this formula, "if God were to become a man," very effectively in his chapter, "The Verification of Christianity by the Supernatural Character of Its Founder," *Protestant Christian Evidences*, pp. 163-83.

Jesus escape this problem? There is cogent evidence that he did. Let's ask three sources: Jesus himself, his friends, and his enemies.

1. Jesus himself possessed a scandalously high estimate of his moral character. He not only forgave sins (Mark 2:5; Luke 7:47), he also predicted that his life would be given for the forgiveness of sins (Matt. 26:28). In a discussion with some opponents, Jesus called them liars and sons of the devil and then asked: "Which of you convicts me of sin? If I tell the truth, why do you not believe me?" The Jews then accused him of being possessed, to which he replied: "I have not a demon; but I honor my Father, and you dishonor me" (John 8:46, 49). Earlier in the same discussion he had asserted: "I always do what is pleasing to him" (John 8:29). On another occasion he told the crowd that he sought only the glory of God and that there was no falsehood in him (John 7:18).[3]

To appreciate this attitude of Jesus, you must contrast it with the confessions of other religious leaders in world history. At the close of his life, the great Confucius said, "In letters I am perhaps equal to other men; but the character of the perfect man, carrying out in his conduct what he professes, is what I have not yet attained to." In the Koran, Mohammed expressly commanded his followers to pray for his sins. And every Bible student remembers that Moses was denied entrance into the promised land because of his sins (Deut. 34:4).[4]

2. Jesus' disciples also shared this high estimate of his moral person. When he came to be baptized, John the Baptist said, "I need to be baptized by you, and do you come to me?" (Matt. 3:14). Peter said, "He committed no sin; no guile was found on his lips" (I Peter 2:22). John appeals to Christians not to sin by saying: "You know that he appeared to take away sins, and in him there is no sin" (I John 3:5). Paul affirmed that, "For our sake he made him to be sin who knew no sin, so that in him we might become the righteousness of God" (II Cor. 5:21). The writer of Hebrews said that Christ was tempted like all men, yet without sin (4:15), and that he was "a high priest, holy, blameless, unstained, separated from sinners, exalted above the heavens" (7:26). Referring to Christ as a sacrificial lamb is a symbolic

---

3. In his *Dialogue Against Pelagius* (3.2), St. Jerome preserves this brief fragment of the lost "Gospel According to the Hebrews": "Behold, the mother of the Lord and his brothers said to him: John the Baptizer baptizes unto the remission of sins; let us go and be baptized by him. But he said to them: Wherein have I sinned, that I should go and be baptized by him? Unless perhaps this very thing that I have said is a sign of ignorance?"

4. See William M. Justice, *Our Visited Planet* (New York: Vantage, 1973), p. 18.

way of asserting his sinlessness (Rev. 5:6), because such a creature had to be without blemish (I Peter 1:19).

This testimony from Christ's disciples is most impressive when you realize that they were all Jews whose minds had been steeped in the Old Testament idea of the universality of sin (e.g., Ps. 14:3; Isa. 53:6). They had lived with Christ in very close quarters for over three years before they finally began to preach to the world that he was the sinless Lord. One of the last things I can imagine a Jew inventing on his own would be the picture of *a sinless man!* The proof for Jesus' sinlessness must have been overwhelming for these men to assert it so confidently.

3. Many of Jesus' enemies give us oblique testimony to his character. Pilate the Roman governor pronounced him innocent three times during the second phase of his trial. Pilate's wife sent an urgent message to her husband during the trial to "have nothing to do with that righteous man, for I have suffered much over him today in a dream" (Matt. 27:19). Herod, tetrarch of Galilee, examined him briefly and agreed with Pilate that he had done nothing deserving death (Luke 23:15). Judas the traitor repented of his treachery and told the Jewish authorities: "I have sinned in betraying innocent blood" (Matt. 27:4). The thief on the cross rebuked his friend for mocking Jesus, saying, "We are receiving the due reward for our deeds; but this man has done nothing wrong" (Luke 23:41). The Roman centurion and others at the cross who watched him die praised God and said that Jesus was innocent (Luke 23:47) and "the son of God" (Matt. 27:54).

But what of his Jewish enemies? Didn't they find many faults in Jesus? Yes, but most of the charges sound like virtues instead of vices. They faulted him for healing on the Sabbath (John 5:16), for associating with the poor and sinners (Luke 19:7), for breaking certain customs like the washing of hands (Matt. 15:2), for placing the inner spirit of the law above the letter (Matt. 12:7), for not being abstemious enough in his eating and drinking (Luke 7:34).

The main accusation—blasphemy—was never proved, only asserted. Even then, they sought to prove blasphemy first by perjured testimony and then by extracting a confession from Jesus himself, a violation of Jewish custom.[5] When the Jews took him to Pilate the charge suddenly changed from religion to politics, from blasphemy to sedition! Pilate dismissed the charge three different times but finally

5. Cf. Matt. 26:57-68; Mark 14:53-65; Luke 22:63-71; John 18:19-24. There are numerous good works on the trial of Christ, but a good short presentation is ch. 24 of Barclay's *Mind of Jesus* (New York: Harper and Row, 1960), pp. 221-38.

gave in when the Jews warned: "If you release this man, you are not Caesar's friend; every one who makes himself a king sets himself against Caesar" (John 19:12).

4. Circumstantial evidence corroborates this personal testimony from Jesus, his friends, and his enemies. If you want to invent a picture of a morally pure man you must have him doing more than *asserting* his purity; you must have him *acting* as if he believed in it. And it is this non-verbal part of the man which is so hard to forge.

Jesus Christ was utterly without any consciousness of sin. He never experienced conversion, reform, repentance, remorse, or guilt. He praised the publican for confession of sins, but never confessed any himself. He never gave the slightest hint that he had ever violated his own conscience, the moral law, or the will of God. He never asked prayer for himself. You would never find him making New Year's resolutions or muttering to himself: "Every day in every way I'm getting better and better."

Even non-Christians admit that Jesus had the closest relation with God that any man has ever known. Yet such intimacy never caused him to utter any painful recognition of his own inadequacy. When Isaiah saw Yahweh in the Temple he said, "Woe is me! For I am lost; for I am a man of unclean lips" (Isa. 6:5). When God spoke to Job, Job said, "I despise myself, and repent in dust and ashes" (Job 42:6). David confessed, "I was brought forth in iniquity, and in sin did my mother conceive me" (Ps. 51:5). Paul called himself the foremost of sinners" (I Tim. 1:15) and cried, "Wretched man that I am! Who will deliver me from this body of death?" (Rom. 7:24). We never hear things like that from the lips of Jesus.

Additional confirmation comes from the fact that Jesus redefined sin in such a way that no human could ever again claim to be blameless. His criticism of moral evil was utterly unsparing; he struck at the very roots of it in the illicit desires of the heart. Moses was against murder; Jesus condemned vindictive anger. Moses was against adultery; Jesus condemned lust itself. Moses said to love your neighbor; Jesus said to love your enemy. Moses said to be good; Jesus said to be perfect (Matt. 5:17-48)! No man in history so radically redefined and exposed human sin. Only God could scrutinize us men in such a searching way. The picture all fits: any man who could so expose sin would also be free of sin himself and could thus forgive sin in others.

Perhaps the best evidence we can offer for thinking Christ sinless is the fact that he allowed his dearest friends to think it. He told them to "follow me," that is, he offered himself as the ideal norm for conduct.

Since he had also told them that they must be perfect even as the heavenly Father is perfect (Matt. 5:48), it follows that he considered himself equal to the Father in moral rectitude. This would be the greatest case of *hubris* in history if he wasn't sinless as he claimed to be.

We're back in the same boat we were in with the claims of Christ, Agnos. If Christ was the best man that ever lived, he would have been very sensitive to the sin in his own person. The best people in the world impress you with their awareness of shortcomings—except Jesus Christ. To think yourself sinless is the greatest of sins—unless it's true. Anyone who would thus claim moral perfection must either be liar, lunatic, or telling the truth.[6]

Aren't we really saying that Christ's character is a miracle, the greatest miracle of all? If all men sin, and Christ didn't, and if a miracle is an exception to the norm, aren't we really saying that his life is the most stupendous miracle of all? Is it any wonder that most unbelievers must flee to some myth hypothesis to escape the clear implication of his sinlessness? We can summarize the argument in syllogistic form this way:

1. If a man is truly good, he will acknowledge his sins, if he has any.
2. Jesus Christ did not acknowledge any sins.
3. Therefore, either:
   a. Jesus Christ was not truly good, or
   b. Jesus Christ had no sins.

Note once again, Agnos: there is no middle ground in your evaluation of Jesus Christ. He was either evil or sinless.

One last point: it's fitting that Christ's ethical ideals were so uncompromising. Assuming God to be the source of all values, would God-in-the-flesh have less than a perfect standard of values? Would he say, "Now, sin just a little"? Christ's values sound absolute and timeless; they're just as hard to keep today as they were when he first uttered them (e.g., turn the other cheek).

Jesus seldom compromised with his culture when it came to values. When Mohammed allowed four wives, that was a compromise with culture. When Moses allowed easy divorce, that was a compromise with culture (Matt. 19:8). When Luther allowed Philip of Hesse to remarry, that was a compromise with culture. But Jesus seemed to go out of his way to offend his culture and to give us the original,

---

6. See Charles E. Jefferson, *The Character of Jesus* (New York: Thomas Y. Crowell, 1908), pp. 330ff.

transcultural ethic. He predicted that everything would pass away except his words.

B. JESUS AND GOD.

If Jesus was sinless, then he could rightfully claim to be the revelation of the perfectly holy God. Many religions think that for the greater glory of God they must prove him unknowable. Not so Christianity. Christians feel that "it is in Christ that the complete being of the Godhead dwells embodied" (Col. 2:9, NEB) and that Christ "reflects the glory of God and bears the very stamp of his nature" (Heb. 1:3). Christ is the explanation, the exegesis, of God's true nature (John 1:18).

Certainly this gives the Christian system a "scandal of particularity," but it also gives the reflective thinker an actual, historical personality to investigate. You can't complain that you have nothing objective to examine. To the Indian or Hindu mind God is near at all times; at any moment you can merge with the Absolute. One who thinks in this way might believe that a historical event can illuminate a truth but never establish it.

With Christianity, the historical Jesus Christ establishes the truth. One must choose between the Indian and the Christian concepts of time and revelation. Either (1) every time and place is equally immediate to God or (2) God has made certain times and places special. Christians insist that unless you orient yourself to the special events, the "great acts of God," especially what God did in Christ, you'll never really gain access to the Eternal Thou. Remember Christ's claim: "I am the way, and the truth, and the life; *no one comes to the Father, but by me*" (John 14:6). Of all the things Christ brought us, we think the most priceless is the disclosure of the loving heart of God.

To the Greeks, God, or the gods, had no heart to speak of. The gods were jealous of man, begrudging even the fire that Prometheus stole to bring to earth. The gods were detached, apathetic, unconcerned about life on earth. The idea of a God with a loving heart was foreign to Greek thought. The idea of God being passionately involved in the human situation was foreign to nearly all classical thought before Christianity.[7]

Didn't the Jewish Yahweh care about men? Yes, but he was still so good and so holy that no man could approach him and look directly

---

7. In his *Confessions* (VII.ix.13), Augustine said, "That the Word was in the beginning and that the Word was with God and the Word was God, this I read in the books of the Neo-Platonists. . . but that the Word was made flesh and dwelt among us, I found not there."

on his countenance (Exod. 33:20). To experience God directly was to die (Gen. 32:30; Judg. 13:22). God was so "wholly other" that no sinner could continue to exist under his wrath. Only the prophet Hosea seems to have glimpsed the mercy of God that Jesus later revealed. Most of the Old Testament would terrify the sinner: "Let sinners be consumed from the earth, and let the wicked be no more!" (Ps. 104:35). "All the sinners of my people shall die by the sword" (Amos 9:10).

In fact, it seems to be an axiom of all religions before Christ that *God deals only with the pure.* This is why most heathen religions, and sadly some forms of Christianity, are based on fear. Jews and Greeks alike knew enough of God's power, knowledge, justice, holiness, and righteousness to fear him, but it took the *Abba* Father of Jesus Christ to teach the world to love God. "Fear not" is often the first thing said when someone in the New Testament is visited of God (Luke 1:13, 30, AV). Jesus brought God so near that his great apostle of love, John, could write, "We need have no fear of someone who loves us perfectly; his perfect love for us eliminates all dread of what he might do to us" (I John 4:18, LB).

To find out that God loves men is surprise enough, but to find out further that he is searching love and self-sacrificing love is indeed mind-boggling. It was a commonplace of all ancient religion that man should sacrifice something to the deity, but the idea that God would sacrifice something for man—this was an innovation. Jesus taught us to think of God as a shepherd searching for a lost sheep, a housewife searching for a lost coin, a kindly father waiting anxiously the return of his prodigal son (Luke 15:1-32). We see that God feels impoverished when men are lost and that he will endure sacrifice at the cost of his only Son to recover them (John 3:16; Rom. 5:8).

To have God revealed so intimately is a great gain in man's moral struggles. Only a father can be loved the way Jesus said to love God. It's hard to love the judge high on his bench, or the powerful king high on his throne. You could say that only those who have discovered God as their Father can really love God the way Jesus said to love him. When Jesus came to earth and healed the sick, fed the hungry, consoled the sad, forgave his enemies, and laid down his life, he was saying, in essence: "God is like that—God loves you like that."

The God of Jesus Christ is a colossal advance over anything before or after him. A personal Father displaces the cold universe of *atheism.* The abstract being of *pantheism* warms into a paternal heart of sacrificial love. The distant, apathetic being of *deism* comes near and bares his soul to us. The many gods of *polytheism* merge into one unitary being whose power, intelligence, and goodness far surpass the

Greco-Roman pantheon. In Christ, for the first and only time in man's history, the idea of God becomes vivid, believable, definite, persuasive.

You might complain that the man who revealed God would eventually eclipse God. One might expect this, but strangely enough, it has seldom happened in the history of Christendom. Christ revealed and interpreted God without superseding God. He enhanced Yahweh's glory without at all lessening his dignity. Christ never broke up the unity of the godhead, because Christians never attributed separate or individual being to him. In Greek and Hindu mythology, such an eclipse did take place when one god claimed to reveal another. Zeus, Indra, and Krishna all rise and then finally overshadow previous deities.[8] In all Christian creeds, however, Christ is still considered ontologically one with his Father.

John Henry Newman once said that great ideas never command us until they are personalized in a great character. Only a person can genuinely reveal another person and if God is a person then the idea of a personal deity could never really reach its full potential until it found lodging in a genuine, historical individual. The moral example of Jesus Christ has for two millennia now repeatedly stirred and shamed his followers with an uncanny power. Lecky, the historian of European morals, claims that, "Amid all the sins and failings, amid all the priestcraft and persecution and fanaticism that have defaced the Church, it has preserved, in the character and example of its Founder, an enduring principle of regeneration."[9]

It is the continual testimony of the Christian community that God is known in Jesus Christ. In Paul's words, "It is the God who said, 'Let light shine out of darkness,' who has shone in our hearts to give the light of the knowledge of the glory of God in the face of Christ" (II Cor. 4:6). No religious leader, no saint, prophet, sage or seer has ever brought God so close to man. No Moslem ever sings, "Mohammed, lover of my soul." No Jew ever says to Moses. "I need thee every hour." No Buddhist ever says, "Fairest Lord Buddha, ruler of all nature."

C. JESUS AND MAN.

Careful! Emphasizing the divinity of Christ has an inherent danger: it tends to belittle his humanity. One of the strangest facts in the

8. See Fairbairn, *Philosophy of the Christian Religion*, p. 540.

9. Cited in James Moffatt, *Jesus Christ the Same* (New York: Abingdon-Cokesbury Press, 1940), p. 110.

history of Christianity is that the first heresy that arose in relation to Christ was the denial, not of his divinity, but of his humanity (see e.g., I John 4:1-3). We should always keep the picture balanced by reciting the great creed: *vere deus, vere homo*, "true God and true man."

The gospel writers make no bones about the humanity of Jesus. Without apology they inform us that he ate, drank, slept, got hungry, got thirsty, got tired, got angry, was in need of human sympathy, sought God in prayer, shrank from death, and finally died. He, like all of us, possessed the attributes of universal man. The writer of Hebrews argues eloquently that Jesus had to become man in order to understand how to help his brethren and to be their "faithful high priest" (Heb. 2:10-18).

The Book of Hebrews has embarrassed some Christians through the centuries, because it stresses so vividly the humanity of Christ. It doesn't embarrass me, Agnos, because I glory in the fact that Jesus was true man. How else could God have revealed himself fully to man? I'm especially touched by the prayer Christ offered in the Garden of Gethsemane just before his crucifixion: "My Father, if it be possible, let this cup pass from me; nevertheless, not as I will, but as thou wilt" (Matt. 26:39). Hebrews says that Jesus "offered up prayers and supplications, with loud cries and tears, to him who was able to save him from death, and he was heard for his godly fear" (Heb. 5:7). Prayer is the highest inward action of the soul and if Jesus hadn't offered genuine prayer the picture of his humanity would have been defective.

But don't let the fact that Jesus was true man mislead you into thinking he was indulgent or permissive with man. No man condemned human sin with greater severity. Yet no man ever had a higher regard for man and for human potential. Jesus kept company with sinners, true, but don't think he ever imitated the behavior of that sleazy crowd or don't think he justified their sin by his companionship. He challenged them at the same time he associated with them. His motto was: hate the sin, love the sinner.

Jesus was the greatest humanist in history, but his was not an anthropocentric humanism, one that denies God and asserts man can save himself by knowledge or behavioral engineering. Greeks favored knowledge and Jews put their trust in moral exertion, but Jesus taught that right living arises spontaneously from a character that has been transformed by God. Only *metanoia* (change of heart, mind) can cause good conduct to flow from the character, just as naturally as fruit comes from a tree. "The good man out of the good treasure of his heart produces good, and the evil man out of his evil treasure produces evil; for out of the abundance of the heart his mouth speaks" (Luke 6:45).

"What Jesus offers in his ethical teaching is not a set of rules of conduct, but a number of illustrations of the way in which a transformed character will express itself in conduct."[10] We see clearly, then, why Jesus came to grief with the champions of the Jewish Law in his day. If he was correct, then the Law was no longer needed and thus the authorities had to stop him from destroying the code which gave Israel her identity. Jesus lived at a time when regard for the "Jewish way of life" and resentment of "heathen culture" were both very high. Doubtless, he seemed to help this inroad of heathen culture by his teaching on the Law. Yet without this new teaching the religion of Christ would never have shaken off the parochial limitations of Judaism and become the world religion that it has.

Jesus was thus one of history's greatest internationalists and egalitarians. His parables show that he was genuinely interested in people, all kinds of people. He enjoyed mixing with various types. He attended weddings and festive gatherings, more often than his critics thought a pious man should. He especially drew criticism when he mixed with the outcasts, the untouchables: tax collectors, prostitutes, Samaritans, and lepers. He defended such outrageous behavior by saying that the sick, not the healthy, need the doctor, and he told the scribes and Pharisees that such people would go into the kingdom of heaven before them (Matt. 21:31).

Jesus taught the value of every individual person, regardless of status, sex, or race. Perhaps his most beautiful parable is that of the Good Samaritan (Luke 10:30-37), the moral of which is obvious: no race has a monopoly on kindness. He chided his apostles for not allowing the little children to come to him. He taught that if God knows every sparrow he certainly knows about every individual human (Luke 12:6, 7). He often spoke of "little ones" or "the least of these my brethren" and stressed how important they are to God (Matt. 18:14; 25:40).

How different this spirit was from the typical attitude of both Jews and Greeks at the time! We have a statement from the Essene *Manual of Discipline* found among the Dead Sea Scrolls which bade members of the sect "to love all the children of light . . . and to hate all the children of darkness, each according to the measure of his guilt." This may have been what Jesus was referring to when he said, "You have heard that it was said, 'You shall love your neighbor and hate your

10. T. W. Manson, *The Teaching of Jesus: Studies in Its Form and Content* (Cambridge: Cambridge University Press, 1967), p. 301. Chapter nine is excellent on this point.

enemy.' But I say to you, Love your enemies and pray for those who persecute you, so that you may be sons of your Father who is in heaven" (Matt. 5:43-45).

If the Jews believed in a religious and moral aristocracy, the Greeks held to a philosophical or intellectual elitism. While Jesus taught that virtue and redemption are possible for all men, Plato taught that virtue in the highest sense is possible only for the philosopher and that the philosophical nature is a plant that rarely grows among men.[11] The entire ancient world was dedicated to aristocracy and elitism. This accounts for the low status of women and slaves in the Roman Empire. The last thinker of antiquity, Plotinus, maintained this aristocratic tone to the very end. Plotinus taught that rapture isn't possible for the "vile rabble," who minister to the needs of more worthy men, but only for the elect spirits who are qualified by superior intelligence for the mystic ascent.[12]

The great Jewish scholar, C. G. Montefiore, says that the most unique thing in Jesus' teaching about God is this idea that "love involves seeking out the lost." Jesus said: seek out the sinner; don't avoid him, search him out; redeem him through pity and love and personal service. Cadoux says that Christ's "respect for women and children, and his eager self-sacrificing quest for the redemption of sinners and enemies, which were a direct outcome of the decision to love one's neighbors as oneself, were admittedly without close parallels in Jewish ethics."[13]

Although Christ seldom traveled outside of Palestine, his love for all men, his concern for all types, his sacrificial death for even his enemies—all these things and more have served to abstract him from his environment and elevate him to the position of the archetypal human, the universal man. Since he lived his life has become, as it were, one of the constants of nature, like the speed of light. His character is considered the highest; his conception of God is still the only notion of deity that most men will tolerate. He struck the catholic ideal; how else can you explain how a swarthy Jew could ultimately dominate the religion of white-skinned Nordics? Christ is the only Oriental that the Occident has ever revered and worshipped.

Even the words of Jesus couldn't be localized but immediately became international. We don't have the teachings of Christ in his mother tongue (Aramaic), as do the Moslems for the precepts of

---

11. *Republic*, Book VI.

12. *The Six Enneads*, Second Ennead, IX.9.

13. Cecil J. Cadoux, *The Historic Mission of Jesus* (New York: Harper, n.d.), p. 117. See also Henry J. Cadbury, *Jesus, What Manner of Man* (London: SPCK Press, 1962), p. 64.

Mohammed. For centuries, the Koran couldn't be translated out of the Arabic language. But from the very first, Christ's sayings came to us in translation and have lived in translation ever since. His words have the mysterious ability to multiply themselves in translation without ever seeming to lose their identity and their vital energy. Christ seems to be at home anywhere, understood in every language, intelligible to every mind, appealing to every heart. We don't say: "Behold the Jew, behold the Galilean, behold the Nazarene." We say: *Ecce Homo!* "Behold the Man!"

D. THE HARMONY OF POLAR TRAITS IN JESUS.

Admiring the character of Christ is like looking through a kaleidoscope: you never seem to run out of patterns to admire. One thing I admire most about him is his well-rounded character, his balanced personality, his systematic harmony of opposite traits. For example,

1. Jesus harmonized strength and tenderness. Most men find it hard to achieve the golden mean between firmness and sweetness, courage and generosity, indignation and control, power and responsibility. Failure to achieve the mean may destroy the effectiveness of a parent.

The strength and courage of Jesus are well documented in the gospels. It is a fatal distortion to picture him as merely mild, sort of velvety and half-feminine. He lashed out at his enemies, calling them "blind fools" (Matt. 23:17) and children of the devil (John 8:44). Mark tells us he grew angry on two occasions: when the Pharisees opposed him for healing on the Sabbath (Mark 3:5) and when his disciples prevented children from coming to him (Mark 10:13-16). We may be sure also that he showed indignation when he cleared the Temple of moneychangers (Matt. 21:12).

It took courage to attack that vile traffic in the Temple, to flout the traditional rules of Sabbath observance, to belittle washing of hands, to associate with prostitutes and tax collectors, to refuse to be made king, to assert messiahship before the Sanhedrin. Jesus obviously struck people as a man of strong will and passionate character. He barked at the evil spirits and rebuked fevers. People said he spoke as one having authority. When the Romans went to arrest him he turned on them and said simply, "I am he," and they fell backward to the ground (John 18:6).

Yet, at the same time, Jesus could be as tender, kind, and generous as the most permissive grandparent. He could weep for a dead friend, Lazarus (John 11:35), feel compassion for a wandering crowd (Matt.

9:36), commiserate with a poor beggar (Mark 10:52), feel love for a young ruler seeking advice (Mark 10:21), enjoy the company of little children (Mark 10:14), make provision for his mother while hanging on the cross (John 19:26, 27). He warned Peter not to make forgiveness a matter of numbers but to forgive without limit (Matt. 18:22). He advised people to "give, and it will be given to you; good measure, pressed down, shaken together, running over, will be put into your lap" (Luke 6:38). He taught it is more blessed to give than to receive and no one in history ever illustrated his own teaching better than Jesus Christ did on that point.

Perhaps the harmony of strength and tenderness can be seen most vividly in the way Jesus used his power. As noted earlier, he demonstrated power over everything—man, disease, nature, the devil and his demons. Yet he never used his power for self-aggrandizement. His miracles were always benevolent, curative, restorative, therapeutic. He was never faced with the problem of power corrupting him. When the soldiers arrested him, Peter tried to defend him by cutting off a man's ear. Christ told him that if he needed help he could summon twelve legions (i.e., about 70,000) of angels (Matt. 26:53). Then Jesus restored the severed ear. What kind of man is this, who would yield to an unjust arrest, not using his powers to defend himself, who would use his power instead to restore the severed ear of an enemy, and who would rebuke Peter for trying to defend him? This quality of self-restraint coupled with boundless power has been called "the masterpiece of Christ."[14]

2. Jesus harmonized dignity and humility. Those who espouse a myth hypothesis need to explain how any legend maker would be so inconsistent as to let a man make such audacious claims to deity and then stoop down like a slave to wash his disciples' feet (John 13:1-20). Such a paradox, to me, is beyond human invention. Paul was deeply impressed by Jesus' humility and told Christians to imitate the mind of Christ, because he didn't seek to retain his equality with God, "but emptied himself, taking the form of a servant" (Phil. 2:7).

Humility is not, as widely believed, the assertion of your own worthlessness. It is rather the willingness to serve, to learn, to make yourself of no reputation, to forget your status and condescend to those of lowly estate (Rom. 12:16). Jesus claimed to be the Messiah and God's special Son yet he associated with all kinds of people and

---

14. Most cultures have a story about a man who suddenly comes into possession of great power through a magic ring, or secret potion, or magic lamp, and then later is corrupted by his power, using it for evil purposes.

served their needs. "Whoever would be first among you must be your slave; even as the Son of man came not to be served but to serve, and to give his life as a ransom for many" (Matt. 20:28). Jesus was free from vanity, pride, ambition, social aspiration, or corrupting power. The Pharisees of his day, like clerics of many cultures, were vain, proud people, who love acclamation and the chief seats in the synagogues, who blew trumpets to call attention to their philanthropy.

3. Jesus harmonized piety and approachability. He had that rare gift of being religious without being sanctimonious, of being pure without being self-righteous. He was sinless himself, but this didn't keep him from loving and working with all manner of humans. Mark says that the common people heard him gladly (Mark 12:37). His sympathy and understanding of sinners rose logically out of his exacting doctrine of sin. If sin is a condition of the heart, then all men are sinners and one must therefore never judge his brethren harshly because he can never know exactly what lies in a man's heart.

Although the story of the woman taken in adultery (John 8:2-11) is probably not part of the New Testament text, most scholars think it is a true incident from the life of Christ. It certainly fits the character of Christ we know from the gospels. When a group of men seized a woman who had been caught in the very act of adultery and asked him what he would do, Jesus wrote something in the sand and then said: "Let him who is without sin among you be the first to throw a stone at her." They all filed away and left Jesus alone with the woman. He dismissed her with the warning: "Go, and do not sin again." Note that Jesus forgave her but reminded her of the reality of her sin.

4. Jesus harmonized self-control and happiness. Sigmund Freud claimed that the conflict between individual desires and social obligations drives many men to neurosis and psychosis, but Jesus seems to have escaped that problem. He showed us that the puritan-playboy dichotomy is a false dilemma. You can be continent without being ascetic, serious without being morose. Conversely, you can be happy without being frivolous, joyful without being intoxicated.

Religion didn't make Jesus gloomy. He was no bloodless saint of the type we meet in El Greco's paintings. He had a warm sense of being a human. He obviously observed nature and society well and loved them both, as you can see by reading his parables. He enjoyed life without apology. He warned people against fasting just for its own sake (Matt. 9:15). No monkish person could ever have gotten the reputation of being "a glutton and a drunkard" (Luke 7:34). Christ would have agreed entirely with the Hebrew toast, "To life!"

You can state this paradox another way: Jesus harmonized body and soul, materialism and spiritualism, realism and idealism, the empirical and the transcendent, this world and the other world. He taught the superiority of the soul and said, "Don't worry about tomorrow," yet he labored to heal sick bodies and fed over 5000 hungry people on one occasion. To him, body and soul formed a psychophysical unit, both of which he came to serve. Heaven and earth, nature and supernature are all one unified order under God. Those with eyes to see can easily discover the transcendent world in and around the world of the senses (John 1:50, 51).

E.   CONCLUSION.

Yes, Agnos, let me assure you that such a man as I've described in this chapter *did* live at one time and lives still. Let me assure you that at least once in man's history a man lived who truly loved, whose supreme joy was ungrudging giving, who lived not to be ministered unto but to minister, who knew how blessed it is to give. Even if this man were only a ghostly ideal like Hamlet, born in the brain of some genius playwright, he would still be the finest ideal in history, the most valuable dream ever dreamed.

But you know that he's more than a dream; you know now how strong is the evidence for his historical actuality. If God were to become man would he be any different from this man? Can any other man in history come as close to your ideal of perfection?

Actually, the farther away you get from Christ the better you can evaluate his greatness, for only at a distance do we see the continuing impact of his person. Those who use a simplistic model of evolution to understand everything will have a hard time explaining how it is that there hasn't been any significant addition to ethical thought since the time of Christ, how it is that no moral character has ever superseded him. It takes a little knowledge of history to appreciate the impact of Jesus' words on the world, but take my word for it, Agnos, the impact has been incalculable. His words have become laws, they have become holy teachings, creeds, doctrines, sermons, consolations, poems, books, greeting cards—all this. But, what is more, as Jesus himself predicted, his words will never pass away!

Jesus Christ pushed every good quality of human character to its utmost limit. We can never go beyond him; he will always be in front of us, beckoning to us, "Follow me." What language can I borrow to praise him enough? He is not just "the Great" like Peter or Frederick or Alexander. He is "the Only." He is beyond our analysis. He confounds all our standards of classification. He bursts all our pigeonholes. He goes off all the charts. He must be more than human!

Suggestions for Further Reading

J. M. Creed, *The Divinity of Jesus Christ* (Cambridge: Cambridge University Press, 1938).

Jack Finegan, *Jesus, History and You* (Richmond, VA: John Knox Press, 1964).

P. T. Forsyth, *The Person and Place of Jesus Christ* (Grand Rapids: Eerdmans, n.d.).

Carl F. H. Henry, ed., *Jesus of Nazareth: Saviour and Lord* (Grand Rapids: Eerdmans, 1966).

Robert C. Johnson, *The Meaning of Christ* (Philadelphia: Westminster Press, 1958).

Howard Clark Kee, *Jesus in History: An Approach to the Study of the Gospels* (New York: Harcourt, Brace and World, 1970).

John Knox, *The Humanity and Divinity of Christ: A Study of Pattern in Christology* (Cambridge: Cambridge University Press, 1967); *The Man Christ Jesus* (Chicago: Willet, Clark and Co., 1941); *On the Meaning of Christ* (New York: Scribner's, 1953).

T. W. Manson, *The Servant Messiah* (Cambridge: Cambridge University Press, 1953).

Wolfhart Pannenberg, *Jesus—God and Man*, trans. Lewis L. Wilkins and Duane A. Priebe (Philadelphia: Westminster Press, 1968).

W. N. Pittenger, *The Word Incarnate* (New York: Harper, 1958).

William C. Robinson, *Who Say Ye That I Am?* (Grand Rapids: Eerdmans, 1949).

Archibald Rutledge, *Christ Is God* (Westwood, NJ: Revell, 1941).

Philip Schaff, *The Person of Christ* (New York: American Tract Society, 1913).

Ethelbert Stauffer, *Jesus and His Story*, trans. Richard and Clara Winston (New York: Knopf, 1960).

Vincent Taylor, *The Person of Christ* (New York: Macmillan, 1958).

JESUS CHRIST AND PROPHECY

"We have found him of whom Moses in the law and also the prophets wrote, Jesus of Nazareth, the son of Joseph" (John 1:45).

Thus did Philip, one of Christ's early disciples, first inform his friend Nathanael, of the advent of the Messiah. Ever since Philip Christians have believed that Jesus Christ was the Promised One of the Jewish Old Testament. Part of our case for Christianity, Agnos, is from prophecy. We believe in Christ because we can't explain his fulfillment of so many Old Testament predictions by mere coincidence, or fraud, or any other naturalistic hypothesis. Here again, we must invoke the transcendent to fully explain him.

A. THE CHRISTIAN THESIS.

Suppose, Agnos, that someone gave you a box of puzzle pieces and asked you to determine if (1) the pieces were all of a single picture or (2) were pieces from several different pictures. How would you settle that question? You'd piece the parts together to see if you could make a single, unified picture of them. If you couldn't, you'd say the pieces didn't make a single picture. The case from prophecy is similar.

The Old Testament has numerous predictions of an Anointed One who would someday inaugurate a new epoch in Israel's and the world's religious history. The Bible is unique among religious books because in constrast to a few vague forecasts it has hundreds of rather specific prophecies. All other peoples in the ancient world (Egyptians, Babylonians, Canaanites) had a circular view of history, which corresponded to the cycle of vegetable life they worshipped. Everything repeated itself anew each year. There was no real progress, only cyclical repetition.

The Jews, however, had a linear view of history, with Yahweh, the God who acts in history, driving developments toward a great future goal in which his will would be realized, the "kingdom of God." Only the Jews looked forward, not backward to a Golden Age. Why didn't any other nation develop this idea of its own selection as the People of the Promise? Why did no other nation gradually unfold a detailed picture of such a Coming One? The Hebrews answer: Yahweh himself spoke to our prophets.

Christians finish off the argument by insisting that only in Jesus Christ can they make sense out of all the messianic predictions of the Old Testament. "All the promises of God find their Yes in him" (II Cor. 1:20). Jesus puts the puzzle pieces together into a coherent picture. Hence, both the *revealing* and the *fulfilling* of the promises belong to the same master plan of the one Intelligence who alone rules history. The same God who prophesied brought it to pass.

We insist that this argument was *not* invented by Christians for apologetic purposes after the New Testament books had been written. You can trace it back to the apostles and back even to Jesus himself. Jesus continually interpreted his mission in the light of messianic prophecy. After his resurrection he explained to the men on the way to Emmaus, "O foolish men, and slow of heart to believe all that the prophets have spoken! Was it not necessary that the Christ should suffer these things and enter into his glory?" Luke adds, "And beginning with Moses and all the prophets, he interpreted to them in all the scriptures the things concerning himself" (Luke 24:25-27).[1]

It is not surprising, then, that the gospels, Acts, and the epistles all speak of Christ as the Messiah, using the terminology of the Old Testament. They used the Old Testament to expound, not to create, the doctrine of Christ as Messiah.When Jesus' disciples explained this pattern of prediction and fulfillment, an explanation that Jesus himself had begun, they just dotted the *i*'s and crossed the *t*'s.

St. Paul was so certain Jesus was the Messiah that he accused the Jews of reading the Old Testament with a veil over their faces. When they turned to Christ the veil was removed (II Cor. 3:14-17). St. Peter spoke of prophecy as "a lamp shining in a murky place" (II Peter 1:19, NEB). Both Paul and Peter used the language of scientific analysis in these statements. An inferior hypothesis is indeed like a "veil" over the face of one who refuses to consider an alternate theory. A

---

1. See also John 5:45-47, where Jesus says, "Do not think that I shall accuse you to the Father; it is Moses who accuses you, on whom you set your hope. If you believed Moses, you would believe me, for he wrote of me. But if you do not believe his writings, how will you believe my words?"

good theory is truly like a "lamp" shining in a murky place, that is, shining into a welter of facts that lack coherence.

The Christian thesis says simply: assume Jesus Christ is the Messiah and you'll make more sense out of the Old Testament, the messianic predictions, than with any other hypothesis.

We assert the unity of the Bible. We insist that both testaments are part of a single choir, an antiphonal choir, both groups singing the same arrangement, written by the same composer. We deny the charge of Nietzsche, that Christians "perpetrate upon the Old Testament an unbelievable philological farce." We deny the charge of liberals, that Christians are guilty of "arbitrary exegesis" when they find Christ in the Old Testament. If Christ is the Messiah, then the Old Testament really belongs to those who believe in him, that is, the church.

Jews have complained ever since Christ that Christians "stole" their Bible and ruined it with the New Testament supplement. But really, isn't it a bit amazing how Christians just took over the Old Testament wholesale, saying that Jesus is the end of the Law, and got away with it? How could we Christians have pulled off such a high-handed act unless there was great plausibility in our thesis in the first place? Could you stick *Mein Kampf* together with the *Imitation of Christ* and fool many people into thinking they form an organic unity? Why have so many millions since Christ believed that the Bible is a unit?

How, then, do we prove Christ is the Messiah? Once again, by building up a case, by examining various messianic predictions and allowing Christ to interpret them, to provide the key to them. If the key fits and unlocks the door then we have a case. I hope as we present the material, Agnos, that you'll take the time to read the passages carefully in context. Only then can you properly evaluate the argument from prophecy. Be like the Jews at Beroea, who, Luke says, "were more noble than those in Thessalonica, for they received the word with all eagerness, examining the scriptures daily to see if these things were so" (Acts 17:11).

B. THE MESSIAH AND HIS AGE.

The best proof that Christians didn't invent the messianic argument is that long before Christ the Jews had a body of messianic literature that agrees substantially with what Christians said of Christ. Both Jew and Christian expected that the Messiah would be a descendant of Judah and David, be born at Bethlehem, be filled with God's Spirit, be a king and priest, rule with justice, bestow peace, have a glorious and enduring kingdom, subject the gentile nations to his law, and so on. In this section we'll look at these common messianic expectations.

1. The lineage of the Messiah is carefully plotted in the Old Testament. Yahweh promised Abraham that he would bless the world through his descendants (Gen. 12:1-3), but this didn't mean that just any Hebrew could be the Messiah. Note the careful selection process: Noah had three sons, but the Messiah was to come through Shem (Gen. 9:26). Terah had three sons, but the Messiah was to come through Abraham (Gen. 12:3). Abraham had two sons, but the Messiah was to come through Isaac, not Ishmael (Gen. 21:12). Isaac had two sons, but the Messiah was to come through Jacob, not Esau (Gen. 28:14; Num. 24:17). Jacob had twelve sons, but the Messiah was to come through Judah (Gen. 49:10). Jesse had eight sons but the Messiah was to come through the house of David (II Sam. 7:16; Isa. 11:1-5; Jer. 23:5, 6; Amos 9:11-15).

New Testament writers mention explicitly about thirty times that Jesus Christ was the son of David (e.g., Matt. 1:1; 21:9; Luke 3:23-31; Rom. 1:3).

2. You'd probably expect the Coming One to be born in Zion, Jerusalem, the capital of Israel and Judah, but no, the prophet Micah picked Bethlehem (Micah 5:1-3). Not just any Bethlehem, but Bethlehem Ephrathah to distinguish it from the city of Bethlehem in the territory of Zebulun. David was a Bethlehemite (I Sam. 20:6) and his father, Jesse, was an Ephratite (I Sam. 17:12). Ephrata was the district in which Bethlehem was located (Ruth 1:2). Thus Micah specified very carefully the exact birthplace of the Messiah, the one "who is to be ruler in Israel, whose origin is from of old, from ancient days" (Micah 5:2).

When Herod inquired where the King of Israel was to be born, the Jews answered him with Micah 5:2. Some Jews who thought that Jesus was born at Nazareth used this verse against his claims (John 7:42).

3. It would be extremely difficult for any messianic pretender to pose as the Messiah because he'd have to fill such a complex role. The Old Testament claims that the Messiah would be a king (Gen. 49:10; Ps. 2:6; Zech. 6:13), and this role was the central one. Yet it also predicts that the Messiah would be a priest, that in the messianic age the royal and priestly dignities would be united.

Psalm 110, a popular messianic text, first speaks of the Messiah as king, but then adds, "The Lord has sworn and will not change his mind, 'You are a priest for ever after the order of Melchizedek' "

(v. 4). Zechariah predicted that "the Branch," a well-known title for the Messiah, would rule as God's king, would build the temple of Yahweh, and yet would "be a priest by his throne" (Zech. 6:9-15).

The Messiah would also be a prophet. Moses predicted, "The Lord your God will raise up for you a prophet like me from among you, from your brethren. . . . And I will put my words in his mouth, and he shall speak to them all that I command him" (Deut. 18:15, 18). The Pharisees sent priests and Levites to John the Baptist to ask if he was this prophet and he denied it (John 1:21). When Jesus fed the 5000 the populace exclaimed, "This is indeed the prophet who is to come into the world!" (John 6:14).

This combination of King-Priest-Prophet shows that the Messiah would be no ordinary sovereign. God smote King Uzziah with leprosy when he tried to usurp the priestly function (II Chron. 26:16-21). How, then, could the Messiah be both king and priest? Because he was to be a different kind of priest, a priest forever—not just for his own lifetime—and a priest after the order of Melchizedek—not the order of Aaron. No king in Israel's history could claim to fill this combination, much less to sit on God's right hand and be a prince forever.

Only in Christ does this unusual triune prediction come true. He was a king, though not of the political order (John 18:36), a priest after the order of Melchizedek (Heb. 5:4-6; 7:1-12), and a prophet (Acts 3:22).

4. The Messiah was to be an extraordinary personality with unusual gifts. Isaiah had the sharpest vision of his personality. The Messiah was to come from the "stump of Jesse."

> And the Spirit of the Lord shall rest upon him,
>   the spirit of wisdom and understanding,
>   the spirit of counsel and might,
>   the spirit of knowledge and the fear of the Lord.
> And his delight shall be in the fear of the Lord.
>
> (Isa. 11:1-3)

Perhaps Moses or Elijah could come close to this description, but Isaiah narrows the vision even more, so that finally only a super-human individual could possibly fulfill it.

> For to us a child is born,
>   to us a son is given;
> and the government will be upon his shoulder,
>   and his name will be called
> "Wonderful Counselor, Mighty God,
> Everlasting Father, Prince of Peace."
>
> (Isa. 9:6)

The child predicted here is patently greater than any prophet, king, or priest that Yahweh ever sent to Israel. Look at his titles: "Wonderful Counselor"—indicating supernatural wisdom and insight; "Mighty God"—a term used only of Yahweh himself (Deut. 10:17; Neh. 9:32; Isa. 1:24; Jer. 32:18); "Everlasting Father"—also used of Yahweh (Isa. 63:16; 64:8).

When John the Baptist sent disciples to ask Jesus if he was really the Messiah, Jesus used Isaiah 35:5, 6 to allay their doubts: "Then the eyes of the blind shall be opened, and the ears of the deaf unstopped; then shall the lame man leap like a hart, and the tongue of the dumb sing for joy." Isaiah foretold literally the miracles of the Anointed One (Luke 7:22).

Christians feel only Christ could fulfill this unusual messianic personality. Only Jesus Christ, the God-Man, could both come from the stump of Jesse and yet be a Mighty God and Everlasting Father with supernatural insight and miraculous powers.

5. One might think that all messianic prophecies speak of a powerful political Messiah. This is true only if you read one strain of predictions. Other strains show that many prophets like Jeremiah and Ezekiel realized it wasn't enough for a king of David's line to come and restore Israel. The core of their messianic message is that for true salvation to come the people must become a new people from within. God must make a new covenant with the house of Israel, not like the Mosaic covenant (Jer. 31:31-34). Yahweh must give his people a "new heart" and a "new spirit" so they will observe his law (Ezek. 36:26, 27).

This new covenant will be taught, not by rote memory using the mind, but by the heart, the emotions. Thus obedience becomes a matter of the inner man. People will no longer teach each other to "know the Lord" because all will know him. God will no longer remember sin, but not because more sacrifices are offered, for sacrifices will cease in that day (Mal. 1:10, 11). People will no longer remember the material paraphernalia of the Mosaic era, such as the Ark of the Covenant (Jer. 3:16).

These prophecies were fulfilled. Jewish sacrifices did pass away and Jesus inaugurated the new covenant with his blood (I Cor. 11:25). The writer of Hebrews quotes Jeremiah 31:31-34 in his careful argument on Christ as the Mediator of the new covenant (Heb. 8, 9).

6. Another prophetic strain emphasizes the universal mission of Israel and the Messiah. Micah and Isaiah picture it with vivid imagery:

It shall come to pass in the latter days
   that the mountain of the house of the Lord
shall be established as the highest of the mountains,
   and shall be raised above the hills;
and all the nations shall flow to it,
   and many peoples shall come, and say:
"Come, let us go up to the mountain of the Lord,
   to the house of the God of Jacob;
that he may teach us his ways
   and that we may walk in his paths."
For out of Zion shall go forth the law,
   and the word of the Lord from Jerusalem.
                              (Isa. 2:2, 3; Micah 4:1, 2).

Someday the entire world will worship Israel's God, say the prophets. Malachi predicted that when the sacrifices ceased the name of Yahweh would "be great among the nations" (Mal. 1:11). Zechariah foretold that the Messiah would "command peace to the nations" and that "his dominion shall be from sea to sea, and from the River to the ends of the earth" (Zech. 9:10). Isaiah saw that even the Egyptians in that age would have an altar to Yahweh (Isa. 19:16-24). Joel shocked his compatriots by predicting that God would someday pour out his spirit "on all flesh," and that new, unusual manifestations would be used by Yahweh. "Your sons and your daughters shall prophesy, your old men shall dream dreams, and your young men shall see visions" (Joel 2:28).

In the Messiah's kingdom salvation would be available to all men, regardless of nationality. Joel said that whoever calls on the name of Yahweh will be saved (Joel 2:32). Isaiah foresaw that God would even accept "foreigners" on his holy mountain and allow their sacrifices on his altar. They need only keep the Sabbath and the covenant. Yahweh wished his house to be called "a house of prayer for all peoples" (Isa. 56:6, 7).

Christ fulfilled such predictions with his universal gospel, in which "there is neither Jew nor Greek, there is neither slave nor free, there is neither male nor female; for you are all one in Christ Jesus" (Gal. 3:28).

7. Another prophetic strain showed that the Messiah would be a peaceful individual with a special mission to the poor and needy. He would be more than just a conquering warrior; he would judge the poor with righteousness and "decide with equity for the meek of the earth" (Isa. 11:4). Isaiah said he wouldn't use force but rather persuasion to bring forth justice:

> He will not cry or lift up his voice,
>   or make it heard in the street;
> a bruised reed he will not break,
>   and a dimly burning wick he will not quench.
>
> (Isa. 42:2, 3)

We've already mentioned the special concern Jesus had for outcasts and the poor. In Luke 4 we read how Jesus used Isaiah 61:1, 2 to set the tone for his life's work. He was to "bring good tidings to the afflicted," "bind up the brokenhearted," "proclaim liberty to the captives," and open the prisons for "those who are bound." Thus in messianic times we note that the poor still exist, but they are close to their Messiah-King; they have a special place in his heart.

The Messiah will also disarm the nations and abolish war. Isaiah and Micah predict that when the word of Yahweh goes forth from Jerusalem, the Messiah shall "judge between many peoples, and shall decide for strong nations afar off; and they shall beat their swords into plowshares, and their spears into pruning hooks; nation shall not lift up sword against nation, neither shall they learn war any more" (Micah 4:3; cf. Isa. 2:4).

Zechariah 9:9, 10 was always considered a clear messianic text by Jewish commentators. Yet they had trouble understanding how the Messiah could be both king and lowly.

> Rejoice greatly, O daughter of Zion!
>   Shout aloud, O daughter of Jerusalem!
> Lo, your king comes to you;
>   triumphant and victorious is he,
> humble and riding on an ass,
>   on a colt the foal of an ass.
> I will cut off the chariot from Ephraim
>   and the war horse from Jerusalem;
> and the battle bow shall be cut off,
>   and he shall command peace to the nations.

The Messianic King is triumphant and victorious, yet he comes humble and riding an ass, not a white horse! Furthermore, he then proceeds to command peace by cutting off implements of war. Matthew quotes this in his gospel (21:4, 5) as being fulfilled on Palm Sunday, when Jesus entered Jerusalem riding an ass. John uses it also (12:15) noting that the disciples didn't understand the fulfillment until Christ had risen from the dead.

These prophecies about the Messiah abolishing war cause Christians some problems. War is obviously still with us. If taken symbolically, the predictions mean that Christ stopped war between nations in the sense of ending national and racial strife in the church.

Some commentators take them literally, however, and say that the cessation of war will occur at the Second Coming of Christ.

8. Both Jews and Christians knew that the Messiah would be preceded by an unusual messenger, Elijah. This remarkable prophecy is found in the last book of the Old Testament, Malachi. First the messenger is described without naming him:

> Behold, I send my messenger to prepare the way before me, and the Lord whom you seek will suddenly come to his temple; the messenger of the covenant in whom you delight, behold, he is coming, says the Lord of hosts. But who can endure the day of his coming, and who can stand when he appears? (Mal. 3:1, 2)

Note carefully that "the Lord" was to appear "suddenly" during the work of the messenger—exactly as Jesus appeared in the midst of John the Baptist's ministry. Note also that Malachi calls the Messiah "the Lord" and "the messenger of the covenant," designations which connect him with the new covenant predicted by Jeremiah. Jesus both appeared suddenly and brought a new covenant (Heb. 8:6).

Note also this strange statement of Malachi, "The Lord . . . is coming, says the Lord of hosts." It reminds you of Psalm 110, "The Lord says to my Lord." The Lord is coming, yet the Lord sends the Lord! Such apparent double talk could only be fulfilled in a person who is divine like the divine Lord who sends him, that is, in the incarnate Son of God, Jesus Christ.

But then Malachi predicts the messenger by name: "Behold, I will send you Elijah the prophet before the great and terrible day of the Lord comes. And he will turn the hearts of fathers to their children and the hearts of children to their fathers" (Mal. 4:5, 6). Matthew and Mark both quote this verse as fulfilled in John the Baptist (Matt. 11:13, 14; Mark 9:11, 12).

There can be no question that John worked an unusual revival in the nation of Israel by his baptizing ministry. He became so popular among the common people that Jesus used his popularity to silence the Jewish authorities in an argument (Matt. 21:25-27). You can't object that John wasn't really Elijah in the flesh, for even the Jews didn't take the prediction in such literal terms. The fact that some people identified Jesus with Elijah (Matt. 16:14) shows that they didn't expect a complete reincarnation of Elijah. John came in "the spirit and power of Elijah" (Luke 1:17) and that was enough to fulfill the prophecy.

Fitting, isn't it? The last verse in the canonical Old Testament promises the Messiah!

C. THE SCANDALOUS PROPHECIES.

So far, we've looked at messianic prophecies that both Jew and Christian largely agree upon. Now let's look at the ones that separate us. Early in the history of the church it became obvious that the Jews were deeply offended at the idea that the Messiah would suffer indignity and rejection by his own people and die on a Roman cross (I Cor. 1:23). Yet already in his earthly ministry Jesus had begun to prepare his disciples for the fact that "the Son of Man must suffer."

But where did any Old Testament prophet say that the Messiah must suffer? In certain moot passages in Isaiah, Zechariah, and the Psalms we find evidence for a "dark side" to the messianic mission, a negative aspect that most Jews were reluctant to acknowledge.

1. The second half of Isaiah (chs. 40—66) is critical to the interpretation of Jesus' mission and message. Scholars of the twentieth century are slowly realizing that the "Servant Songs" of Isaiah give us the most important clue to Christ's messianic consciousness.[2] Jesus plainly identified himself with the Suffering Servant of Isaiah (e.g., Mark 10:45; Luke 22:37). But just who was this Servant and how do we know he was the promised Messiah?

We don't know for sure, of course, but we have the authority of Jesus Christ that this is the proper explanation of the Servant Songs. Even without Christ's authority, however, we have some evidence that the Servant is similar to the Messiah. Some Jewish commentators identified the Servant with the Messiah. He has certain traits that other prophecies assigned to the Messiah: (1) he is called the sprout or the shoot, (2) he is equipped with the Spirit of God, (3) he brings light and Torah (instruction), (4) he brings justice to the nations. So far there is nothing embarrassing about him, but gradually, in the second and third songs, we hear of the Servant's sufferings. He complains that he has labored in vain, that sceptics have smitten him on the back and cheek, that they have pulled out his beard—a terrible insult to an Oriental!

Then finally in the fourth song we learn that the Servant dies and is resurrected and we come to understand the meaning and purpose of the suffering Yahweh brought upon him.

---

2. The four Servant Songs are: Isaiah 42:1-4; 49:1-9; 50:4-11; 52:13—53:12. Commentators differ as to exactly what verses are incorporated in each of the first three songs but there is no dispute on the fourth. A careful reading of these songs will reveal that they do stand out from the background of the book. They aren't arbitrarily constructed as some charge.

Who has believed what we have heard?
    And to whom has the arm of the Lord been revealed?
For he grew up before him like a young plant,
    and like a root out of dry ground;
he had no form or comeliness that we should look at him,
    and no beauty that we should desire him.
He was despised and rejected by men;
    a man of sorrows, and acquainted with grief;
and as one from whom men hide their faces
    he was despised, and we esteemed him not.

Surely he has borne our griefs
    and carried our sorrows;
yet we esteemed him stricken,
    smitten by God, and afflicted.
But he was wounded for our transgressions,
    he was bruised for our iniquities;
upon him was the chastisement that made us whole,
    and with his stripes we are healed.
All we like sheep have gone astray;
    we have turned every one to his own way;
and the Lord has laid on him
    the iniquity of us all.

He was oppressed, and he was afflicted,
    yet he opened not his mouth;
like a lamb that is led to the slaughter,
    and like a sheep that before its shearers is dumb,
    so he opened not his mouth.
By oppression and judgment he was taken away;
    and as for his generation, who considered
that he was cut off out of the land of the living,
    stricken for the transgression of my people?
And they made his grave with the wicked
    and with a rich man in his death,
although he had done no violence,
    and there was no deceit in his mouth.

Yet it was the will of the Lord to bruise him,
    he has put him to grief;
when he makes himself an offering for sin,
    he shall see his offspring, he shall prolong his days;
the will of the Lord shall prosper in his hand;
    he shall see the fruit of the travail of his soul and be satisfied;
by his knowledge shall the righteous one, my servant,
    make many to be accounted righteous;
    and he shall bear their iniquities.

Therefore I will divide him a portion with the great,
    and he shall divide the spoil with the strong;
because he poured out his soul to death,

and was numbered with the transgressors;
yet he bore the sin of many,
and made intercession for the transgressors.

(Isa. 53)

A careful analysis of this fourth song will show to an unveiled mind that it speaks clearly of the vicarious suffering, death, resurrection, and exaltation of Jesus of Nazareth. The prophet admits that his *kerygma*, his proclamation, is so unusual that many won't believe it, that kings will be startled and shut their mouths over it (Isa. 52:15—53:1). Nevertheless, the death of the Servant is the manner in which Yahweh reveals his "arm," his power.

The Servant is a man of humble station. He has no grandeur or reputation. He is even repulsive in appearance, sick, unclean, unfit for community life, "stricken" like a leper. Yet with all this, the Servant is pronounced *blameless!* They nevertheless put him to death with unjust methods; they kill him without legal proceedings. He doesn't protest. No one cares what happens to him. Even in death he is classed with the criminals.

Then the prophet discovers that Yahweh planned the Servant's sufferings. It was God's will to bruise him, to make him a "sin-offering" for us. There can be no question about this offering; it is the trespass-offering or guilt-offering of the priestly code, which is distinguished from all other offerings by the stress it puts on satisfaction and compensation. The prophet finds the explanation of his suffering in God's purpose for Israel's salvation. He died, not for his own sins, but for ours.

Most ordinary prophets do their greatest work in preaching; the Servant does his greatest work in dying.

Then comes the most unusual part—Yahweh raises the Servant! He can't remain dead, for a just God must reward such unusual piety. Yahweh prolongs his days and allows him to see the "fruit" of his efforts, his spiritual children, those who benefit from his death. Yahweh says, "I will divide him a portion with the great, and he shall divide the spoil with the strong" (53:12).

Then comes the final meaning of all the Servant Songs. God's miracle in raising him causes many to "be accounted righteous" (52:11). We now see that the Servant was in the right. We see Yahweh restore his greatness and his honor. We're deeply touched by his unparalleled patience in suffering and by his substitutionary death for us. The great miracle causes us to share the view of the Servant which the prophet has discovered. The staggering psychological effects of the Servant's work produce a change of heart in everyone who shares the prophet's discovery.

This Suffering Servant is the true redeemer of Israel. He will truly restore Jacob to Yahweh, because only he can remove the thing that separates them—sin (Isa. 59:2). When Jesus came to Israel he taught people that bondage to sin is far worse than bondage to any man (John 8:33, 34). He was merely interpreting Isaiah 53. Small wonder that this little chapter is now called "the bad conscience of the synagogue" and is no longer read in Jewish assemblies.

Many people try to wiggle out of Isaiah 53 by saying you can interpret the Servant some other way. This is true, but most other interpretations lead to incredible difficulties.

a. **The Collective Interpretation** says the Servant is Israel, the nation. But this suggestion makes Isaiah 53 a shambles. The prophet, who is obviously a Jew, uses "we" and "us" to distinguish himself from the "he," the Servant, who dies for everyone's sins. Moreover, no Hebrew prophet would ever say that Israel suffered patiently, much less that Israel was sinless and could die for anyone's atonement. Did Israel as a nation ever die, get buried, experience a resurrection, and then become a light to the gentiles?

b. **The Individual Interpretation** claims that the prophet was talking about some great Israelite in the past who had suffered in God's service. Many have been suggested—Hezekiah, Uzziah, Jeremiah, Job, Moses, or Zerubbabel—but none of these fill the bill. Many Hebrew prophets suffered for their work, but their suffering didn't involve atonement followed by a resurrection which empowered them to bring true religion to the gentiles. If the Servant was some unknown saint that the prophet wished to glorify in verse, he would have been rather crushed, I think, when his hero died and failed to rise again so that his death had no significance for the gentiles.

c. **The Autobiographical Interpretation** holds that the prophet was talking about himself. If so, it's hard to see how he could depict his own death and resurrection and how he could speak of his death as an atonement. Some have suggested that the prophet had a high fever when he spoke of his own resurrection!

I agree, Agnos, that the Servant Songs of Isaiah are mysterious, but I see no sense in revelling in mystery when we have an adequate explanation of the Servant in Jesus Christ. Jesus was lowly in origin, he had God's Spirit, he encountered opposition, he was unjustly convicted, he didn't protest his mistreatment, he was executed with criminals, he died an atoning death, he was raised by God, and he became a light to the gentiles. Can anyone else in all history fit the picture so well?

2. The prophet Zechariah also has some mysterious prophecies that show the dark side of the messianic mission. We've already referred to the paradox of the coming king being "humble" and riding into Jerusalem on an ass (Zech. 9:9). Zechariah predicted that with the coming of "the Branch" (a sure title for the Messiah) God would "remove the guilt of this land in a single day" (Zech. 3:8, 10). This suggests some cataclysmic event to effect a sudden atonement; it reminds you of the once-for-all nature of the atonement of the Servant. One of the basic themes of the Book of Hebrews is the once-for-all atonement wrought by the death of Jesus Christ (Heb. 9:28).

Zechariah 11 discusses how the Messiah will be related to his "flock" or nation, both to the good and to the evil. Verses 8-11 show that some of the people detest the Shepherd (Messiah), whereupon the Shepherd annuls the covenant, an action which makes the poor people realize that this event is "the word of the Lord." Then in verses 12-14 the Messiah asks them to pay for his services and they pay him thirty pieces of silver, the price of a slave. This paltry sum shows in what low esteem they hold the Shepherd. The Lord tells him to cast the silver "to the potter." This strange passage is alluded to by Matthew (27:5-10) and it has some amazing parallels with the life of Christ. Jesus was the Good Shepherd (John 10:11); he caused the flock Israel to polarize over him; the side that detested him bought him from Judas the betrayer for (exactly!) thirty pieces of silver; the money was cast to the potter; and the covenant was annulled.

Another strange prediction about the Shepherd reads like this: "Awake, O sword, against my shepherd, against the man who stands next to me, says the Lord of hosts. Strike the shepherd, that the sheep may be scattered" (Zech. 13:7). Since the sword is a symbol of judicial execution, the prophet is saying that Yahweh will execute the Shepherd. At once you want to say that the Shepherd must be evil, but no, he's called "my fellow" (KJV) or "the man who stands next to me." "My fellow" implies one who has a very close community of interest with God, perhaps even a Son of God. But why would Yahweh slay his fellow? Why did Yahweh allow the Servant to die (Isaiah 53)?

I can't answer these questions without Jesus Christ. Jesus himself referred to this very passage as fulfilled by his death on the cross (Matt. 26:31, 32). He was the slain Shepherd, his disciples the scattered flock.

The Jews had trouble with many of these predictions. As a matter of fact, some of them who had hopes of a glorious Messiah but who also gave these dark passages a messianic interpretation had to postulate two Messiahs—one the son of Joseph, who had suffered and died, and the other the real Messiah, the son of David, who would conquer and reign. Occam's Messianic Razor shows that one Messiah—Jesus Christ, who both suffers and reigns—will explain all these prophecies.

3. Psalm 22 reads as if David wrote it at the foot of the cross. Jesus uttered the first verse from the cross: "My God, my God, why hast thou forsaken me?" (Matt 27:46). I can count at least twelve clear references to Christ in this short passage: (1) he was scorned and despised by men (v. 6); (2) people mocked his faith in God (vv. 7, 8); (3) his birth had been in God's plan (v. 9); (4) he was surrounded by evil men, "bulls," a "lion," and "dogs" (vv. 12, 13, 16); (5) his bones were out of joint and clearly visible—a standard result of crucifixion (vv. 14, 17); (6) his heart was collapsed within him (v. 14); (7) he had a terrible thirst (v. 15); (8) his enemies pierced his hands and feet (v. 16); (9) they divided his garments among them (v. 18); nevertheless, (10) God delivers him from this situation (vv. 22, 24); (11) he lives to tell future generations of God's greatness (vv. 22, 31); and finally (12) "all the ends of the earth" and "all the families of the nations" (v. 27) shall honor God for his deliverance. Read the gospels and note the parallels.

No king, prophet, or priest of Israel had ever suffered the mistreatment described in this psalm. Nor could any Hebrew ever imagine his personal deliverance from death becoming the occasion for the world's conversion. Psalm 22 and Isaiah 53, therefore, are best explained by Christ's resurrection.

Psalm 16:9-11 also has David speaking of a resurrection: "Therefore my heart is glad, and my soul rejoices; my body also dwells secure. For thou dost not give me up to Sheol, or let thy godly one see the Pit." An extraordinary statement, this, because in David's day no one was certain of life after death. Yet David calmly asserts that death will have no lasting power over him, that he won't stay in Sheol, that his body won't decompose. As Peter argued on Pentecost (Acts 2:25-32) and Paul argued at Antioch (Acts 13:35-37), David couldn't be referring to himself, because he died and was buried and is still in the tomb. David was referring instead to the Messiah, Jesus the Christ, who came forth from the tomb.

Thus, the "bright side" of the Messiah and the "dark side," when joined together, make a mysterious tangled web that puzzled many Jewish commentators. How could the Messiah be so many things at once: King, Priest, Prophet, Shepherd, Suffering Servant, Sin-offering, vicarious victim? Perhaps this was God's way of making sure that no one could artificially fulfill all these visions until he should come who had the key. "The very fact that the threads of the Old Testament seem hopelessly tangled," says Ramm, "and yet are so beautifully un-tangled in the life of Christ is further proof that beneath the letter of Scripture is the unerring guidance of the Holy Spirit."[3]

One thing is certain, Agnos: when you get to the New Testament, to Christianity, you're struck by its *finality* and *universality*. With the gospel of Jesus Christ we're no longer in the presence of mere prepara-tory institutions and anticipatory predictions. We expect no further religious developments in the future. We will hear no additional prophecies of a Coming One, a great Branch, a new covenant. He has already come and his religion covers the earth as waters cover the sea. He is the true glory of his people Israel, the light to lighten the gen-tiles. After him you have only—his *second* coming!

D. THE FULLNESS OF TIME.

If the argument from prophecy is correct we know that God con-trols the chronology of history; he brings things to pass according to his plan. The New Testament tells us that Christ came when the time was ripe. Jesus began his ministry with the announcement: "The time is fulfilled, and the kingdom of God is at hand" (Mark 1:15). Paul told the Galatians, "When the time had fully come, God sent forth his Son" (Gal. 4:4), and he told Titus that God revealed Christ "at the proper time" (Titus 1:3).

Can we show that Christ came at an auspicious time in world his-tory? Definitely yes. Let's divide our analysis into two parts: mental and physical.

1. God prepared men's minds for the coming of Christ. He sent Christ at a time when ideas, ideology, philosophy, and attitudes were right.

a. God prepared the Jews, as we've seen, with many messianic prophecies describing the Christ, his lineage, his birthplace, his titles, his work. Anyone reading these prophecies correctly would expect a Deliverer, a new covenant, a sharp change in Israel's history. The Jews didn't know exactly when he would come, but Isaiah 11:1 sug-gested it would be when the stump of David was unimportant and

3. *Protestant Christian Evidences*, p. 119.

Genesis 49:10 suggested it would be before Judah lost her sovereignty.[4]

As the first century B.C. came to a close there were many groups in Israel looking for the Messiah or the kingdom of God, "the consolation of Israel." You can understand the excitement, therefore, when John the Baptist suddenly appeared in Israel in the fifteenth year of Tiberius Caesar preaching repentance in preparation for the Coming One. No one had seen such a prophet for four hundred years. His message had the ring of conviction and authority. He urged a new birth, a change of mind. He warned that descent from Abraham proved nothing; God could make children of Abraham out of the rocks. He predicted the Messiah would come soon after him, separating the good from the worthless as a farmer separates the wheat from the chaff (Matt. 3:1-12).

b. God prepared the gentiles mentally for the coming of Christ. He sent Christ at a time when human reason was in the doldrums, when speculative philosophy was at a low ebb. The Hellenistic period of western philosophy, which started with Alexander the Great, has been called "a failure of nerve."[5] It was a time of cynicism, scepticism, and ideological despair. Gone were the days of Plato and Aristotle, who constructed huge, speculative systems of thought. The thinkers of the Hellenistic period—the Stoics, Epicureans, Cynics, and Sceptics— were convinced that abstract Truth was impossible for the human mind to achieve. What, then, was the goal of human thought? Just happiness, individual felicity, personal contentment, achieved either by unlimited sensual pleasures (Epicureans), or by a return to nature (Cynics), or by a lofty inner ethical code (Stoics). For such people, a firm word from God brings great joy.

Christ came when the old classical religions of the Roman Empire were bankrupt. The Greco-Roman pantheon failed to unify the empire and the Caesars had to institute emperor worship as a unifying force. Many common people flocked to new mystery religions from Egypt and the East in their search for meaningful religion, for a personal savior and individual immortality. When the Christian gospel began to spread among the people it showed an amazing capacity to satisfy this craving for personal salvation and immortality.

4. A very plausible interpretation of Daniel 2 and 7 would also lead one to expect the Messiah to come during the Roman Empire. The fourth part of the great statue Daniel saw in ch. 2 and the fourth unnamed beast he saw in ch. 7 both seem to refer to Rome. The previous three would be: Babylon, Medo-Persia, and Macedonia.

5. See ch. 4 of Gilbert Murray's *Five Stages of Greek Religion* (New York: Columbia University Press, 1925).

Christ came, therefore, when the Mediterranean world was in a "spiritual vacuum," a point acknowledged even by non-Christian historians. He came when many people recognized their need for a savior. "Blessed are the poor in spirit," he said, "for theirs is the kingdom of heaven" (Matt. 5:3).

2. God prepared the physical world for the coming of Christ. He guided politics, economics, linguistics, and social events to create an auspicious time for his Son to enter history.

a. The Roman Empire had barely rounded out its eastern limits when Christ appeared. Pompey conquered Palestine in 63 B.C. and the land was scarcely subdued and organized politically by the time Jesus was born, somewhere between 7 and 4 B.C. We can't stress enough the fact that Christ came to earth during the most peaceful period of human history, the Pax Romana, the "Roman peace." The previous century was one long civil war in the Mediterranean basin. But from the accession of Octavian (Augustus) in 27 B.C. to the death of Marcus Aurelius in A.D. 180 the Mediterranean world enjoyed almost unbroken tranquility. Only two local conflicts, both involving the Jews, marred this period of peace and political stability.

Once the gospel began to spread Christian evangelists found they had easy access to all parts of the empire; they had good Roman roads, well-established sea lanes, the protection of Roman troops, the Roman navy, and Roman courts, as well as substantial religious freedom to spread their views.

b. Christians also found that Roman imperialism helped the spread of Christianity by fostering the unity of the human race. If Christ had come three centuries earlier, when the Greeks dominated the eastern Mediterranean, the gospel would have had rough sledding against the racism, the cultural, linguistic, and intellectual snobbery of the Greeks.

The Romans weren't the greatest egalitarians in history, but they did hold to a rough notion that "all men are men, under the skin," an idea that slowly liberalized their institutions. By A.D. 212 the Emperor Caracalla had made all free residents of the empire full citizens. Christians preached a similar universal message: all men are men, all men have sinned, and all men therefore need the God-Man, Jesus Christ, to save them.

c. God prepared the world linguistically. He saw to it that when Christ came a good vehicle existed for the preservation of his word—

the Greek language. Of course, God could have used any language on earth for his revelation, but you can mention certain features of the Greek language that seem to make it specially suited for revelation: (1) it had a large general vocabulary, (2) it had a large theological and philosophical vocabulary, (3) it had a long history with many great works of literature composed in it, (4) it was flexible and precise. Most important, however, (5) it was the *lingua franca* of the ancient world, the second language of most educated people. If Christ had come in the fourth century B.C. there would have been no such language for the gospel. All the New Testament (with the possible exception of the original Matthew) was composed in it.

E.   CONCLUSION.

But you say, "All that could be a coincidence!" Yes, I suppose it could, but when I find one man who claimed so much fulfilling so easily so many Old Testament prophecies, when I find him coming at a time when theological, philosophical, ideological, political, economic, and linguistic conditions were so auspicious—when I find all this, I have to judge the coincidence theory very weak.

Don't you get tired, Agnos, of explaining away all the evidence as a coincidence? The design in the universe, the nature of man, the claims, miracles, and character of Christ, the prophecies he fulfills, the fullness of time—is it all coincidence?

Don't you get tired, Agnos?

Suggestions for Further Reading

Willis J. Beecher, *The Prophets and the Promise* (New York: Crowell, 1905; Grand Rapids: Baker, 1963 [reprint]).

F. F. Bruce, *The New Testament Development of the Old Testament Themes* (Grand Rapids: Eerdmans, 1970).

Charles N. Cochrane, *Christianity and Classical Culture* (London: Oxford University Press, 1944).

Charles H. Dodd, *The Old Testament in the New* (Philadelphia: Fortress, 1963).

Alfred Edersheim, *Prophecy and History in Relation to the Messiah* (New York: Randolph, 1885).

Paul Heinisch, *Christ in Prophecy*, trans. William G. Heidt (Collegeville, MN: Liturgical Press, 1956).

E. O. James, *In the Fulness of Time* (London: SPCK, 1935).

Sigmund Mowinckel, *He That Cometh*, trans. G. W. Anderson (New York: Abingdon, 1954).

Helmer Ringgren, *The Messiah in the Old Testament* (London: SCM Press, 1956).

Harold H. Rowley, *The Unity of the Bible* (Philadelphia: Westminster, 1955).

THE RESURRECTION OF
JESUS CHRIST

Agnos, we've reached the Achilles' heel of the Christian faith, the jugular vein of the entire system—the resurrection of Christ. If our evidence falters here, our whole case is in dire straits. It would be similar to a key witness dying in a big court case. St. Paul stated it correctly at the very beginning of the Christian era: if Christ didn't rise from the dead, then we Christians are the most pitiful group in the world (I Cor. 15:19). The Resurrection isn't just a pretty optional extra of Christian theology, invented by some Pollyanna theologian to give a happy ending to the tragic death of Jesus. No! The Resurrection is the linchpin of our complete system. Remove it and the whole structure of Christianity collapses.

There is no question that Jesus' enemies felt that his death was the final refutation of all those preposterous claims we examined in chapter 13. If the cross was the last thing we knew about Jesus we would judge him a failure. His death would have justified the Sanhedrin in executing him for blasphemy. But if God raised him from the dead then his claims have been dramatically vindicated. We still face the same dilemma today as the Jews right after Easter morning: either Christ was all he claimed to be and is therefore still alive or he was a liar-lunatic and the Jews should be commended for killing him.

Before we look at the evidence for the Resurrection, let us recall that faith is not knowledge but reasonable trust. You could never study the Resurrection scientifically, because you can't investigate it directly, empirically. Remember: proof in theology and history doesn't mean that you have the object at direct disposal. It means rather that you have some dependable indirect knowledge of it. I feel that the resurrection of Jesus Christ is as certain as any event from ancient history, more certain than most. This doesn't mean, however, that I can prove it perfectly. If we may use a courtroom analogy again, the event really happened; it is objective; but our present apprehension of it is only indirect, remotely objective.

As our custom is, we shall divide the evidence into direct and indirect, eyewitness evidence and circumstantial evidence. Some events in history have more of one kind than the other, but the Resurrection has abundant evidence of both kinds.

A. EYEWITNESS EVIDENCE FOR THE RESURRECTION.

Luke the historian tells us that Jesus showed himself alive after his passion by "many infallible proofs" (Acts 1:3, AV). The word for proof *(tekmērion)* means "a sure sign or token." It implies the strongest type of legal evidence, a demonstrable corroboration. Obviously, Luke was trying to tell us that Jesus appeared enough times to enough people in the forty days between his resurrection and ascension to convince a normal man that he had conquered death. When we look at the appearances recorded in the New Testament we can see that no one ever harmonized them into an official list with a definite chronology. One can only guess what the original order might have been.

Several appearances occurred on Easter Sunday. The women who planned to anoint the body first saw an angel at the tomb and then met Christ on the way back (Matt. 28:1-10). Some time later, Jesus appeared to Mary Magdalene in the vicinity of the tomb (John 20:11-18). This was probably Mary's second visit to the sepulcher, since she is mentioned in the original group of women. Then Jesus appeared to two disciples, one named Cleopas, on the road to Emmaus, a town about seven miles from Jerusalem (Luke 24:13-35). He appeared also to Peter the same day, although we have no information about the circumstances (Luke 24:34; I Cor. 15:5). When Cleopas and the other disciple returned to Jerusalem, they found the eleven apostles gathered together. They told them of the appearance on the road to Emmaus, and the others said, "The Lord has risen indeed, and has appeared to Simon!" (Luke 24:34). At that very time, Christ appeared to the entire group of apostles, with the possible exception of Thomas (Luke 24:36-40; John 20:19-23).

John tells us that eight days after this Jesus appeared to the same group with Thomas present (John 20:26-28). At an undesignated time he appeared to several disciples at the Sea of Galilee, while they were fishing (John 21:1-23). Then he appeared to more than five hundred people at once, on a mountain in Galilee (Matt. 28:16-20; I Cor. 15:6). Sometime between resurrection and ascension he appeared to his blood brother James (I Cor. 15:7). Finally, he appeared to all the apostles at Jerusalem, immediately before the ascension from the Mount of Olives (Luke 24:50-52; Acts 1:3-8).

Note certain characteristics of these appearances which strengthen their evidential value.

1. Notice that the appearances stress the *physical* or *empirical* aspects of Christ's person. The women take hold of his feet (Matt. 28:9); he eats bread with the men at Emmaus (Luke 24:30); he eats fish on the shore of Galilee (John 21:12); he challenges Thomas to handle his body (John 20:27); he reassures the disciples that he is not a ghost: "See my hands and my feet, that it is I myself; handle me, and see; for a spirit has not flesh and bones as you see that I have" (Luke 24:39).

2. Note carefully that the first appearances were to *women*, not to the apostles! That's why the apostles were naturally suspicious at the first reports; women were considered so unreliable as witnesses that they weren't allowed to testify in Jewish courts. This fact militates strongly against the Myth Hypothesis; if the resurrection accounts were later manufactured out of whole cloth by the church to strengthen faith, it is unlikely that Jews would have included women in the story, certainly not as the very first eyewitnesses. It would be like a pre-Civil War southerner fabricating a myth about his own white race and giving pre-eminent place to Negro testimony.

3. Note that the record of the appearances has a variety and a spontaneity you would expect in such a situation, where several people see the risen Christ and run off in all directions to report the event. There are quite a few puzzles and discrepancies in the narratives, as unbelievers have always pointed out, but the amazing thing is that the church left them there in the gospel record. No one has ever been able to completely harmonize them, but far from discrediting the stories, these alleged contradictions strengthen the account by showing that no harmonizing instinct worked them over. No attempt was ever made to fabricate an official story free of all difficulties.

Any student of history knows that contradictions in the record don't destroy an event. For example, the Greek historian Polybius and the Latin historian Livy have Hannibal crossing the Alps by completely different routes, routes which can't be harmonized by any stretch of the imagination, yet no one doubts that Hannibal arrived in Italy (just ask Fabius!). There are startling discrepancies in the accounts of the Battle of Waterloo as given by Wellington, Marshall

Ney, and Napoleon, yet who in his right mind doubts that this battle occurred? A great event involving many witnesses usually generates such divergent accounts.

The same is true in a law court. Any good lawyer or good judge knows that if eyewitnesses agree in detail they probably have been coached by their lawyers. Differences in detail sometimes prove the authenticity and independence of personal witnesses. Several witnesses with small differences are preferable to one witness whose story can't be compared with anything else. Furthermore, the circumstantial data often clear up the differences among the witnesses and authenticate the account of the central event. We will see that this is true of the Resurrection.

We still have one more eyewitness, and a star witness at that—Saul of Tarsus, better known as St. Paul. What would you think, Agnos, if the President of the United States should suddenly defect to the Communists? Or the Pope should become a Protestant? Or Hitler should become a Jew? Well, only some such bizarre improbability could match the colossal conversion of Saul the Pharisee to Jesus Christ. Saul was a brilliant Jew, trained by the Old Testament specialist, Gamaliel. He was a fanatical opponent of the new faith, threatening, imprisoning, and executing Christians from Jerusalem all the way to Damascus (Acts 9:1, 2; 22:3-5). Any man who could write two-thirds of the New Testament, especially such masterpieces as Romans and Galatians, deserves our careful attention when he talks about his conversion.

And what does Paul say? Simply that Christ met him in some form on the road to Damascus, questioned his motive for persecution, caused him to be blind for three days, and commanded him to proceed to Damascus where a disciple named Ananias received him and three days later baptized him (Acts 9:1-22; 22:6-16; 26:1-23). All this took place some four to seven years after the ascension of Jesus. So shocking was this *volte-face* that the Christians of Damascus couldn't believe it, nor could the disciples in Jerusalem (Acts 9:21, 26). From then on, Paul preached the resurrected Christ until the day of his death, always reminding people that he had "seen the Lord" (I Cor. 9:1). In I Corinthians 15:3-8 Paul gives what seems to be a semi-official list of the appearances of Christ. This may be the oldest document the Christian church possesses:

> For I delivered to you as of first importance what I also received, that Christ died for our sins in accordance with the scriptures, that he was buried, that he was raised on the third day in accordance with the scriptures, and that he appeared to Cephas, then to the twelve. Then he appeared to more than five hundred

brethren at one time, most of whom are still alive, though some have fallen asleep. Then he appeared to James, then to all the apostles. Last of all, as to one untimely born, he appeared also to me.

Paul wrote this statement around A.D. 51, though he may have been in possession of this list long before. The First Epistle to the Thessalonians is even earlier and there we find this statement: "Since we believe that Jesus died and rose again, even so, through Jesus, God will bring with him those who have fallen asleep" (4:14). Just as we used Paul to destroy the interpretation which the Myth Hypothesis gives to the claims of Christ, so also we can use him to destroy its interpretation of the Resurrection. I Thessalonians was written about two decades after the Resurrection and that will destroy forever any theory which says that the Christian church hatched its Easter myth over a lengthy period of time or that the sources were written several decades after the event occurred. Paul's writings, which came before all four gospels, give the death blow to any myth hypothesis.

B. CIRCUMSTANTIAL EVIDENCE FOR THE RESURRECTION.

Evidence, like a person, walks on two legs better than one. Eyewitness testimony is best corroborated if circumstantial data help it along. Witnesses can lie, but cold hard facts remain the same. Circumstantial evidence is mute, non-verbal testimony, in contrast to the spoken testimony of eyewitnesses. It usually consists of conditions which strongly imply that such and such an event occurred. For example, what caused the enormous hole in Arizona known as Meteor Crater? You may suggest several hypotheses:

1. A small boy threw a firecracker on the ground.
2. A family of gophers dug the hole.
3. A violent volcanic explosion blew out the hole.
4. A large meteor fell and made the hole.

Anyone can see that #3 and #4 are the two most likely hypotheses to explain the effect; #1 and #2 are obviously impossible. Now, the same thing is true of Christ's resurrection: we have a large "hole" in history, a great explosion two millennia ago that must be explained. Any cause you suggest must do justice to the effect. I maintain that only the Resurrection does justice to all the following circumstantial evidence.

1. There is, first of all, the fact that Jesus predicted several times in his ministry that he would rise from the dead (Matt. 16:21; Mark 9:1,

10; Luke 9:22; John 12:32, 34). When the Scribes and Pharisees asked for a sign, he gave them the "Sign of the prophet Jonah." He said the Son of Man would be in the bowels of the earth three days and nights, thus alluding to the fact that a violent death would be followed by an unusual return (Matt. 12:39, 40). I personally would be suspicious if the event had taken Jesus by surprise. These pre-Passion predictions gave the event an "antecedent probability" that it would otherwise have lacked. We should give these predictions the same consideration a lawyer gives to the background of a defendant whose deed seems to fit in with a previous pattern of behavior.

2. The Resurrection fits the character and the claims of Jesus which we've already analyzed. That there was some antecedent probability for his rising becomes more apparent when we contemplate at length his unusual claims and his unparalleled character. You may say that you've never seen a dead man come back to life. You're right, neither have I. But then—we've never seen a man like Jesus either! "No man ever spoke like this man!" (John 7:46). When I meditate at length on his claims and his character, I want to shout, "This man must not remain dead!" His uniqueness helps me to believe in this unique event.

The enemies of Jesus were obviously impressed by his resurrection predictions. Why did they post a guard at the tomb to forestall it?

3. The Resurrection explains the mysterious predictions in the Old Testament we examined in the last chapter. It especially explains the passages in Isaiah, Zechariah, and the Psalms that depict the Messiah suffering for the sins of many, being bruised, smitten, and punished by Yahweh. How, without the Resurrection, could it happen that the Suffering Servant would after his sacrifice "see his offspring" or "prolong his days" or "see the fruit of the travail of his soul" (Isa. 53:10, 11)?

4. A very strong piece of circumstantial evidence is the empty tomb. How do we know the tomb was empty? First, we have the testimony of the eyewitnesses (Matt. 28:6; Mark 16:6; Luke 24:3), but even if we lacked this we would have a very strong case for the empty tomb. We can use the coherence method of proof and show that all the facts are inconsistent with an occupied tomb. If Christ's body was still in the tomb, why didn't the Jews recover it and stop the apostles from preaching the Resurrection after Pentecost? How could they have continued preaching the Resurrection in and around Jerusalem if the body lay in the tomb just outside the city walls?

Most religions honor the remains or the final resting place of their founders but there's not a trace in any New Testament book or any post-apostolic document of anyone ever going to pay homage at the "shrine of Jesus Christ."

5. The emptiness of the tomb is confirmed by another piece of circumstantial evidence: *the silence of the Jews.* This is one of those rare cases where the argument from silence is almost devastating. We can be sure that the authorities in Jerusalem would have used any possible means to stop the preaching of the Resurrection recorded in the early chapters of Acts (e.g., 2:24, 32; 3:15; 4:10, 33; 5:30). But the Jews never did affirm that the tomb was occupied, though that would have been the most damaging thing they could have done. No, they said the next best thing, that the body had vanished, stolen by the disciples. Everyone around Jerusalem admitted that the body had disappeared from the tomb; the only question was: How did it disappear? Instead of refuting the Resurrection by producing the body, all the Jews could do was to throw the apostles into jail (Acts 5:18).[1]

Agnos, if you claimed that the Resurrection was preached in Jerusalem while the tomb was still occupied it would be as incredible as the claim that a man walked the streets of Berlin unmolested in 1941 carrying a sign, "Hitler is a Devil."

6. Any theory which competes with the Resurrection must explain what transformed the lives of Christ's apostles around the time of the Resurrection. We know they didn't expect the Resurrection and were sceptical of the first reports from the women. What dispelled the darkness of his tragic death that hung over them like a black cloud? If Christ didn't appear to them, what changed them?

What changed Simon Barjona from the coward who dodged the questions of a maid during the trial into Peter the fearless preacher who defied the Sanhedrin by preaching Christ all over Jerusalem? What changed James, the sceptical blood brother of Jesus, into James the Just, a leader of the early Jerusalem church? What changed Saul of Tarsus, the arch-Pharisee, the greatest enemy of the faith, into Paul the Apostle to the Gentiles?

1. An archaeological discovery called "the Nazareth Inscription" may also be evidence for the empty tomb. Most scholars think it dates from the time of either Tiberius (14-37) or Claudius (41-54). It is an ordinance of Caesar decreeing death for anyone guilty of "violation of sepulcher," that is, disturbing or removing the remains of bodies laid in tombs. All previous Roman edicts on grave violation set only a large fine as punishment and one naturally wonders what serious infraction led Rome to stiffen the penalty. See F. F. Bruce, *New Testament History* (London: Oliphants, 1971), pp. 285ff.

Pascal once said, "I readily believe those witnesses who get their throats cut." Myths don't inspire very many martyrs, Agnos. Most of the original apostles died a martyr's death for the message of Christ's resurrection. If they deceitfully tried to spawn a new faith on the world, would they have gone on to give their very lives for it? When a man undergoes persecution, contempt, beatings, prison, and death for a message, he has a good motive for reviewing carefully the grounds of his convictions. It is extremely unlikely that the original disciples of Jesus would have persisted in affirming the truths they affirmed if Jesus hadn't actually risen. The first century in Palestine witnessed many self-styled Messiahs. Why did none of them have the staying power of the simple carpenter from Nazareth?[2]

7. Finally, only the Resurrection can adequately explain the existence of the Christian church, perhaps the strongest circumstantial evidence we possess. After you account for the belief of the apostles, you must then explain the belief of all those who accepted it from them. How in the world, without the Resurrection, could the frightened followers of a crucified "Messianic Pretender" have become the nucleus of a militant church, a community which has now endured for nineteen centuries? You may be prejudiced enough to reject everything found in the New Testament but you can't possibly pass off the church as legend. By A.D. 64 it was already a potent force in the Roman Empire, as one can see from secular sources.[3] This church must be explained.

Without the Resurrection certain things about this church can't be explained. For example, how could the eleven apostles seriously insist that any new apostle must be a witness of the Resurrection (Acts 1:21, 22)? How in the world did the rite of baptism come to have the meaning it had in the early church, that of being "buried with" Christ and "raised with" Christ (Rom. 6:1-6; Col. 2:12)? How did the Lord's Supper become a feast of such joy to Christians, a feast in which the cross took on a new, redemptive significance?

What caused Jewish Christians to transfer their worship from Saturday to Sunday and to call the latter, "the Lord's Day"? What caused Jewish Christians to accept Jesus as the Old Testament Messiah, especially when the Law clearly said that a man hanged on a

2. Josephus in *Jewish War* (II.13.4.259) and *Antiquities* (XX. 8.6.170) tells of a certain Theudas, who in A.D. 44 told a crowd he could divide the waters of the Jordan, and of an unnamed Egyptian messiah who assembled 30,000 Jews and claimed that at his command the walls of Jerusalem would fall down.

3. See e.g., Tacitus, *Annals*, XV. 44; Josephus, *Antiquities*, XVII.33; Suetonius, *Life of Claudius*, 25.4; *Lives of the Caesars*, 26.2; Pliny the Younger, *Epistles*, X.96.

tree is cursed of God (Deut. 21:23)? What caused Jewish Christians to modify their historic monotheism and enlarge the Godhead by granting deity to Jesus (Phil. 2:6)? What caused Jewish Christians to call Christ "Lord" *(kurios)*, a term used in the Old Testament for Yahweh? What broke the back of history and gave us B.C. and A.D.?

I can't answer any of these questions, Agnos, without the Resurrection.

You can tell how I feel if you imagine yourself as a space traveler who went to Mars from 1900 to 1919. World War I changed the course of all history. On your return to Europe in 1919 you might not know what had happened but you would know that *something big had happened*. You would ask: Where did Poland come from? What happened to the Turkish, Romanov, Habsburg, and Hohenzollern Empires? How did the Bolsheviks get control of Russia? What killed 13 million people? How did America and Japan get control of most of the world's trade? If someone then told you about the Great War you would be satisfied.

I feel the same way about the Resurrection. Let's now examine some of the alternate theories and see if any of them can explain the evidence.

C. ALTERNATE THEORIES.

A good defense lawyer protects his client from the accusations of the prosecuting attorney by showing that the incriminating evidence can be explained by some hypothesis other than his client's guilt. In this case, any alternate theory must explain *all* the evidence— eyewitness and circumstantial—as well as or better than the Resurrection. None of them does as good a job as the Resurrection. Of the five theories we shall examine, two try to explain the empty tomb, two explain the appearances, but only one proposes to explain them both together.

1. The Stolen Body Theory is the oldest competing theory on the empty tomb. According to Matthew, the Jews bribed the soldiers guarding the tomb and said, "Tell people, 'His disciples came by night and stole him away while we were asleep.' "[4] Since that time,

---

4. Matt. 28:13. We know this was the standard answer of the Jews to the Resurrection because Justin Martyr in his *Dialogue with Trypho*, 108, written around A.D. 150, reported that the Jewish authorities even sent specially commissioned men across the Mediterranean Sea to counter Christian claims with the assertion that the disciples stole the body of Jesus. See also Tertullian, *Apology*, 21.

others have suggested that the theft was the work of the Jews, or Joseph of Arimathea, or Pilate, or the Romans.

Two problems face any stolen body theory: (1) motive and (2) execution. What motive would any of these people have for stealing the body? The apostles? How could this group of cowering, defeated disciples have summoned the courage to attack the tomb guard, break the Roman seal, and make off with the body? Jesus didn't spend his time welding the apostles into a "Mission Impossible" team. The Jews? Why would they want to steal it? They had insisted on the guard in the first place to stop this very thing (Matt. 27:62-66). Pilate or the Romans? These pagans had no desire to believe in the Resurrection; the Roman seal on the tomb was their god and their religion.

Even if you find a motive for theft, it would have been very difficult to pull it off. This is especially true if the guard was a Roman one, for any Roman soldier found sleeping on duty was subject to court-martial and death. It is possible that it was a Jewish guard, but there are three good reasons why I think it was a Roman guard: (1) the word for guard *(koustodia)* is a Greek word built on a Latin root, (2) the Jews wouldn't have to ask Pilate for permission to use their own temple guard, and (3) in the bribing of the guard a risk of punishment from Pilate was implied. Whether the guard was Roman or Jewish, however, we can say with certainty that the Jews did everything possible to prevent a theft that could be interpreted as a resurrection.

And that brings us to that nasty argument from silence again: if someone stole the body why didn't the Jews just produce the body on Pentecost and stop the preaching of the Resurrection? Why didn't they at least get some witnesses to say they had seen the body after the alleged resurrection? Why didn't the Sanhedrin use this theory when the preaching started? It offered nothing to contradict the preaching of the Resurrection—nothing except prison for the preachers.

2. The Wrong Tomb Theory explains the empty tomb in terms of a misunderstanding on the part of the women. According to Professor Kirsopp Lake,[5] the women visited the wrong grave on Easter morning. A young man there directed them to the correct spot by saying, "He is not here; see the place where they laid him," which is a corrected reading of Mark 16:6. Lake suggests that someone later added the words, "He has risen." An astonishing suggestion, this, that the story of the empty tomb goes back to a mistake of a few women. It

5. *The Historical Evidence for the Resurrection of Jesus Christ* (New York: G. P. Putnam's Sons, 1907), pp. 250-53.

makes the whole course of Christian history seem like a massive inverted pyramid, balanced precariously on the apex of a very trivial occurrence. Lake's reconstruction of the text is a clear example of special pleading: you could rebuild hundreds of Bible verses to fit your pet hypothesis if you wanted.

This theory has numerous problems. Why did everyone in the group forget the location of the tomb in just a few days? There was no reason for the mistake, since the spot was a private tomb, not a public cemetery. Furthermore, we're told that the disciples ran to the tomb once they heard it was empty. Did they run to the same wrong tomb? Did everyone go to the wrong tomb? If so, then the body was still in the *right* tomb and would have been found eventually, either by some disciple who hadn't lost his senses yet, or, most certainly, by the Jewish authorities who wanted to squelch the preaching of the Resurrection. Even if you make the incredible assertion that the women, the disciples, the Jews, and the Romans *all* went to the wrong tomb, surely Joseph of Arimathea, owner of the plot, would have cleared up the puzzle. Or had Joseph lost his mind also? Remember: it's the duty of a theory to explain puzzles, not multiply them. This theory only multiplies them.

Both the Stolen Body Theory and the Wrong Tomb Theory try to explain only the empty tomb; they make no attempt to explain the recorded appearances of Christ. Consequently, they can't stand alone but must be joined with a sub-theory of some kind to explain all the data of the case. If someone stole the body that still doesn't tell us what the disciples *saw* between Easter and Pentecost. It certainly doesn't tell what Saul of Tarsus saw on the road to Damascus several years later. The next two theories work on the appearances.

3. The Hallucination Theory seeks to explain the appearances of Christ as private phantasms, as subjective experiences, as internal visions seen within the mind but bereft of any external, objective referent. An hallucination is a morbid, pathological condition of the mind in which the person is conscious of a perception without any impression having been made on his external sense organs. Ordinarily, we say that a "true experience" is one that we share with other people whereas illusions or hallucinations are experiences that are essentially private and unshared. All of us see the grey elephant in the circus parade, but only the drunk sees the pink elephant on the chandelier.

Now, if the resurrection appearances were hallucinations in this general sense, we are again faced with a number of enigmas.

a. Hallucinations usually occur only with particular kinds of personalities, such as high-strung, imaginative, or unstable people. But Jesus appeared to common housewives, prosaic fishermen, practical tax collectors, logical Pharisees—a wide variety of personalities. It's not likely they all had the hallucinogenic personality.

b. Hallucinations usually are very individualistic because their source is the private subconscious. They come one at a time. Thus it is unlikely that a group of disciples, especially a group 500 strong, would all see the exact same person at the exact same time.

c. Hallucinations are seldom misinterpretations of the external object (that is called a *delusion*). Hence, this theory can't explain how it happens that on three separate occasions the vision of the Christ was not immediately recognized as Jesus (Luke 24:13-31; John 20:15; 21:4).

d. Hallucinations usually occur in people who have had psychological preparation, induced by such things as special drugs or plants, strong ascetic practices, or deprivation of food, drink, and sleep. If the disciples had been in such a receptive mood we might be persuaded to accept this theory, but none of them expected the Resurrection. They doubted the first reports of the empty tomb. When the women visited the tomb Easter morning they were expecting to anoint a dead body, not discover a risen Christ.

e. Hallucinations usually occur in auspicious *places*, such as a sacred grove or a spiritual sanctuary of some kind. But Christ appeared in a variety of places: on a lake shore, on a mountain, near the tomb, in both Jerusalem and Galilee, on the road to Emmaus.

f. Hallucinations usually occur at auspicious *times*, such as night, early morning, or twilight. But Jesus appeared to people at several different times of the day: early morning, broad daylight, evening and night.

g. Finally, hallucinations customarily recur over a rather long time with some regularity. Sometimes they even increase in frequency. Bernadotte (Charles XIV), King of Sweden, was regularly besieged by a woman in a red cloak during his daily ride. The second Earl Grey was constantly haunted by a gory head that he could dismiss at will. But with the resurrection appearances the visions stop all at once; after forty days no one claimed to see Christ again in the flesh. The appearances to Stephen and Paul (Acts 7:56; 9:3) don't seem to have been bodily appearances. If the visions of Christ had no objective source, no external referent, why did they stop so suddenly? What caused *all* the disciples to stop hallucinating at the same time? Why didn't the Christophanies multiply in the Book of Acts? The church had plenty of crises to call forth more visions.[6]

4. The Objective Vision Theory or the "Telegram Theory" is a strange halfway house for those who recognize the weakness of the hallucination theory but don't want to go all the way to the orthodox position. This theory says that the appearances of Jesus were truly visions, but objective visions, that is, they were messages ("telegrams") sent to the grieving disciples by the direct intervention of God to reassure them that Jesus was still alive, albeit in a glorified, spiritual form.

This theory is small comfort to someone who wants to avoid the supernatural, because it is more miraculous than the Resurrection itself. Its greatest difficulty, however, is that it attributes deceit to God and Jesus. If the appearances were just incorporeal visions why the emphasis on the physical elements of the body of Jesus? Why did Jesus eat a meal with the disciples (Luke 24:43)? Why did he say that a spirit has no flesh and bones (Luke 24:39)?

Furthermore, no Jew in the first century would have believed in a resurrection that was "totally spiritual." If Jesus' body was still rotting in the grave it would have been impossible to start a church in Jerusalem based on the Resurrection. To a Jew, resurrection meant the restoration to life of the total person, body, soul, spirit and whatever else personality entails. The Jewish belief in resurrection was so crudely physical that some people believed that a man would rise wearing exactly the same clothes as those in which he was laid in the tomb.[7]

All four theories examined thus far have crippling difficulties. They explain neither the empty tomb nor the appearances very well and they certainly don't explain the two together. If you say someone stole the body, then you have to say something else about the appearances, e.g., that the disciples all hallucinated. Anytime your basic theory must have a sub-theory to prop it up it weakens the main theory. What you need to beat the Resurrection in this battle is an alternate theory that explains both empty tomb and appearances simultaneously.

---

6. Even Hugh J. Schonfield, in his strange theory of the Resurrection, admits that the disciples saw something objective, a young man they mistook for Jesus (*The Passover Plot* [New York: Bantam Books, 1965], p. 172).

7. See II Baruch 49:2-4; II Maccabees 7:11; 14:46; *Sanhedrin* 90b.

5. The Swoon Theory is the only alternate theory that can provide a plausible solution to this problem. It maintains that Christ really didn't die, that he merely "swooned" and passed into a state of semi-consciousness that was mistaken for death. This unusual condition was brought on by the ordeal of trial and crucifixion—beating, loss of blood, exhaustion. Once inside the cool tomb, however, he started breathing the spices on his body and revived, got out of the tomb and showed himself to his disciples.

I can't deny that this theory could fly a long way—if we could just get it off the runway! That's the trouble, however, it crashes as soon as it tries to leave the hangar. It must prove that Christ didn't really die but the evidence for that fact is almost insurmountable. Roman crucifixion teams did their job well—they had a lot of practice. John testified that his side was pierced with a spear and that blood and water gushed out—an indication that the heart had probably ruptured and filled the abdomen with blood (John 19:34). In all the observation and handling of the corpse between crucifixion and burial you'd think that some observant soul would have noticed if there had been a spark of life in Jesus' body.

But, allow for the moment that Jesus swooned and was interred in that condition. This theory asks us to believe that after the grueling ordeal that caused the swoon, Jesus could lie for thirty-six hours in a cold, stuffy tomb, sealed away from fresh air, breathing stale air filled with spices, with no food, drink, or medical attention, and then find the stamina to extricate himself from eighty pounds of spices wrapped tightly around his body, push away a stone that intimidated several women,[8] assault the Roman guard, walk for miles on pierced, wounded feet, and then pass himself off to the disciples as the Lord of life and the conqueror of death! I don't care if this theory was the favorite of eighteenth-century rationalists, it's quite a draft on credulity.

If Jesus just swooned, he would have explained this to the apostles later on. He wouldn't have allowed his followers to spread the resurrection message if it hadn't really happened. Furthermore, if this theory is true, what finally happened to Christ after the Resurrection? Is the story of the Ascension mere fabrication? Did Jesus retire after the church got started? Pray tell, then, how did his disciples get away with preaching a resurrected and ascended Christ when he was just in retirement? Why didn't he come forward when the church started

---

8. In the Codex Bezea version of Mark 16:4 there is a gloss concerning the size of the stone that sealed the tomb: "And when he was laid there, he [Joseph] put against the tomb a stone which twenty men could not roll away."

Which Theory Explains ALL the Evidence?

The Theories ↓ The Evidence →	EMPTY TOMB	APPEARANCES	LIVES OF THE APOSTLES	THE CHURCH
1. RESURRECTION	Yes	Yes	Yes	Yes
2. STOLEN BODY THEORY	Yes	No	No	No
3. WRONG TOMB THEORY	?	No	No	No
4. HALLUCINATION THEORY	No	Yes	No	No
5. OBJECTIVE VISION THEORY	No	Yes	?	?
6. SWOON THEORY	Yes	Yes	?	?

growing and give it guidance to meet the problems we see in the Book of Acts? The Swoon Theory must tell us what finally happened to Jesus Christ. If he lived on after his resurrection and died a natural death, I don't see how the Christian church could have started or progressed as it did.

Thus it turns out, Agnos, that the only theory which tries to explain both tomb and appearances is almost as weak as the other theories. There doesn't seem to be any theory that can compete with the Resurrection for uniting all the available data in a coherent picture. You can see this very well by studying the chart on page 241 which summarizes our investigation.

D. HUME AGAIN!

"Wait just a minute," says David Hume. "I don't care if all the alternate theories *sound* weak, there must be *some* alternate theory that's true, because we know for sure that dead men don't come back to life. Even if these theories are hard to believe, the resurrection is even harder to believe. Therefore, there must be some alternate theory that's true."

By now, Agnos, you can see through this philosophical trick. We pointed out in chapter 11 on miracles that Hume assumes the very thing to be proved when he defines a miracle as an event "contrary to experience." Contrary to whose experience? If Hume answers, "to my experience," that hardly matters since there may be many things in heaven and earth and history not dreamt of in Hume's personal experience. If he adds, "and contrary to all men's experiences," he has begged the question, for *that* is the very thing under dispute. If a miracle occurred, it certainly wasn't contrary to the experience of the man who experienced it!

If Hume says that the testimony of the *majority* must determine what happens in history, he's made an untenable use of the democratic method. You don't determine history that way. Actually, Hume has left the realm of history and jumped into metaphysics. He is now affirming that all events must be repetitious, that *something can't happen only once!* But this is a philosophical, not a historical canon, and Hume's argument claims to be historical.

Actually, Hume and all those since him who have parroted this argument fail to recognize that in their rush to avoid one irregularity they end up believing in another irregularity. If, for example, you deny the Resurrection you obligate yourself to suggest an alternate theory that will account for all the evidence as well as, or better than, the Resurrection. But, as we have seen, all alternate theories are wellnigh incredible. The hallucination theory is just as "contrary to experience" as the Resurrection. Hallucinations seldom appear to crowds, they seldom occur to all personality types, they seldom are misinterpreted, and they seldom stop all of a sudden.

If, then, both the miracle (the Resurrection) and the alternate (hallucination theory) are contrary to experience, why would Hume prefer the alternate to the miracle? He certainly couldn't say he rejected all unusual events, because the hallucination theory, or any alternate, is unusual. He could only say that the Resurrection is a bit "more unusual" or "more irregular" than the hallucination theory. It is, then, a difference in degree, not in kind. I personally feel that the degree of difference between them is very small, but, just for the sake of argument, let's grant that there is an appreciable difference. We can still defuse Hume's argument against miracles by taking a different tack.

The most basic flaw in Hume's argument is that he assumes a fundamental worldview from which to attack miracles and then he assumes further that *his* worldview is the rudimentary worldview of *everyone*. After analysis, his metaphysic turns out to be a kind of common sense Scotch realism. Hume had no right to presuppose that his worldview is common to us both, no more than I have a right to assume that "revelatory theism" is common to all men. The fact is, there is no such thing as a "basic worldview," a lowest-common-denominator metaphysic that "all sensible men believe in."

To repeat the message of chapters four and five, worldviews are like glasses; you view the data of experience *through* them and you usually prefer the glasses that present the most coherent picture of the data. You don't look at data with no glasses at all, for then the world of experience would have no order at all. It would be nothing but "a blooming, buzzing confusion." Recall the words of A. N. Whitehead: "The true method of philosophical construction is to frame a scheme of ideas, the best that one can, and unflinchingly to explore the interpretation of experience in terms of that scheme."[9]

This means that all men bring to the interpretation of experience—and this includes historical events—a "perceptual set," an organized corpus of preconceptions. It's not wrong to begin your investigation of something with a theory, for one never starts these things from scratch. We always beg *some* questions. What's wrong in this serious game of worldviews is to cling to a theory that has proved to be inferior in explanatory power. It's not wrong to grind an axe; what's wrong is to keep grinding when you know your poor metal won't sharpen.

9. *Process and Reality* (New York: Macmillan, 1967), p. x.

Anyone has a right to assume an explanatory hypothesis for a body of data if he is in the process of "building up a case." In court, for example, we grant each lawyer his postulate (guilt or innocence) so long as he's arguing that it smoothly explains all the evidence. After both postulates have assumed themselves to be true and explained the data, each in its different way, then we, the jury, decide which theory makes the better case. *We don't allow either lawyer to begin the process assuming that his postulate is the only possible explanation.*

It wasn't wrong at first for Hume to approach miracles with a naturalistic preconception; what was wrong was to hold to that bias when it failed to adequately interpret irregular events in history (miracles). If you must espouse the hallucination theory to keep from believing in the Resurrection then you've made your naturalistic preconception into a Bed of Procrustes. Your hypothesis has become a prejudice. You would think that if a man embraces something as unlikely as the hallucination theory to avoid the Resurrection he might consider the possibility of altering his worldview to embrace the miraculous.

Let's try it! Take off your naturalistic glasses and assume, for the moment, the metaphysic of revelatory theism. Assume you believe in a personal God who reveals himself in history and confirms his revelation by signs and wonders (Heb. 2:4). Now, given that metaphysic, what is so offensive about the Resurrection? As Paul asked Agrippa, "Why is it thought incredible by any of you that God raises the dead?" (Acts 26:8). The Christian worldview has the advantage of not only incorporating the Resurrection coherently into its network of evidence but also of throwing doubt on the alternative, the near-miracle of the alternate theories.

Once you understand the Christian position, Agnos, you can see that we're just as opposed to the uncaused, irrational event as the naturalist. That's the whole point; if you grant revelatory theism the Resurrection isn't uncaused and irrational. It has a cause and its purpose is very rational. It fits perfectly into the Christian worldview, whereas the near-miracle is a problem for Hume's naturalism. What I'm saying is, grant Christian theism and our irregularity (the Resurrection) becomes rational, but grant Hume's naturalism and his irregularity (the hallucination theory) is still a problem for his system.

Either way you go, you've got the problem of harmonizing an irregularity into your total system. The hallucination theory is a bigger "break" in the scheme of naturalism than the Resurrection is in the scheme of revelatory theism. Those who say the Christian believes the more irregular event are simply wrong; they have fallen for Hume's trick that we all have a basic worldview which deifies regularity. If Yahweh, not Order, is God, then the Resurrection isn't irregular.

It's gratifying to note that this fine point was perceived by the great John Stuart Mill, one of the finest minds of the last century. Mill, who was certainly no friend of Christianity, noted in his *System of Logic* (II, 110) that the most Hume's argument proves is that no evidence can prove a miracle to an atheist or a deist. Defining a miracle as an event "contrary to experience" is simply like saying, "A miracle is contrary to a naturalist's experience," which is like saying, "Naturalists don't like miracles." This really isn't news to me.

Agnos, I think you can perceive by now that if you reject the resurrection of Jesus Christ you must end up embracing an alternate theory that is as incredible as the Resurrection. If you do that you'll be saying: "My miracle, but not yours!"

E. THE MEANING OF THE RESURRECTION.

It only remains to sum up the major implications of the Resurrection of Jesus Christ. The long historical argument we launched in chapter 9 is now at an end. If our reasoning has been correct, we can truly say, "God was in Christ" (II Cor. 5:19), indeed, "God *is* in Christ," for the strongest proof the Christian has for the Resurrection is the living experience he has of the risen Christ in the Christian fellowship. Let's summarize the results of our study thus far.

1. If Jesus rose from the dead, then we have a vindication of righteousness, of cosmic optimism. We know that man isn't just an accident in a backwater. We know that there is a Friend behind phenomena, not a "Vast Imbecility" as Thomas Hardy complained. Jesus called him Father, or better, *Abba* Father. We know that goodness has a meaning, that virtue has a central purpose in this cosmos. We know that sacrificial love will endure and will conquer.

2. If Jesus rose from the dead, we know that death, the great enemy of meaning, has been defeated. The Resurrection confirms all Christ's claims, but especially the claim to be the author and giver of eternal life. In St. Paul's words, Christ "abolished death and brought life and immortality to light through the gospel" (II Tim. 1:10). If Jesus was "true man" and if he ascended to heaven, then his manhood ascended with him and therefore our manhood too will someday be taken into the heavenly places. Resurrection and Ascension prove that manhood is destined for heaven and not for an entropic catastrophe in an impersonal universe.

3. If Jesus rose from the dead, we have the final capstone placed on the revelation of God in history (Heb. 1:1-4). This means that the Resurrection is the terminal proof for the authority of the Bible. If Jesus rose from the dead, then the whole Bible falls into your lap in one neat apologetic package, because Jesus is the Son of the same Yahweh who spoke from Genesis to Revelation. He reached back and confirmed the Old Testament retrospectively (Luke 24:44); he reached forward and confirmed the New Testament prospectively (John 14:26).[10]

If Jesus Christ rose from the dead the whole picture of theistic revelation hangs together. The whole Bible hangs together. History hangs together. The universe hangs together.

Suggestions for Further Reading

J. N. D. Anderson, *Christianity: The Witness of History* (Downers Grove, IL: Inter-Varsity, 1972).

Floyd Filson, *Jesus Christ the Risen Lord* (New York: Abingdon, 1956).

Michael Green, *Man Alive* (Downers Grove, IL: Inter-Varsity, 1968).

William M. Justice, *Our Visited Planet* (New York: Vantage, 1973).

John Warwick Montgomery, *History and Christianity* (Downers Grove, IL: Inter-Varsity, 1964).

Frank Morison, *Who Moved the Stone?* (London: Faber and Faber, 1930).

Richard R. Niebuhr, *Resurrection and Historical Reason: A Study of Theological Method* (New York: Scribner's, 1957).

Ramm, *Protestant Christian Evidences*, ch. 7.

Michael A. Ramsey, *The Resurrection of Christ* (Philadelphia: Westminster Press, 1946).

Albert Roper, *Did Jesus Rise from the Dead?* (Grand Rapids: Zondervan, 1965).

Wilbur Smith, *Therefore Stand* (Boston: W. A. Wilde, 1945; Grand Rapids: Baker, 1969 [reprint]), ch. 8.

W. J. Sparrow-Simpson, *The Resurrection and Modern Thought* (New York: Longmans, Green and Co., 1905).

John R. Stott, *Basic Christianity* (Grand Rapids: Eerdmans, 1957 [revised edition]), ch. 4.

Merrill C. Tenney, *The Reality of the Resurrection* (Chicago: Moody, 1972).

10. For an unusually cogent presentation of this argument for Biblical authority based on Christ, see John W. Wenham, *Christ and the Bible* (Downers Grove, IL: Inter-Varsity Press, 1972).

JESUS CHRIST AND THE PROBLEM OF EVIL

And now, Agnos, what about evil?

The duty of the Christian apologist is to remove rocks on the road to commitment. So far, I think I've shoved several big ones into the gutter. But one monster stone still remains, blocking our path, the problem of evil. We can't bypass it. We can't shut our eyes to it, because rational religion is never a matter of believing after you've shut your eyes. Rational religion is trusting beyond the very best you can see with your eyes fully open.

The existence of evil presents some evidence that weighs against the Christian's belief and he must come to terms with it. It is possible that the existence of evil might prove that my faith is wrong. I might have to give it up *if* the force of evil seems intellectually and morally stronger than the presence of God. Whether evil is this strong or not is always an individual viewpoint. I write this chapter, therefore, in a very personal vein; it represents my individual response to the problem.

A. FROM A PROBLEM TO A MYSTERY.

Our first task is to slay that paper dragon of unbelief which says that evil is an outright contradiction to Christian theism. Many moderns have argued that evil makes our entire system incoherent. We admitted in chapter four that inconsistency would kill a world-view quicker than anything and we must therefore meet this charge.

Let me say first that I feel deeply the problem of evil. Like all Christians, I've had those moments when I wanted to ask, "Is God really there?" Having learned to love the Father of Jesus Christ, I am prompted by the evil in history to ask, "What's a nice God like you doing in a universe like this?"

Nevertheless, when I look at the problem of evil with cold, sober logic there is really no contradiction in the idea that a perfectly good God could allow evil in his creation. The usual objection posits three propositions:

1. God is all good.
2. God is all powerful.
3. Evil exists in his creation.

The argument runs that it is impossible for all three of these propositions to be true at the same time. The three statements are "incompossible," impossible together. Since the Christian affirms all three, he is inconsistent.

I reply: it *is* possible for all three propositions to be true at the same time. There is nothing in the meaning of all three statements that makes them incompossible. There are several ways of reconciling divine purpose and evil, any one of which is possible, i.e., internally consistent. If God allows evil, it may be for a very good reason unknown to us. The fact that we don't know the reason is psychologically and philosophically interesting, but hardly a contradiction.

We're back to square one, Agnos. We started this book pointing out that only an omniscient being can really be a dogmatic atheist. We notice here also that only a person who knows everything can really say that evil is a fatal contradiction to Christianity. You would have to know that all the proposed ways of reconciling the existence of evil and divine purpose are false to say that "evil destroys God." You would have to prove something like, "God would *never* allow suffering," or "God would have created *only* blessed men." Are you prepared to prove this?

I needn't have an elaborate theory on the origin of evil to believe that theism is a consistent worldview. In mathematics, we have good arguments for the notion that *pi* is a definite number, though we don't know what it is. In theology, too, it's possible that God is justified in permitting evil, though we don't know what his reason is. (In fact, I'd be a bit surprised if theologians *did* know all about God's reasons for doing certain things.)

All we've done so far is reduce evil from a contradiction or problem to a mystery or puzzle. A problem you solve and forget; a mystery you learn to live with.

B. THE SNARE OF HEDONISM.

You'll never learn to live with evil if your thinking is distracted by the siren voice of hedonism. Any worldview that makes pleasure the supreme good will always judge a world of suffering like this one bad. If we start with a "playboy metaphysic," if we assume that existence is supposed to be an eternal picnic, we'll never get to a solution of the problem of evil. Hedonism must take a back seat in negotiating the problem.

Some people say, "If God really loved us, he would never let anyone suffer." But when you try to mix (1) God and (2) your own desires, you get into the problem of having two ultimate principles. "No one can serve two masters" (Matt. 6:24). Two ultimate principles won't synthesize; one will eventually govern the other; you must subordinate one to the other. Since man isn't omniscient and may not fully understand the purpose of pain, it seems reasonable to make pleasure subordinate to God.[1]

I know this may go against your psychological grain, Agnos, since we're all more or less brainwashed by modern secularism and hedonism. I must insist, however, that any reasonable discussion of evil start by making pleasure subordinate to God. When you say, "God would create a painless world," you're overlooking the fact that there are values other than mere happiness, such as freedom, creativity, personal growth, moral struggle, and achievement—things that are often acquired only at the price of conflict and frustration. Any teacher knows that you have to set up a situation of some resistance to stimulate the student to find the answer for himself. Knowledge obtained from struggle is always appreciated more than spoonfed knowledge.

If true happiness consisted merely of a perennial stream of agreeable feelings and sensations, I think it would soon become the most wearisome of states, a nauseating monotony. Have you ever noticed that sometimes the very people who complain of evil in this life are the same people who complain that heaven would be monotonous? Doesn't this show that, down deep, none of us really believes in the eternal picnic?

The problem of evil reminds us of the problem of miracles. The naturalist dislikes miracles because they are exceptions to law; they disturb uniformity. The hedonist dislikes pain because it disturbs his uniform pleasure. The deist says God wouldn't break his own law; the hedonist says God wouldn't allow evil. All three—deist, naturalist, hedonist—err because they have a perspective too narrow. In all three

---

1. A recent book, *The God I Want* (London: Hodder and Stoughton, 1967), is a good illustration of making the individual ego and its pleasures the ultimate principle. Couldn't God just as easily write a book entitled, *The Man I Want?* Indeed, hasn't he done just that in the Scriptures?

cases you claim to know what the Almighty would do, whereas you really can't say what he would do, unless you're omniscient. You can only say what you'd *like* for him to do.

Hedonism does have a partial truth—it guards us against masochism. It proves that suffering, if allowed by God, must be instrumental, not ontological. Suffering must be the *means* to some good end, determined by God, not the *end* of existence. I agree with the atheist that purposeless pain would surely be evil. A woman laboring in childbirth will forget the pain when the child is born. But no sane woman would want the pain to last forever with no purpose.

C. HISTORICAL RESPONSES TO EVIL.

Man has reacted to evil in a variety of ways throughout history. His reactions stretch all the way from the bleakest pessimism to the shallowest optimism. We'll find, as usual, that a *via media* is probably closest to the truth.

1. Pessimism is the response of people who feel that evil is so strong it is the very essence of being. The real is the irrational. The bad in life far outweighs the good. This is the worst of all possible worlds. Arthur Schopenhauer in the West and Buddha in the East are examples of this pessimism which says that reality is so absurd we should merely labor to enter Nirvana.

Such pessimism, however, is rare. It seems to run contrary to common sense. We instinctively take for granted that good is the rule and evil the exception. Most of us are glad to be alive; suicide is still rare; critically ill people usually fight for life; old folks don't ask to be killed; laughter still rings out from the ghetto. This instinct to cling to life is our basic religious impulse. We really want to believe that "being is gracious."

2. Naturalism has no genuine solution to the problem of evil. Indeed, the problem logically shouldn't bother a naturalist at all. If nature is all there is, and if nature is impersonal and non-axiological, the presence of evil in nature wouldn't disturb a consistent naturalist. Both evil and good are just impersonal data to be noted, not explained. As a human being, you might be perplexed by the widespread suffering in creation, but as a naturalist you wouldn't demand any special explanation of evil. You would only say that all things—nice or nasty—are caused by the same blind mechanism that accounts for the universe.

This, incidentally, is why we find no elaborate theodicy (explanation of evil) among the ancient Greeks. If Zeus and his family is the best theology you can muster you'll probably not be troubled by the problem of evil. The problem doesn't even arise unless you believe in an all-good, all-powerful God. The first mature theodicy in world history, the Book of Job, appeared among the Hebrews, whose God was perfect in power and morality.

All this leads to a puzzle: if the modern world is really so secular, why the widespread concern over the problem of evil? Why do people demand that we Christians explain it? Could it be that, down deep, people really have a preference for theism (and optimism) and want it to be true? If naturalism were true, I'd be puzzled at why this animal, man, worries so much about evil!

From now on, all the responses to evil are religious in nature.

3. Legalism solves the problem of evil by saying that all pain and suffering are merely just punishments for sin. Job's friends used this theory on him during his suffering. They concluded that his sin must have been heinous to merit such calamitous sufferings. When Job protested that he had done nothing to deserve such pain, friend Eliphaz chided him for arrogance:

> What do you know that we do not know?
>> What do you understand that is not clear to us?
> Both the gray-haired and the aged are among us,
>> older than your father.
> Are the consolations of God too small for you,
>> or the word that deals gently with you? (Job 15:9-11)

Job's friends were really the arrogant ones; they naively assumed that if God were personally present he would say nothing different from what they were saying. We've had many thinkers in history who felt they were speaking for God while pontificating on evil. As a matter of fact, Jesus Christ flatly denied the theory that suffering is always the result of evil (Luke 13:1-5; John 9:1-3).

But you ask: Doesn't the Bible teach that sin causes suffering? Yes, but that's not the same as saying, "All suffering is caused by sin." The proposition (a) "if you sin, you will suffer" is not identical with (b) "if you suffer, you have sinned." To go from (a) to (b) is the fallacy of "false conversion." (E.g., the statement, "if I'm Chinese, I'm human," does not at all prove the statement, "if I'm human, I'm Chinese.")

4. Pantheism or monistic idealism declares that evil isn't really a problem, just an illusion. This response to evil is very old, but its most modern form is Christian Science, which teaches that all evil is merely "an error of mortal mind." If you will but view all things "under the aspect of eternity," evil will vanish. Evil is only a mental error, a subjective notion in the mind of the sufferer that disappears when right thinking is restored.

This solution to evil fairly enrages someone who is suffering unjustly. No matter what else we may think of evil, we must never deny its existence nor consider it a necessary aspect of a perfect world. Certain medieval theologians used to argue that Hell was necessary so that Being could have all possible variations, so that no possible *kind* of being would be left out. To me, this is a perverse species of theological romanticism. If evil has a purpose, it surely must be more than just to provide aesthetic variety. If pantheism were true, you'd be sad when evil disappeared; you'd want it to remain eternally to enhance the variety of Being!

Pantheism really doesn't explain evil. Even if evil is a mental error, it is still a fact, a datum. You haven't helped by proving it mental; you've just changed the adjective. Why is there *mental* evil? If evil is just a nightmare, why does the nightmare occur? Regardless of its true nature, evil is a fact, an instance of actual experience, a true occurrence. To call it illusory still leaves it on the level of fact, exactly where it was before. It remains to be (1) explained in your worldview and (2) overcome in your devotional life.

I must admit that pantheism makes one good point: we'll never understand evil until we take a *total* view of things. Evil will always disturb an agnostic or a logical positivist because such thinkers refuse to go into metaphysics. If you insist on the blinders of positivism, if you refuse to leave the plane of the bare empirical, you'll never get a handle on the problem of evil. We must judge evil in the light of our fullest truth, not our "most certain" truths.

5. Theistic Finitism boldly assaults the problem of evil by affirming frankly that God is limited in power (not in goodness) and therefore can't thoroughly eradicate evil from the universe. Sometimes this idea is expressed in a thoroughgoing Cosmic Dualism, which posits two eternal, fundamental and yet antagonistic principles in the universe—God and Evil. Sometimes Evil is personalized in Satan, the Devil or Adversary, sometimes it is simply called "the Given" or "the Surd." In any case, evil is outside God's power; he must struggle with it forever.

One must admire the courage of a thinker who will resort to such a drastic hypothesis to solve the problem of evil. I feel, however, that such a thinker has been falsely impressed with the faulty dilemma we discussed in Section A. He has assumed that either God's goodness or his power must be denied to account for evil. You needn't sacrifice either, in my judgment, unless you're prepared to claim omniscience.

Theistic Finitism, like hedonism, falls into the error of having two ultimate principles in its system. If evil is as ultimate and as eternal as God, we may well ask, "How do we know that God will ultimately triumph?" What right do we have to believe that good will finally win? Why join with God in the struggle?[2]

6. Instrumentalism is the mainstream Christian answer to the problem of evil. This position says that evil is a necessary aspect, a needed defect, in an otherwise good universe. This gives us a dualism, but it's only a relative or temporary dualism. God will ultimately be victorious over evil. In history, however, God allows and uses evil as an *instrument* for his various purposes. Since we can't always see his purpose for suffering, this solution presupposes a large measure of faith or trust in God.

The key to understanding the instrumental solution lies in the nature of human freedom. Christians feel that God "permitted" evil in the creation because this was the only way he could really create a moral being like himself.[3] A moral universe demands a moral order that can be broken. If you ask, "Why doesn't God intervene every time someone chooses to do evil and prevent injury to an innocent party?" we answer: intervention in this sense would be the same as destruction! If you suspend a will in its choice you destroy that will. If God did this, it would be like making a race of automata—robots, not men.

But then, you logically ask: "Why didn't God make a world where men could exercise free will (even choose evil) without hurting anyone else?" Our answer? Such a world seems incompossible. How could God make a world with creatures social yet free, gregarious yet morally autonomous, and still avoid undeserved suffering? It would seem that you can't have togetherness and moral freedom without

2. See the excellent critique of Theistic Finitism in Gordon Clark, *Christian View of Men and Things*, ch. 6.

3. Unbelievers sometimes amuse themselves with questions like, "Could God create two mountains without a valley in between?" or "Could God make a rock he couldn't lift?" or "Could God think up something he couldn't do?" Such questions may disturb the simple, but they really don't even get off the runway, because they are contradictions in terms. Such questions strictly don't exist. It would be like asking, "Could God _____?" If your question amounts to a contradiction, there's nothing in the blank, because the human mind can't negotiate such a question. God is limited to the possible. He can't work a contradiction, but then, a contradiction is not a *thing*. Strictly speaking, a contradiction cannot exist.

undeserved suffering. If you insist on a world where no one ever suffers unjustly you'll have to become a pessimist, because this world certainly isn't like that.

We can illustrate the instrumental solution with many aspects of everyday life. Very often, intense suffering strengthens the character. Victory, in almost anything, requires opposition, a negative aspect. Knowledge acquired through struggle is appreciated more than spoonfed learning. Competition, hardship, and struggle have molded many a great man: Erasmus, Beethoven, Milton, Franklin Roosevelt. If life were an eternal tea party most people would be soft and lazy.

Of all the responses to evil, the instrumental theory offers the most hope. But it too, in my estimation, isn't enough to provide a completely satisfactory intellectual solution to evil. Much suffering seemingly has no purpose at all. Much of the pain in history helped no one in particular. You can't possibly blame man for most natural evils like earthquakes, tornadoes, tidal waves, and germs.

To get a better handle on evil, I suggest we look one more time at Jesus Christ.

D. HOW JESUS CHRIST HELPS THE PROBLEM.

It is fitting that Christ should help us on the problem of evil; he's helped us understand the universe so much already. Even with his help, however, we'll see that his solution is more devotional than intellectual. Historically, it is interesting that when western man let Christ drop out of the traditional theodicy the result was ultimate dismay. When deism came along and rejected the Bible, miracles, prayer, providence, and redemption, that left just the rational God of Tom Paine and Voltaire staring into the face of the grimmest evil. God made the world yet allowed sin to enter it and then wouldn't lift a finger to save his creation from evil!

No wonder Voltaire despaired of ever really solving the problem of evil. No wonder some deists finally became outright agnostics and atheists. Most deists just hid their heads and repeated the stale formula of Leibnitz and Pope: "Everything is for the best in this best of all possible worlds." If deism had left Jesus in the traditional solution things wouldn't have seemed so bad.

1. Jesus helps us with the problem of evil, first, when we note that he shared man's attitude toward the problem of pain. He suffered as much as any man yet he never pontificated on the problem. He never talked about the origins of evil. He never said that good men wouldn't suffer. He refused to blame evil on the angels, on Adam, or even on the

individual exclusively. He knew that suffering doesn't always improve character. To him, evil was the enemy, the stranger, the mystery—and we must fight it. He loved God's creation, but you'd never catch him saying, "This is the best of all possible worlds."

When Jesus stood at the tomb of his best friend, Lazarus, he was "deeply moved in spirit and troubled" (John 11:33). The root of the verb used here means "to snort," like a horse. Jesus was so agitated by the death of his friend that his disciples could see it in his physical appearance. The shortest verse in the Bible is John 11:35, "Jesus wept." In some ways it's also the longest verse, for it tells us that Jesus, God in the flesh, could sorrow, like any of us, at the loss of a loved one. "Because he himself has suffered and been tempted, he is able to help those who are tempted" (Heb. 2:18).

2. Jesus helps us with the problem of evil by bringing God into his suffering creation. Since Christ suffered and died for our sins, we know that our Creator cares for our pain. When deism kicked out Christ, it also kicked out the compassionate God who suffers with his creatures. We have no aloof deity, like Allah of Islam, who isn't personally involved in human suffering.[4] In a way that still remains mysterious, even to Christians, God involved himself through Christ in the pain of creation. He is, in T. S. Eliot's terms, "the Wounded Surgeon." No one could improve on the words of Dorothy Sayers:

> For whatever reason God chose to make man as he is—limited and suffering and subject to sorrows and death—He had the honesty and the courage to take His own medicine. Whatever game He is playing with His creation, He has kept His own rules and played fair. He can exact nothing from man that He has not exacted from Himself. He has Himself gone through the whole of human experience, from the trivial irritations of family life and the cramping restrictions of hard work and lack of money to the worst horrors of pain and humiliation, defeat, despair and death. When He was a man, He played the man. He was born in poverty and died in disgrace and thought it well worth while.[5]

Man needs more than just a savior; he needs a suffering savior. He needs a captain who understands him, who has gone through man's common trials (Heb. 2:10-18; 4:14-16). When Jesus gets too closely identified with God, then men often turn to Mary to find understanding. This is why Christians must never loose sight of the human side of Jesus.

---

4. See J. N. D. Anderson, *Christianity and Comparative Religion* (London: Tyndale Press, 1970), pp. 84, 85.

5. *Creed or Chaos?* (New York: Harcourt, Brace, and Co., 1949), p. 4.

3. Jesus gives us a handle on evil when we realize that in his life *love caused suffering!* The most ethical man in history died as a criminal. Surely, then, Jesus knows about injustice. Isn't it strange, Agnos, that Jesus Christ, who gladly took up a cross, has become the standard for human morality? If the cross of Christ became history's finest example of self-giving love, how could suffering really contradict love? The cross of Christ proved that God (Christ) didn't seek the greatest pleasure in life, but the path of redemptive love. God is not a hedonist.

This thought actually brings our whole book to a climax. We started out showing that nature has some hints of God, but we pressed on to show that God must reveal his nature fully to us in history, and finally in Jesus Christ, the highest revelation of all. The innermost nature of God—love, his heart—came out clearly in the redemptive death of his Son. After God revealed his love in Christ, even the Friday on which he died is now called "Good Friday." Even the evil that killed Jesus could be called, as it was in the old Roman service at Easter, "a happy fault." Even the sin that brought on his death could be called by St. Augustine, *O felix culpa*, "Oh blessed guilt, that did deserve so great a redeemer!"

I'm sure by now, Agnos, all this is getting much too mushy for you. You probably want to say, "Please, turn off the melodrama." I must tell you, however, that no argument ever devised for the truth of Christianity affects me like the death of Jesus Christ. When I hear him forgive his enemies from the cross, when I contemplate that my sins caused his death, I want to say with Job, "I despise myself, and repent in dust and ashes" (42:6). Such love is beyond me. I must invoke the transcendent to explain it.

Job saw God in a whirlwind of questions. I see God in the death of Christ. In both cases, we have a vision of God, not an intellectual solution to evil. And that, I think, is all God wants us to have in this life.

4. God has promised, however, that someday evil will disappear (Rev. 21, 22). Evil belongs to history; it is not in the eternal constitution of things. The Bible informs us plainly, not about the origin of evil, but about its destiny. It is destined to be totally overcome at the Second Coming of Christ. Christ gave it the death blow in his resurrection; he will deliver the *coup de grâce* when he comes again.

In the meantime, God's grace is sufficient for us (II Cor. 12:9). The cross gives most Christians the strength to live with the confusion, ambiguity, and mystery of evil. We trust God not to give us more than we can bear (I Cor. 10:13). When we finally reach the ultimate confusion—death—we try to face it, not as a wall, but as a door, a passageway into the higher, fuller, truer history. Only those who have seen God in Christ and have acquired a certain "knowledge through suffering" can truly view death in this way. To those who lack this knowledge, these remarks must be deeply offensive.

E. CONCLUSION.

Agnos, I said Jesus *helps* us with the problem of evil; he doesn't completely solve it. The best solutions come in learning how to overcome evil, not how to understand it. If you're the compulsive rationalist who insists that everything in your worldview be a "clear and distinct idea," then I can't help you with evil. If everything has to be deductive or empirically immediate, then suffering will forever remain a problem for you.

Jesus helps, yes, but the problem still won't go away. It stays with us Christians, chained to our ankles like an iron ball, a constant reminder that we don't know everything in this life, that faith isn't knowledge, that hope isn't fruition. In the final analysis, you must choose to believe either that evil destroys God or that God will someday destroy evil.

Let me remind you that all worldviews have problems. Evil is our problem. But problems don't destroy a worldview, because all systems have them. Evil is a mystery, an internal perplexity in our faith, but it doesn't bring down the whole system. One loose bolt doesn't necessarily collapse the whole machine.

If you choose naturalism you have the problem of explaining the good in this impersonal, non-axiological universe. You can't explain the good by materialistic determinism. You must choose whether good or evil shall be the enigma in your philosophy. If you choose God in Christ, he can give you (1) an adequate explanation of good and (2) a handle on the problem of evil.

Suggestions for Further Reading

Carnell, *Introduction to Christian Apologetics*, chs. 16, 17.

Nels F. S. Ferré, *Evil and the Christian Faith* (New York: Harper, 1947).

John Hicks, *Evil and the God of Love* (New York: Harper and Row, 1966).

C. S. Lewis, *The Problem of Pain* (New York: Macmillan, 1948).

Ramm, *The God Who Makes a Difference*, chs. 8-10.

Trueblood, *Philosophy of Religion*, ch. 17.

THE PROBLEM OF SIN [1]

You think our book should end here, don't you, Agnos? You're wrong—we have one more rock to remove, the largest rock of all. This rock, however, doesn't lie in the road. It lies within you. We've pushed many obstacles into the ditch on the road to commitment and I hope we've also made it possible to slip past that monster called evil. But there is still an obstacle that may keep you from walking that road of commitment to Jesus Christ. That obstacle is your own sin.

"Aw, come on now," you object, "what could sin have to do with the sufficiency of the evidence?" Very much, Agnos, very much indeed. You recall from chapter three that your "perceptual set," your epistemological filter, can determine what you accept or reject in a worldview? I firmly believe that the real cause of unbelief is not the absence of evidence but the presence of sin. Berkeley's words fit here: "We have first raised a dust and then complain that we can't see."

A. HOW SIN RATIONALIZES.

If you were to ask most non-theists why they became what they are, they'd reply, "That's easy! I chose atheism objectively, after a careful, dispassionate examination of all the relevant evidence."

Really? I wonder.

I have a sneaking suspicion that this is just a front. I suspect that a lot of "hidden persuaders" gnaw at one's mind when he is forming a worldview. Friedrich Nietzsche suggested that to understand a man's whole philosophy you look first at his ethics. Find out how he wants

1. This article appeared, in slightly altered form, in *Christianity Today*, XVIII:3 (Nov. 9, 1973).

to behave and then examine the rest of his thought. You may find a cause-and-effect relation that you didn't expect.

I agree with Nietzsche. I think that many unbelievers have an ethical prejudice when they choose a life philosophy. As Cornelius van Til was fond of saying, "A sinner has a sinner's ax to grind." He really doesn't want Christianity to be true, hence he searches out objections and rejoices when he finds them. Aldous Huxley was honest enough to admit this:

> I had motives for not wanting the world to have meaning; consequently assumed that it had none, and was able without any difficulty to find satisfying reasons for this assumption. . . . For myself, as, no doubt, for most of my contemporaries, the philosophy of meaninglessness was essentially an instrument of liberation. The liberation we desired was simultaneously liberation from a certain political and economic system and liberation from a certain system of morality. We objected to the morality because it interfered with our sexual freedom.[2]

Sigmund Freud argued that man believes in God to escape the loneliness that comes with separation from his real father.[3] Let's take the Freudian shoe and put it on the other foot. Let's argue that man *disbelieves* in God when he wants to find a secular alternative to guilt and sin. Freud said theism is a widespread neurosis; I say atheism is a widespread escape mechanism.

No person is without guilt. Alleviating the sense of guilt is a daily problem for the psychiatrist; everybody does *something* to get rid of it. The Christian is convinced that both his sin and his guilt are taken away when he believes in Jesus Christ. The unbeliever also, in a sense, holds to a doctrine of "justification by faith." Or better, justification by antifaith. The thing he erects as his metaphysical ultimate is the thing in which he places his trust, devotion, and obedience. His life philosophy is what takes away his guilt and neutralizes his sin. Once he has chosen a secular, naturalistic philosophy he can say with Paul (Rom. 8:1), "There is therefore now no condemnation for those who are in _____." Fill in the blank with your secular alternative!

Filling the blank is simple. In these times when there is a smorgasbord of non-religious worldviews to choose from, the sinner

---

2. *Ends and Means: An Inquiry into the Nature of Ideas and into the Methods Employed for Their Realization* (New York: Harper, 1937) pp. 312, 316. St. Augustine also illustrates this point on how sin can foul up the operation of the analytical process. Augustine, who had a serious problem of self-control, was on the threshold of conversion when he cried out, "Give me chastity and continency, but do not give it yet" (*Confessions*, VIII. 7).

3. *The Future of an Illusion* (New York: Doubleday, 1957), pp. 39, 40.

can easily select a theory that makes his sin a function of something other than his own will. He consciously or unconsciously passes the buck to something outside of himself—to nature, matter, or society. He must never choose Christian theism, for that would require belief in individual choice and personal responsibility, and such a belief would dramatize his sin, not remove it. He must choose a theory that allows him to say, "I can't help it."

What are some of these secular alternatives that relieve the sense of sin?

1. **The philosophy of humanism** neutralizes sin by asserting that moral error is usually a result of mere ignorance. "Knowledge is virtue," as the ancient Greeks said. Now ignorance usually results, not from basic moral culpability, but merely from lack of opportunity. Give a person the opportunity to get a good education, to increase his knowledge, to train his mind, and he will eventually conquer his bad behavior. The voluntary wrongdoer doesn't really exist.

This optimistic view of man afflicted many thinkers of the eighteenth-century Enlightenment. In his *History of Human Progress* (1794), the Marquis de Condorcet wrote that "no bounds have been fixed to the improvement of human faculties," and that "the perfectibility of man is absolutely indefinite." Jean Meslier claimed that "men are unhappy only because they are ignorant; they are ignorant only because everything conspires to prevent them from being enlightened; and they are wicked only because their reason is not sufficiently developed."[4]

Even the careful thinker, Immanuel Kant, expatiated on the *Perpetual Peace* (1795) that would come when enlightened statecraft directed the political affairs of men. H. G. Wells felt that it was "in the power of scientists to produce a world encyclopedia for dissemination of their knowledge to all, which will compel men to come to terms with one another." Note the naive conviction that *knowledge compels.* Before the twentieth century the hope was widespread that the Christian doctrine of Original Sin would slowly expire on the altar of human dignity.

"The dignity of man!" Today the words die on our lips. Despite Kant, Condorcet, and Wells we've seen the Reign of Terror, two world wars, Fascism, Hitler, the Stalin Purges, Auschwitz, and the Final Solution, the bomb. Not many people still believe in the essential goodness of man, although this brand of humanism is always an option for escaping the reality of sin. An unbeliever nowadays will

4. See Will Durant, *The Age of Voltaire* (New York: Simon and Schuster, 1965), p. 615.

more likely neutralize his guilt with some form of behavioral determinism, whether biological, psychological, or social.

2.   Biological determinism dodges the issue of personal sin by attributing misconduct to some malfunction of the physiological organism. The body gets the blame. Man is merely what he eats. Sometimes man's problems are too easily explained as the unfortunate legacy of his animal background, as in the popular but pseudoscientific works of Robert Ardrey *(African Genesis, Territorial Imperative)*.

Other people explain human aggression and associated urges in terms of an evolutionary lag in the growth of the human brain. This theory says that the neo-cortex, the "new brain," the locus of purely human faculties, grew so quickly as man evolved from the primates that it couldn't completely establish control over the "old brain," the seat of the animal instincts, the sources of irrational or impulsive behavior.

By most purely biological accounts, sinful man is merely an evolutionary miscarriage, a biological freak. As G. K. Chesterton quipped, "One of the animals just went off its head."

3.   Psychological determinism focuses on a more specific section of the human organism, the hereditary drives in the Id or the Unconscious. Freud branded forever on the modern mind the idea that some mysterious, hidden realm—call it passion, emotion, instinct, unconscious force—is the true reality and that it mightily determines who men are and how they act. Freud's view led to a tragic depreciation of the conscious part of man and a widespread feeling that human nature is predominantly irrational. This pessimism has contributed heavily to the growth of Fascism, authoritarianism, and thought control in the modern world.

Fortunately, this gloomy view subsided somewhat as the twentieth century wore on. Psychologists in recent decades have emphasized anew the autonomous activity of the individual, the purposive, future-oriented motivation of the self. Many contemporary theories of personality stress that in the normal person conscious desires probably have more power than Freud thought. Human beings are a good deal less rational and innately virtuous than the optimists of the Enlightenment felt, but I doubt if they are as morally blind and hopelessly unreasonable as Freudian pessimists of this century think.

The main point to remember is that Freud's system had no way to make man responsible for his problems. He could still say, "I can't help it."

4. Sociological determinism takes the searchlight off the individual man and blames all human problems on the structure of society. Thinkers like Karl Marx and J. J. Rousseau felt that man is born free, innocent, and without the profit motive, but that some mysterious process always develops evils in society.

Classical Marxism (not necessarily revisionist Marxism) teaches that all immorality arises from the multi-class organization of society that has dominated history: master and slave, lord and serf, bourgeoisie and proletariat, have and have-not. Hence, when the classless society arrives after the great revolution and all men become members of the same class (proletariat), sin will die out, because the socio-economic structure that nourishes it will be gone. When evil vanishes the state also vanishes, because men will no longer need force to keep down antisocial behavior.

Rousseau and other Enlightenment philosophers insisted that a "cultural lag" or an inertia in social and political institutions causes man's moral problems. "Man is born free but everywhere he is in chains," wrote Rousseau. But just how he first got into chains, or why he remains in chains, is somewhat of a mystery. A sociological determinist always finds plenty of people to blame. Kings, priests, nobles, capitalists, czars, police, bureaucrats—someone is always fouling up the works. Before the French Revolution many critics repeated the great one-liner of Holbach, that society would never be right until "every king is strangled with the guts of every priest!"

B. IMPLICATIONS OF SECULAR ALTERNATIVES.

Sinful man thus shows great ingenuity in his efforts to fabricate secular alternatives to explain sin and remove guilt. When one surveys all these salvation surrogates, certain general features of all non-Christian secular explanations stand out.

1. All alternatives destroy the essential paradox of human nature, the balance between dignity and wretchedness. Humanism upholds the dignity of man but without the balancing ingredient of fallenness. Conversely, most forms of determinism admit the wretchedness of man but lose sight of his potential dignity. Man is seldom as good as some want him to be, nor as evil as others think him to be.

Christian theology has an appreciation of both the heights and the depths of human nature. God created man in his own image and placed him a little lower than the angels (Ps. 8:5). No matter how low man sinks he still retains the capacity to respond to the divine initiative. As Pascal said, man is, at the same time, "judge of all things, a ridiculous earthworm, who is the repository of truth, a sink of uncertainty and error; the glory and the scum of the world."[5]

2.   All secular alternatives make human sin a *natural* fact, rather than a *moral* fact. They make sin a function of something other than the self, the ego that judges. Humanism makes sin a function of the intellect. Determinism makes it a function of either body, Id, or society. In all cases, the guilty will is exonerated and sin is thrown into the material, scientific realm of the *is*, rather than into the spiritual transcendent realm of the *ought*.

We've noted many times that naturalism logically has no axiology, because empiricism can never verify a value. Scientific method handles only concrete data; it can't negotiate a problem in axiology. Hence, a consistent naturalist must treat sin just as he treats disease, temperature, and chemicals, as a concrete datum to be manipulated according to purely physical laws.

3.   By thus reducing sin to a simple concrete datum, all four alternatives lend themselves to human self-therapy, to social engineering. And when sinful man tries to heal himself, the attempt leads to all kinds of ethical quackery. Man, says the unbeliever, can save himself, but *only* if he turns over his life to the educator, or the nutritionist, or the psychiatrist, or B. F. Skinner, or Chairman Mao.

4.   Finally, all forms of determinism dehumanize man. They take away his sin, true, but only at the price of reducing him to the status of a natural fact, a chunk of matter, a machine, a mere animal—in short, an object, not a subject. Skinner hit the nail on the head when he entitled his manifesto of behaviorism, *Beyond Freedom and Dignity*. He might just as well have added: *Beyond Humanity, Selfhood, and Personality*, because this is what behaviorism requires.

Christianity teaches that man's problem isn't really a brain lag or a culture lag, but a will lag, an ego lag. The problem of sin is in man himself, in the deepest, most essential part of his being, at the very core of personality—in his will. This will, as Luther argued against Erasmus, is in bondage prior to God's regeneration of it. It refuses to live according to the divinely ordained law of its being, the law of

5. *Pensées*, #246. Many keen thinkers have been impressed with the realistic assessment of human nature that one finds in Christianity (e.g., Pascal and Reinhold Niebuhr). This anthropology is so full of insight that it is a type of proof for the faith. See Pascal, *Pensées*, #433; Niebuhr, *Beyond Tragedy: Essays on the Christian Interpretation of Tragedy* (London, 1938), pp. 265f.

love. It refuses God and chooses itself, no matter how favorable the physical or social conditions may be.

C. GOOD NEWS!

If Christianity is true, then no amount of body engineering, education, psychiatry, or social engineering can really solve our behavior problems, because none of these really attacks the problem of sin at its roots. Help must come from someone who can renew man's heart and transform his will (Rom. 12:1, 2). Where does a good man get his good behavior? Jesus answers: "The good man out of the good treasure of his heart produces good, and the evil man out of his evil treasure produces evil; for out of the abundance of the heart his mouth speaks" (Luke 6:45).

By now, Agnos, you should see the advantages of the Christian worldview. If you can face the truth that you are to blame for your own sins, then *Jesus Christ can remove both sin and guilt without dehumanizing you!* To me that's gospel, good news. Choose any secular theory, however, and you're less than the man you were created to be. All secular alternatives to Christ leave you both unsaved and dehumanized. Only in him can you both remain human and be justified from sin and freed from guilt.

THE FINAL PROOF

The final proof of any pudding, Agnos, is in the eating. "Taste and see" (Ps. 34:8) is the ultimate test of any worldview. I can lead you to Christ, but I can't force you to commit your life to him. A momentous decision like that must be very personal and very private. I can promise you, however, that commitment to Christ brings you the final proof of the Christian faith. The final proof is an inward, spiritual testimony that comes only with decision and obedience.

If a person hasn't committed himself to Christ yet, he may find this final proof difficult to understand. But this is only natural since you appreciate fully the strongest evidence for any worldview only from the inside. For example, a secular musician can analyze and admire the musical technique of Bach's *B Minor Mass*, but only the Christian, whether musician or not, can recognize its profound religious significance. The Christian knows that he isn't just arbitrarily reading certain notions into the piece, because Bach wrote the music to glorify Christ.

Sir Arthur Eddington made the same point when he drew a distinction between (1) symbolic knowledge and (2) intimate knowledge. He compared spiritual sensitivity (intimate knowledge) to a sense of humor—you either have it or you don't. If a man hears a joke and misses the point, no amount of scientific explanation of the structure of the joke is likely to compel laughter.[1] The difference here is between *cognition* and *recognition*.

1. *The Nature of the Physical Universe* (New York: Cambridge University Press, 1928).

A. SUMMARY OF OUR CASE.

Before we present the final proof, which lies in commitment, we should summarize the whole book up to now. We have argued that naturalism commits the fallacy of reductionism and thus fails to adequately explain certain features of our universe and human history. We feel you must go beyond the reductive categories of naturalism to explain nature, man, history, and Christ.

We argued that you should believe in an absolute being to explain contingency and an intelligent being to explain design (ch. 6). You should believe in a moral-aesthetic being to explain man's special nature (ch. 7). You must invoke the transcendent to explain the accuracy of the Bible (ch. 10), the miracles of Christ (chs. 11, 12), the claims of Christ (ch. 13), the character of Christ (ch. 14), the prophecies fulfilled in Christ and his timely advent (ch. 15), the resurrection of Christ (ch. 16), and the problem of evil (ch. 17). Finally, you may appeal to the Biblical view of man and sin to explain the problems of unbelief (ch. 18).

Our general argument has been that Christian theism makes more sense out of reality than does naturalism. It is a more coherent worldview. If theism is wrong, then we have a contingent universe with no everlasting source, design without a designer, a moral-aesthetic man hatched by an amoral, non-axiological universe. Worse, we have one of history's most gifted nations, the nation from which came the greatest book in the history of man, producing a string of demented people called prophets, culminating in that greatest fraud of all, Jesus Christ, who somehow started a group dedicated to an illusion that has persisted to our own day. These implications of naturalism are too much to stomach—intellectually.

Why not stop here? Why not let the case for Christianity rest as it is at this point? Because it is incomplete. Nothing is really *certain* yet. Most people reserve the word "certain" for either (1) deduction or (2) the empirically immediate, and our evidence is neither. God is still a theory and Christ is still just a remote historical figure—before commitment.

Could you live and die for something, Agnos, that is only highly probable? I couldn't—unless I had a certitude from some source other than the mere external, objective evidences we've discussed so far.

Now, as a matter of fact, millions of Christians for hundreds of years have had the kind of certainty that gave them the courage to live and die for Jesus Christ. Where did they get it? From the objective evidence? No, because, as I've admitted all along, it is never demonstrative. Where then? I can only conclude they got it from God himself, or, more accurately, from the Holy Spirit.

B. THE INTERNAL WITNESS OF THE HOLY SPIRIT.

Yes, Agnos, God himself is the final proof! I don't mean that he comes to you in a special revelation, an epiphany, but that he undergirds his objective revelation in Scripture and in Christ with an internal psychological certitude. This inner certainty, created by God himself, is the psychological equivalent of deduction and empirical immediacy. With the inductive, objective evidences we can never say, "It is certain," but with the Holy Spirit in us we can say, "I am certain," or, as one great Christian said, "I know whom I have believed" (II Tim. 1:12).

Sometimes the New Testament attributes this divine assistance in understanding to God himself. When Peter confessed that Jesus was the Messiah, Jesus congratulated him: "Simon son of Jonah, you are favoured indeed! You did not learn that from mortal man; it was revealed to you by my heavenly Father" (Matt. 16:17, NEB). Peter's recognition of Jesus' messiahship arose, not out of superior external evidences, but with the help of God. Jesus' own brother James had more objective data on him but lacked Peter's insight into his true mission.

Usually the New Testament attributes the divine inner certitude to the working of the Holy Spirit.[2] The things the Spirit reveals can only be understood with the help of the Spirit (I Cor. 2:6-16). The Spirit removes the veil so that the Jew can see Christ in the Old Testament (II Cor. 3:14-17). He enables you to assert, "Jesus is Lord" (II Cor. 3:16). He helps us address God as "Abba! Father!" (Gal. 4:6; Rom. 8:15). He functions as a seal or guarantee of our final redemption (II Cor. 1:22; Eph. 1:13). When the Christian receives the Spirit he gets an abiding teacher, not just a momentary flash of insight (I John 2:27). With the inner testimony of the Spirit the Christian possesses *plērophoria*, certainty, full assurance, complete conviction (Col. 2:2).

If you find this hard to understand, Agnos, don't feel badly—Jesus' disciples also found it puzzling at first. Jesus said to them, "He who has my commandments and keeps them, he it is who loves me; and he who loves me will be loved by my Father, and I will love him and

---

2. A book on apologetics isn't the place to dwell at length on the doctrines of the Trinity and the witness of the Holy Spirit. For an excellent introduction I would start with Ramm's *Witness of the Spirit* (Grand Rapids: Eerdmans, 1959). Richardson shows that the doctrine of the witness of the Spirit was held by most Christian theologians from the very beginning (*Christian Apologetics*, pp. 211f.).

manifest myself to him (John 14:21). But one puzzled apostle asked, "Lord, how is it that you will manifest yourself to *us*, and not to the *world?*" (John 14:22).

Isn't it really the same question today? How can Christians see God in Jesus Christ and non-Christians miss him altogether? Jesus answers the question: *"If a man loves me, he will keep my word, and my Father will love him, and we will come to him and make our home with him"* (John 14:23). In another place, Jesus said, "I'm not teaching you my own thoughts, but those of God who sent me. If any of you really determines to do God's will, then you will certainly know whether my teaching is from God or is merely my own" (John 7:17, LB).

St. Augustine (as usual) said the same thing. Love, he said, is the key to learning—anything. Without a sympathetic internal disposition to the material you're studying, you'll never learn anything about anything. That's why we teach courses in art and music appreciation. A man once went all the way through the Louvre in Paris and remarked sarcastically to the doorman at the end, "I didn't see a thing in there!" The doorman smiled and replied courteously, "Don't you wish you could have?"

The Scriptures teach that man has a spiritual faculty which is deeper than his regular cognitive powers, a faculty which sin has distorted. God is hidden from most men, but the pure in heart see him (Matt. 5:8). If you don't perceive him, you may just have dull ears (Matt. 13:15), or darkened eyes (Rom. 11:10), or a darkened mind (Rom. 1:21), or a hard, impenitent heart (Rom. 2:5), or a veiled face (II Cor. 3:15). You may have suppressed the truth (Rom. 1:18).

The Scriptures also teach that when a man turns to God he receives an internal testimony (I John 5:10), his eyes are enlightened (Eph. 1:18), his heart is opened (Acts 16:14), his veil is removed (II Cor. 3:15), he understands the Old Testament (Luke 24:27), he discerns spiritual things (I Cor. 2:13), and he acquires the very mind of Christ (I Cor. 2:16).

Naturally, you protest like Nicodemus, "How can this be?" (John 3:9). I don't know. We may never know the *how*. Not even Jesus tackled that question. He just told Nicodemus: "Look at the wind. You see its effects but never the thing itself. It's the same when the Spirit causes the new birth. Forget about the *how*; rejoice in the *effect!*"

You could say that the Holy Spirit personalizes and contemporizes the revelation of God. He makes the Bible read like a personal letter to you. He makes God more than a theory to you. He makes Jesus Christ contemporary with you.

All this shouldn't really surprise a psychologist; he knows that your perceptual set determines what you see or don't see. Because of different perceptual sets some people see beauty, some see logical concepts, some see the point of a joke, some see ethical issues—and *some see God!*

C. THE HOLY SPIRIT AND EVIDENCES.

Logically you should now ask: "If the final proof is the Holy Spirit, why fuss with all the objective evidence we've covered in this book?"

Good question. The Scriptures teach that the Spirit works *with* the Word (I Thess. 1:5). The Spirit testifies, not to himself, but to Christ (John 16:14). His work, therefore, presupposes the external Scriptures and the historical Jesus Christ. In the final analysis, faith is a creation of God, a miracle of the Holy Spirit, but it arises in relation to historical realities, to actual facts. You can't have the faith apart from the facts.

It would be a waste of time to discuss the issue, "Could the Spirit work apart from the Word?" because the New Testament definitely teaches that he *will* not. We have no right to conclude, therefore, as some fideists do, that apologetics is unimportant just because the witness of the Spirit is the final proof of Christ.

The best distinction I've found to explain the relation between Spirit and Word, inner and outer witness, is the necessary and sufficient cause. Recall that a necessary cause is a condition *without which* the effect will not occur, while a sufficient cause is a condition *with which* the effect will occur. A necessary cause can prevent the effect by its absence but can't, without a sufficient cause, cause the effect by its presence. If a room is full of light and you ask, "What causes this illumination?" I can point to a hole in the ceiling as the necessary cause of the illumination. But the sufficient cause is the sun shining through the hole. The hole could prevent the illumination by its absence but couldn't, without the sun, cause the illumination merely by its presence.

Now, the external evidence, in my estimation, is a necessary cause of belief, but not the sufficient cause of belief. If the external evidence were faulty, that would justify unbelief, but even when it is good it doesn't compel belief. God himself, the Holy Spirit, is the sufficient cause of belief, but he uses the evidence as he works. With this distinction we can see the importance of the evidence and we can justify writing long books on it.

Paul says the Word is the "sword of the Spirit" (Eph. 6:17). This is a helpful metaphor because it ties Spirit and Word together in their work. We note, however, that the Spirit is the dominant partner in the arrangement; the Word is the instrument of the Spirit. The Spirit converts through the Word and apologetics helps by removing the unbeliever's defenses so the Spirit can strike with his sword.

Isn't it really the necessary cause, the objective evidences, that unbelievers complain about? Don't they usually say things like: the Bible has errors, Jesus never lived, Jesus was only a prophet, you can't prove miracles, and so forth? Don't they say, "I'll believe if you can show me _____," the conditional clause focusing on some aspect of the objective evidence? Well, if this book is a success, Agnos, our necessary cause is in pretty good shape.

If our necessary cause is in good shape, then we must conclude that the real (sufficient) cause of unbelief lies in the unbeliever himself, as the Scriptures teach. Please don't ever forget the illustration I just used: the sun can fill a room full of light *if . . . if* there is an opening in the ceiling.

You, dear Agnos, are that opening for the light. You are the crucial cause of your own belief. God can lead you to his son, Jesus Christ, by using the evidence presented in this book . . . *if* your mind isn't closed against him.

"No one is so blind as the one who *will* not see."

YOU, THE JURY

Our journey is over, Agnos.

You've been an excellent traveling mate and I thank you for that. But we must now part company. The next chapter is all yours, and it's the most important chapter of all—decision. God has sent you a card through Jesus Christ. It has R.S.V.P. on it. How will you respond?

You've reached that crucial point where you must pass from intellectual curiosity to personal commitment. It's like the moment when you actually strap yourself into a glider after listening to arguments proving that "gliders can really fly." Or like taking a ride in a bathysphere after admitting it would be safe to go down into the ocean in such a vessel.

You may have more objections to Christianity. I can't possibly answer them all. No one can. The river of life won't stop for you to acquire perfect knowledge. You should decide for Christ now. Sometimes we must dare in order to know. The man who determines to do God's will is the one who will know (John 7:17). Christianity must be lived to be fully understood. You can't borrow faith second-hand from the pages of a book; you must finally discover your faith in an act of radical commitment to Jesus Christ.

Some people think you have to take an oath on the Bible as well as on St. Thomas' *Summa Theologica* and Calvin's *Institutes of the Christian Religion* to become a Christian. Wrong. You start by trusting Jesus Christ; systematic theology can come later. St. Anselm put it right: "Some men seek for reasons because they do not believe; we seek for them because we do believe." That is, once you're a Christian you'll still study and study hard, because our knowledge is always incomplete. As long as we live, we'll always be believing in order to understand, or, to understand better.

But now—I seem to hear a voice from beyond saying, "Okay, Hoover, you've had your say. Now shut up! Be still, and know that I am Yahweh!"

My words must end, Agnos. Philosophy has done all it can. It's time for all talk to phase out, to die in the silence of decision, *your* decision. For all decision is finally made in silence.